POISON
TEA

POISON
TEA

☆ ☆ ☆ ☆ ☆ ☆ ☆ ☆ ☆ ☆ ☆ ☆ ☆ ☆ ☆ ☆

HOW BIG OIL AND BIG TOBACCO

INVENTED THE TEA PARTY AND

CAPTURED THE GOP

☆ ☆ ☆ ☆ ☆ ☆ ☆ ☆ ☆ ☆ ☆ ☆ ☆ ☆ ☆ ☆

JEFF NESBIT

THOMAS DUNNE BOOKS
St. Martin's Press
New York

THOMAS DUNNE BOOKS.

An imprint of St. Martin's Press.

POISON TEA. Copyright © 2016 by Jeff Nesbit. All rights reserved. Printed in the United States of America. For information, address St. Martin's Press, 175 Fifth Avenue, New York, N.Y. 10010.

www.thomasdunnebooks.com

www.stmartins.com

The Library of Congress Cataloging-in-Publication Data is available upon request.

ISBN 978-1-250-07610-6 (hardcover)

ISBN 978-1-4668-8747-3 (e-book)

Our books may be purchased in bulk for promotional, educational, or business use. Please contact your local bookseller or the Macmillan Corporate and Premium Sales Department at 1-800-221-7945, extension 5442, or by e-mail at MacmillanSpecialMarkets@macmillan.com.

First Edition: April 2016

10 9 8 7 6 5 4 3 2 1

To the members of the "relentless, positive storm" family.

You know who you are, and why it's important to wake up every single day with the

courage to change the world around each of us and make it a better place.

CONTENTS

☆ ☆ ☆

Introduction

☆ ☆ ☆

The Tea Party Movement—
Sudden Appearance or Calculated Move?

How did today's Tea Party movement really come to be? Did it suddenly appear in 2009, as the widely publicized, grassroots response to Barack Obama and health care reform? Was it indeed a spontaneous movement, founded by well-intended citizens concerned about the future of America? People who decided they'd had enough of increased taxation and government intervention in the private sector and were determined to at last do something about it? Was it truly CNBC news commentator Rick Santelli's famous rant from the floor of the Chicago Mercantile Exchange and his reference to the Boston Tea Party that lit the spark for this new American Revolution and became a rallying cry against a strong federal government?

Or was the true purpose and history behind the Tea Party movement something far different? Was it even an expansive, carefully strategized effort over two decades by two of the planet's wealthiest individuals, the tobacco industry, and corporate interests to form a series of political coalitions and remake government to support their own interests, as well as seize control of one of our two national parties and ultimately gain both the White House and Congress?

Americans are passionate about their politics. They owe it to themselves to know the truth—including the real motives, calculated strategies, and long-range plans behind the scenes of a seemingly populist political movement. The Tea Party's central aims are well understood—to retain cherished personal, constitutional freedoms; the ability to pursue the American dream of hard work that leads to wealth; and a debt-free future for the next generations. But those goals are shockingly disparate to the real ones of those who strategized the development of the Tea Party precepts years earlier—to protect big oil and tobacco profits (under the guise of battling taxes, regulations, and government intervention in corporate lives, built around a seemingly broad base of followers) and to develop a network that is now a dominant force in American politics.

I was present in the room at the beginning of a shocking alliance between representatives of the world's largest private oil company and the planet's largest public tobacco company creating the outlines of a national political grassroots movement that dovetails precisely with the aims of the Tea Party. I understood what I was witnessing because I've worked in senior public-affairs positions at two federal science agencies and a GOP White House.

This startling proposal was for a powerful alliance between two individuals who, if their fortunes were combined, would likely represent the wealthiest person on earth, and one of the wealthiest industries on the planet. The end goal? To create an "Allied Forces" grassroots political movement to seize control of one of America's two national parties. That goal has been relentlessly carried out step by step ever since, largely unnoticed by the American public.

This book begins with my firsthand knowledge of the opening move in a long game that is only now coming fully into view. Much of the rest of the untold story is on display in careful searches of 14 million internal tobacco-industry documents released since 2003. The balance of the book's contents—obtained through firsthand knowledge of some of the events, reputable observation, interviews, and painstaking research—is an effort to answer questions such as:

- What if the wealthy and the powerful could carefully orchestrate and fund the long rise of the Tea Party movement beginning in the mid-1990s, yet lead the American public to think it was a spontaneous response to populist anger?
- What if there is a carefully shielded alliance with a clear aim to break Washington? An alliance that has relentlessly been carrying out that plan for decades, under the guise of something completely different?
- What if the wealthiest individuals and industries on earth established a maze of front groups to attack all taxes and regulations in general in order to hide their real goals: to protect their own interests through the efforts and political machinations of such groups?
- What if one family used its vast wealth to slowly remake the entire landscape of American politics—including all levels of government, from local to national—by building a hard-edged conservative movement that despises and undermines national government in the belief that it is of little use?
- And what if these alliances and efforts were strategic and could be followed step by step to reveal a master plan so broad in scope that it could direct key decisions in America?

Poison Tea uncovers the truth, history, and the hidden motives and secrets of the people pulling the strings behind the curtains of big oil, big tobacco, and the creation of the Tea Party movement. It presents new information that will surprise Democrats who are pro big-government solutions as well as Republicans who are worried as they watch their party being hijacked by a vocal minority.

It reveals the Tea Party not as a sudden emergence due to reactionary movements against big government but rather the behind-the-scenes, secret strategy of wealthy corporations and individuals that began in the early

1990s to control the GOP. It uncovers the hidden alliances made to further that purpose. And it details the steady progress of remaking one of America's two political parties. *Poison Tea* is for all those who care about the true nature of the national political discussion in the country today.

1

☆ ☆ ☆

An Unholy Alliance

The spring of 1993 was a lousy time to be associated with the Republican Party in Washington, DC. Bill Clinton had just stormed into the White House. The Democratic Party controlled both houses of Congress. Even undersecretaries of powerful cabinet departments from the Bush administration discovered that they were unloved, unwanted, and unemployed in the nation's capital.

That included me. I'd worked at the White House as the director of communications for Vice President Dan Quayle, an Indiana Republican, during the second half of the elder Bush's term as president.[1]

In 1993 DC had few open doors for refugees of the losing Bush White House. Defeat had been sudden and unexpected, and plenty of folks like me found themselves on the street with bleak job prospects in a place that had become a one-party town.

So I did what many others did in that spring of 1993 in the nation's capital: I began consulting. My first client was a think tank that I'd never heard of—a small outfit with big dreams and a curious checkbook.

At the time, no one knew much about Citizens for a Sound Economy (CSE). Its chairman, Jim Miller, had been President Reagan's budget director. Two of the colleagues I'd worked with at the White House on the Competitiveness Council that Quayle chaired, David McIntosh and Nancy Mitchell, had both decided to sign up at CSE. They brought me along for the ride as CSE's communications director while I built up my consulting practice. Paul Beckner, the young president of CSE, was intense, driven, and clearly ready to take on the one-party town. He viewed the political landscape in 1993 as an opportunity—a tabula rasa—to remake national politics in ways that tilted much more toward the Libertarian side of the table.

When I'd asked about funding for CSE, it had taken a while to get a clear answer. But, eventually, it became obvious when Rich Fink showed up at critical strategy sessions and spoke with unblinking certainty about what Charles Koch was interested in and wanted done without question. Though few have heard of Rich Fink, he's been in the inner circle of the Koch brothers' movement-building efforts for decades, influencing the creation and actions of Koch-funded front groups.

CSE was, in effect, a wholly owned subsidiary of Koch Industries,[2] the second-largest privately owned company in the United States, with interests in manufacturing, trade, and investments. CSE hoped, and planned, to expand its reach to other funders such as oil, pharmaceutical, and tobacco companies. But at the time, CSE largely survived on the philanthropy and political aims of the Koch brothers, Charles and David, who owned the mammoth private corporation based in Wichita, Kansas, named after their family.

Stated simply, Koch Industries was the largest private oil company in the world in 1993 and still is today. For example, annual revenues in 2010 were estimated to be $100 billion.[3] But the company had humble beginnings and a great deal of familial conflict along the way.[4]

Fred Koch, the son of a Dutch immigrant, was born in Texas at the start of the twentieth century. At that time, the extraction of fossil fuels—specifically coal and oil—was the economic engine driving the advent of the industrial revolution.

America alone had seven hundred thousand coal miners when Fred was born. King Coal was at its apex. Oil exploration wasn't far behind. Truly significant sums of money were available to industry titans with access to banking capital, manufacturing synergies, and coordinated distribution.

But Fred Koch wasn't part of that elite club. Despite his impeccable academic training, he was more an outsider looking in the plate-glass windows built by inherited wealth in America. After graduating from MIT with a degree in engineering, he became a partner in a company called Winkler-Koch in Wichita.

When Fred Koch invented a new thermal cracking process that could convert crude oil into gasoline, it opened the potential for even more oil exploration.[5] It made possible turning difficult or dirty crude oil into consumer products, such as gasoline for automobiles or jet fuel for airplanes.

The innovation should have propelled him into the inner leadership circle of the biggest companies in the refined-oil business. It didn't. Those industry titans wanted nothing to do with his process to refine crude. In fact, they sued Fred Koch and his business partner for patent infringement, forcing them out of business temporarily. The corporate successors to the breakup of the Standard Oil monopoly had no need of Fred Koch's groundbreaking technology. More than enough money was to be made without innovation.

That's when Fred Koch looked overseas for other markets, taking his method of refining crude to Joseph Stalin's Soviet Union. There he made his initial stake, building refineries and refining oil from Stalin's fields. From 1929 to 1932, Fred Koch built fifteen plants in Russia based on his thermal cracking technology, until Stalin, in one of his infamous purges, killed several of Fred Koch's coworkers. That experience not only caused him to grow disenchanted with doing business with Stalin, but instilled a lifelong fear of a Communist takeover in the United States, as well as a suspicion of governmental motives.

One reason Fred Koch's business history with Stalin isn't entirely clear and straightforward is that it is deeply enmeshed in his anticommunist diatribes years later as he helped found the John Birch Society. Fred Koch didn't immediately criticize Stalin when he left Russia. Instead he formed what became Koch Industries, grew the business, and only later began to publicly denounce the birthplace of his family business. Not until the 1950s, as the Birch Society was being formed, did Fred Koch write a bestselling pamphlet that denounced Communism in the strongest possible terms and drew upon his years of doing business in Stalin's Russia.

Fred would pass his antigovernment ideology on to his four sons—Frederick, Charles, and twins David and Bill. He claimed that both the Democratic and Republican Parties had been infiltrated by Communists and warned that someday even the US president would be a closet Communist. Later, David Koch would tell Brian Doherty, an editor of the Libertarian magazine *Reason,* that his father constantly told the Koch children what was wrong with government. "It's something I grew up with—a fundamental point of view that big government was bad, and imposition of government controls on our lives and economic fortunes was not good."[6] Those beliefs provided a foundation for Charles and David Koch that would influence every area the brothers touched—politics, business, and culture.

Fred Koch moved to Wichita, Kansas, as World War II was under way and founded an engineering company with new partners. That company eventually became Koch Industries, and he spent twenty years building it up. He also made another smart move—buying a minority stake in a refinery near the Canadian border. The Pine Bend refinery in Minnesota refined twenty-five thousand barrels of Canadian crude every day. Over the years as Koch Industries grew, the importance of the Pine Bend refinery—and its ability to take millions of barrels of Canadian crude and turn it into gasoline and jet fuel for consumer consumption—became apparent. It created Fred Koch's first ability to truly compete with the big oil-refining titans who had once been so threatened by his thermal cracking innovation. It also made Koch Industries a lot of money.

Any of his four sons could have inherited that family business, but only two followed him long-term into that business—Fred Koch's Rock Island Oil and Refinery Company (which was later renamed Koch Industries). Frederick, the oldest son, refused to go to MIT and chose instead to study law and drama, so was disowned by his father and partially disinherited. When Fred died in 1967 of a heart attack, thirty-two-year-old Charles was the clear choice to take the reins since he'd already been working with his father for a number of years.

Later, David and Bill would join Koch Industries. However, Bill lived in his twin's shadow, and reportedly his ventures regularly lost money. By 1979, David was put in charge of his own division, Koch Engineering, which later became Koch Chemical Technology Group.

After an attempted family coup in 1980—Bill, Frederick, and some investors tried to gain control of Koch Industries from Charles—the board fired Bill. That launched a lengthy feud between the brothers, which was not resolved until 2001. Yet, through all the family turbulence, under Charles's leadership, Koch Industries became more than two thousand times the size of the company that Fred Koch had built.

But what I didn't know when I began consulting for Citizens for a Sound Economy was what any of the connections between CSE and the Koch brothers were really all about. What was the endgame? Today, we know. Charles and David Koch—who, if their individual fortunes were combined in one place, would quite possibly represent the wealthiest person on earth— have almost certainly spent or raised more than a billion dollars to successfully bend one of the two national parties in America to their will. The long rise of the Tea Party movement was orchestrated, well funded, and deliberate. Its aim was to break Washington. And it has nearly succeeded, as America saw in the debt-ceiling debacle of 2011, prompted by the Republican Party's demand that the president negotiate over deficit reduction in exchange for an increase in the maximum amount of money the US Treasury is allowed to borrow. There are no mistakes or accidents in the Tea Party movement. Its leadership has made certain of that.

For instance, Nancy Mitchell (now Nancy Pfotenhauer) ran Koch Industries' DC office and became president of the Kochs' Americans for Prosperity (AFP) as CSE was beginning to dissolve into its new entities in 2003–4. She helped to shepherd AFP through the CSE and CSE Foundation split, when the CSE Foundation was officially renamed AFP, and then assisted in directing AFP to prominence. She was also John McCain's most articulate economic spokesperson during his bitter presidential campaign in 2008 against Barack Obama. David McIntosh—a brilliant GOP strategist who won a seat in the House in Newt Gingrich's 1994 revolution and became one of just two freshmen House subcommittee chairs—helped orchestrate antiregulatory attacks against the FDA's tobacco investigation after leaving CSE and winning his House seat. He now cochairs the conservative Tea Party coalition, the Conservative Action Project, with Reagan's attorney general Ed Meese to lead the charge against Obamacare.[7]

Charles and David Koch and others in the donor network they've created through Freedom Partners—a new 501(c)(6) group that includes more than two hundred donors gathered together by the Kochs, by their own accounts—spent $250 million in 2012 on core groups that coalesced around a plan to defund Obamacare by shutting down the government, according to a *New York Times* investigation—though Koch Industries' spokesmen vigorously dispute this assertion. Wayne Gable, who has run Koch's DC office and has served on countless Koch think tank boards, is the chairman of Freedom Partners. Throughout its steady evolution at every critical juncture, the network has been directed by Rich Fink—described by those who have worked inside the network as Charles Koch's political brain and policy enforcer.

"The Koch brothers are using their vast wealth to remake all levels of government, from local to national," Larry Jacobs, who directs the Center for the Study of Politics and Governance at the University of Minnesota, told me. "They often use their money—like a venture capitalist—to build an effective, hard-edged conservative movement by investing in established figures like Wisconsin's Scott Walker and in initially small insurgencies like the Tea Party. Not since the robber barons of a century ago have we seen such vast wealth used so effectively to remake the landscape of American politics."

I met David Koch a few weeks into my consulting project in that spring of 1993 as the small band of folks at CSE was trying to determine where to drive their stakes into the ground. I'd never met him previously, but I'd heard his views often during family discussions. My brother-in-law had been a special assistant and the traveling press secretary for the Libertarian Party's 1980 presidential candidate, Ed Clark, and had interacted considerably with Clark's vice-presidential running mate, David Koch. And my father-in-law had been the Libertarian Party's national treasurer at the time as well—and attempted to become its national chairman in 1981. We'd argued—quite a lot—about the aims of the Libertarian Party movement, and whether it would ever manage to become part of the mainstream national political discussion.

For instance, they'd described how the Kochs had moved the Cato Institute, a Libertarian think tank, from the West Coast to the East as part of a complicated political chess match to gain more power in the eastern states, and thus Washington, DC. The Koch brothers didn't want to just enter the political fray; they wanted to direct it in myriad ways through a national political party. However, when that move failed to get the desired results, the Kochs recognized that they would need to change the national political landscape from the inside.

While the Kochs clearly didn't much like party politics, they chose the Republican Party as the likeliest target of opportunity for the Libertarian brand. At the center of every one of our family discussions was the notion that Libertarian advocates such as the Kochs despised nearly everything about the national government. In their political utopia, there would be no national government—or one that was a small fraction of its size and scope today. At a minimum, the Kochs hoped to create a movement within the Republican Party that reflected their own philosophy—that the best government was a very limited government.

CSE was a hybrid. Its foundation was a C-3—a nonprofit organization engaged in educational activities—while its main organization was a C-4, which can work more directly on political activities. It was built to be a political, grassroots advocacy group that would dovetail its C-4 activities with

C-3 nonprofits (such as the Cato Institute) around Washington. The problem, though, was that, despite tens of millions of dollars in effort, CSE and other like-minded Libertarian organizations had no real political grassroots reach to them and a permanent seat at only a handful of important Republican Party tables in Washington. All that CSE and others, fueled by the Koch brothers' funding and political ideology, had to show for their efforts were costly astroturf efforts and a few largely ineffectual think tanks and academics on their payroll.

Rich Fink and Charles Koch had grand plans to change that. But it would require a new political paradigm . . . one that combined antitax front groups in a number of states to deliver grassroots muscle; elite academics and intellectuals at dozens (and eventually hundreds) of American universities to provide the safe, intellectual foundation behind the movement; propaganda efforts in state capitals; and a national coordinating group to knit the effort together and supply oxygen to it. Fink had a master plan, and others were quick to rally behind it.

"We need boots on the ground," Fink would say emphatically in every strategy session on building a network that lived beyond costly astroturfing. Fink always made it clear that he and the Kochs didn't trust the instincts of pro-business interest groups and traditional Republican politicians in Washington, but he was also willing to find allies wherever they might be to deliver results. The ends could justify the means.

While the Kochs were judicious in their funding, they were obviously playing a long game. They were patient with their money, and they had lots of it to spread around to acolytes at universities and organizations that proved their worth. They didn't set up CSE with a one-year grant and then ask for deliverables and status reports every few months.

Instead, CSE was fully born, and fully funded, by the Kochs to set up the basic infrastructure of the network that would become known as the Tea Party movement. Fink and the Kochs have said on several occasions that they didn't create or control the Tea Party movement. But what is now obvious from documents released as part of tobacco industry litigation settlements, IRS tax forms, nonprofit reports, and several public-health-journal research efforts is that they deliberately planned, funded, and built the pieces behind the movement years before its success.

One of my first assignments as a consultant in early 1993—as President Bill Clinton planned his first budget submission to Congress—was to join the CSE leadership on a New York fund-raising trip to meet with a huge corporate partner with vast experience in building real political muscle who could help CSE reach beyond Koch oil money for their new grassroots efforts. We visited Philip Morris.

As we walked into the tobacco giant's imposing headquarters in New York, I considered whether I should tell CSE about my relentless efforts over the past three years to convince the FDA to declare jurisdiction over the tobacco industry. Philip Morris knew what I'd been up to with Commissioner David Kessler (my former boss) at the FDA. Philip Morris's senior government affairs officials knew we'd come quite close to getting the leadership at the Department of Health and Human Services—including Secretary Louis Sullivan—interested.

But there wasn't time. We headed to one of their main conference rooms. We were met by several of Philip Morris's state-based government affairs experts, all of whom had significant experience in building coalitions with an eye toward blocking regulations they didn't like at the state level. The concept that CSE put on the conference table, which was quickly taken up by the Philip Morris staff, was a bit shocking to me. They proposed an unholy alliance—Philip Morris money commingled with Koch money to create antitax front groups in a handful of states that would battle any tax that moved. It would make no difference what kind of tax—the front groups could battle cigarette excise taxes in the Northeast and refined-oil fees at the coasts. Any tax, for any purpose, was bad—and these front groups would tackle them all, with Philip Morris and the Kochs behind them.

It made good business sense—and good political sense as well. You could relabel just about anything as a tax, and heaven knows the American public hates taxes. This, at its core, was the beginning of the American Tea

Party revolt against the power of the government to pay for its programs. They could recruit average citizens from a variety of ideological groups to their cause. They would work side by side with corporate-directed workers and employees, providing real boots on the ground when enough activists weren't readily available. And no one would be the wiser—or even care— that these "grassroots" antitax groups would be jointly created and funded by the largest private oil company and the largest cigarette company in the world.

What didn't become public until nearly twenty years later was that these themes of a Tea Party antitax, antiregulation, and antigovernment revolt were then developed almost simultaneously by two of the largest tobacco companies—Philip Morris and R.J. Reynolds—under the guise of political and business coalitions to fight excise taxes of all sorts, including cigarette taxes. In successive phases in the 1990s, with the Kochs' CSE as its core mobilization network partner, Philip Morris and RJR helped create state-based antitax and antiregulation propaganda campaigns such as Get Government Off Our Back, Enough is Enough, and the Coalition Against Regressive Taxation.

Before that first deal in early 1993 was wrapped up, however, more se-nior Philip Morris officials joined the meeting. One of them knew me and my efforts to convince the FDA to regulate the tobacco industry. He stopped the meeting and ushered us out of the room. I was never invited back into these discussions, and I knew that it was only a matter of time before my consulting contract with CSE would end.

But I still had time to watch one more episode in the beginning of the transformation of CSE from an unknown hybrid advocacy think tank carrying out Charles Koch's wishes in Washington to, years later, the much more well-known Americans for Prosperity.

When President Clinton's first budget was submitted to Congress, it con-tained a novel idea to tax carbon emissions—a BTU tax that Vice Presi-dent Al Gore and others had been proposing as a method to start combating global climate change.

When Clinton's budget arrived in Congress, Rich Fink walked into the

American Petroleum Institute with a check in hand for several million dollars. That funding, he told API's leadership, was available if they'd match it and allow CSE to take on just the BTU issue in Clinton's budget. API said yes, and the single-minded campaign to target the BTU tax began in earnest.

CSE created the content of the relentless attack ads in media in key states, all with an eye toward demonizing the BTU tax. In the end, they only had to flip a single senator—Democratic moderate David Boren, who represented the swing vote on the Senate Finance Committee. CSE took out one full-page ad after another in Oklahoma's daily newspapers to hang the BTU tax around Boren's neck. It worked. Boren capitulated quickly, the BTU tax was pulled from Clinton's first budget, and CSE and the Kochs had their first significant victory on the new political playing field they had created for themselves with help and guidance from Philip Morris and the American Petroleum Institute.

Today, the "BTU tax" legend has grown to near-epic proportions among Democratic political operatives and leaders, who have essentially forgotten what actually happened (or never truly knew in the first place).

What looked to be an easy victory on one issue became a lightning rod for discontent over the Clinton administration in general, since the BTU tax was attacked as a job destroyer. Clinton's message that energy taxes were more beneficial to the country than other taxes because they fought pollution never reached the general public. Opposed from all directions—inside and outside Washington, including through grassroots protest rallies—members of Congress who favored the tax ended up being silent and passive. Many of the House Democrats who supported the BTU tax were "BTU'ed"—Washington speak for those who weren't reelected in 1994 because they'd voted for a controversial proposal. It was a lesson for the Democratic Party that even taxes based on sound economics and ecology could be killed because of political favoritism.[8]

The truth here is simple. Rich Fink and Charles Koch detested the concept of a BTU tax and donated considerable sums to make it toxic for anyone who came near it. In so doing, they forged a partnership and created the framework for successful action in a political realm for the first time in their lives.

But the other truth—unknown for many years—is that their alliance with the tobacco industry is what truly made the emerging Koch political empire a force to be reckoned with and firmly planted the seeds of what has become the modern Tea Party movement, which will select the Republican nominee for president in 2016.

2

☆ ☆ ☆

The Playbook

In recent years, progressive organizations such as the Center for American Progress (CAP), the Center for Media and Democracy, and the Center for Public Integrity have issued a number of reports in an effort to track the far-flung and seemingly disconnected Koch network.

"The Kochs have [waged] a 20-year campaign . . . to distort science [and] orchestrate fake grassroots campaigns," CAP said in a report attempting to trace the rise of the Koch network in parallel with the Tea Party movement from the 1990s up to today.[1]

The Kochs founded CSE in 1984 to "create grassroots support for deregulation, corporate tax cuts and other right wing, corporate causes," CAP said. At roughly the same time, the Kochs created what would become the Mercatus Center at George Mason University to "train hundreds of academics in [their] ultra-libertarian theories."

More than a decade later, the CAP report said, "court documents [from the Legacy Tobacco Documents Library] reveal[ed] that Philip Morris and the tobacco industry rent[ed] Citizens for a Sound Economy" in a $2 million campaign to "educate and mobilize consumers, through town hall meetings, radio and print ads, direct mail, patch-through calls to the Capitol switchboard, editorial board visits, polling data, meetings with Members and staff and the release of studies and other educational pieces."

CSE's prime target through much of that time was Dr. David Kessler at the FDA, who declared that the federal agency had jurisdiction over the tobacco industry and would regulate the sale and marketing of cigarettes to minors—starting a fight that would wind through the federal court system, lose 5–4 at the Supreme Court, but eventually become law at the start of the Obama administration.

"CSE and the other corporate front groups in that network threw everything at us that they had in their arsenal as we began to investigate the tobacco industry," Dr. Kessler told me. "It was a deliberate campaign—from lobbying and congressional oversight to public campaigns and protests—to try to keep us from regulating nicotine and cigarettes."

What Dr. Kessler and others involved in the FDA wars with the tobacco industry dealt with and witnessed mirrors the Tea Party movement's methods, tactics, and strategies today nearly perfectly.

Political movements take years to build and reach maturity. The "Reagan Revolution" was born from the ashes of Goldwater's defeat and the shame of Nixon's crimes. The Clinton years were made possible by strategic decisions (after Walter Mondale's crushing 1984 defeat) to move the Democratic Party to the center and avoid special-interest politics that had paralyzed the party.

As a Knight-Ridder reporter in its Washington bureau, for instance, I spent three days in a hotel suite in 1985 with Jesse Jackson's confidants as Democratic National Committee (DNC) chairman Paul Kirk systematically replaced the special-interest DNC vice chairs in an effort to unify the party and orient it toward the center. I wrote an inside account of the bitterly contested fight. Jackson's surrogate as DNC vice chair—Richard Hatcher, then the mayor of Gary, Indiana—was the last holdout. They fought to the end but lost. Roland Burris, who would later be appointed to Barack Obama's Senate seat after the 2008 presidential election, replaced Hatcher as the DNC vice chair as the party began to move to the center after Mondale's defeat.

Rich Fink knows this history of the DNC better than almost anyone else in America and has systematically built a movement around Charles and David Koch's wish to direct a national political party. "He's a true believer. But he has always been the guy with the plan, who had the backers to make it happen," said a former senior official with one of the key organizations Fink built with substantial funding from the Kochs.

Fink has been close at hand at every major juncture of the step-by-step strategy to build a Koch network of "boots on the ground" to seize control of the GOP's agenda—from the creation of the Mercatus Center, which serves as the hub of a far-flung academic network; to the creation of CSE, first chaired by Ron Paul; and then to the creation of its spin-off, Americans for Prosperity.

"Richard Fink and his ideas helped build the Koch brothers' political empire," Gabe Elsner, who authored a Checks and Balances Project report on Fink's central role in creating the vast Koch network over the past twenty years, told me. "He's their political strategist, close confidant, and employed by Koch Industries—which goes to show that their political efforts are part of the Koch Industries' business model. But hardly anyone has ever heard of him—and even fewer know of his history as a pay-to-play operative for Big Tobacco."

Whenever a new entity begins with substantial core funding from Charles and David Koch, Fink is there to see that it gets started as they intend. Then, as it succeeds, he moves on to the next network puzzle piece. What's more, according to those who've been in that network, Fink is the central player in a system across all of its many entities to "test" someone at one job to see how well he or she performs. If people do well, then they become eligible to move on to other parts of the network. Basically, once you're in and you've proven yourself, you're in for the long haul.

Most are well aware today of the Kochs' substantial influence inside the Republican Party. They organized and spent vast sums in a half dozen key swing state races that flipped the US Senate to the GOP in 2014. Recent estimates have pegged the cost of that attempt to take the Senate at more than $400 million. There will almost certainly be an even bigger, unprecedented campaign in 2016 to finally win the White House. In fact, the Kochs' donor network pledged to raise nearly a billion dollars toward that effort.

"But the Koch-funded front groups' involvement in the tobacco industry over the years has largely gone unreported," Elsner told me. "In 1999, for instance, major tobacco companies were accused of a mass conspiracy to deceive the public about the dangers of smoking. The Justice Department filed a racketeering lawsuit against them. To fight it, the tobacco companies called on their most important allies for support—specifically, the Mercatus Center and CSE, both of which Fink created for just this sort of purpose."

That effort is detailed in internal tobacco industry memos in a plan called the "mobilization universe," Elsner said. Philip Morris tasked CSE and Mercatus to coordinate roles in order to blunt the federal racketeering case with Tea Party–styled protest rallies, letters to the editor, speeches, policy reports, and congressional lobbying. It was one more in the evolution to today's network—tested with tobacco funding in a big DC fight.

The Mercatus Center, over time and by design, has become the central hub for a network of hundreds of academics at nearly three hundred American universities. According to others working at the university near the nation's capital, Mercatus operates independently of George Mason. "Mason has a live-and-let-live attitude. Most people at Mason barely know it exists," one longtime academic at the university told me. "The affiliation of Mercatus with Mason is very loose and strictly arm's-length."

However, Mercatus is linked to grassroots organizers through the State Policy Network. The SPN has created and funded think tanks across the nation and was an $83 million empire as of 2011. Their member organizations claim to be nonpartisan and independent, but an investigation by the Center for Media and Democracy revealed that SPN and its think tanks are "major drivers . . . of the American Legislative Exchange Council (ALEC) . . . backed corporate agenda in state houses nationwide, with deep ties to the Koch brothers." The SPN grew significantly while Obama was running for president in 2008—a year before the alleged spontaneous-combustion birth of the Tea Party in the spring of 2009. SPN also has close connections with the Franklin Center for Government and Public Integrity, which directs propaganda in state capitals across the United States, and Americans for Prosperity.

Efforts to fight taxes on the tobacco industry's behalf continued from CSE to Americans for Prosperity, up until the spring of 2009 and beyond when the Tea Party movement became more broadly known. AFP state chapters campaigned against cigarette taxes in four states (South Dakota, Texas, Kansas, and Indiana) in 2006, Elsner said. Those efforts were funded by several tobacco groups. AFP opposed an indoor-smoking ban in Texas in 2007. It fought cigarette taxes in Virginia in 2009. And AFP fought cigarette taxes in California in 2010.

The political grassroots playbook is nearly always the same—built by Rich Fink and the Kochs with substantial tobacco funding over the past twenty years.

Obama's election in 2009 was the excuse to put in motion everything they'd learned over the years, Fink said in an October 2012 interview with two reporters for the local *Wichita Eagle*—the only extensive interview he's ever given on motivations behind the rise of the Koch political network.[2]

In that interview, Fink said that Obama's election was finally their moment to much more prominently take on regulatory and government spending. He portrayed the Kochs' decision to challenge Obama, create a political grassroots network with key pillars funded by the Koch donor network, and help fuel the Tea Party movement as a decision they'd reached reluctantly. He said they'd first actively considered and decided to pursue it in 2009. He didn't mention the substantial effort prior to that time.

So the Kochs jumped in that spring of 2009, Fink said, and committed to spending essentially whatever it would take. As with all successful propaganda built around a simple, elegant story, it wasn't the entire story.

3

☆ ☆ ☆

A Critical Bridge: Ron Paul and the "Patriot" Movement

H ow" many of you people want to pay for your neighbor's mortgage that has an extra bathroom and can't pay their bills? Raise your hands! President Obama, are you listening?" Rick Santelli, an on-air editor, called out to the CNBC audience on February 19, 2009, while he stood on the floor of the Chicago Board of Trade.

All around him the floor erupted with hearty boos of agreement. Santelli claimed that through the bailouts and stimulus package, the government was promoting bad behavior. He railed against subsidizing "losers' mortgages" and asked, why not "reward people that could carry the water instead of drink the water?" Santelli concluded his speech by asking that all capitalists join him in July for a new tea party on the shores of Lake Michigan.[1]

In those few minutes, Americans who were frustrated with higher taxes and the resulting fewer dollars in their pockets—which, if we're honest, is quite a few of us—found a voice in the "rant heard round the world." It wasn't only those on the trading floor that Santelli riled up. It was average Americans in general. Those who didn't particularly care for the Obama administration in the first place could rally around an antigovernment movement. They cheered in their living rooms and blogged about Santelli's courage in speaking the truth they had felt but not been able to put into words.

Rick Santelli has been heralded publicly since with being the "father" of the modern Tea Party movement because of his "off-the-cuff" monologue. As he told *Businessweek* in 2014, "I was fed up, the country was fed up . . . the country was a tinderbox, and I said something that lit the fuse." Within hours a Web site called ChicagoTeaParty.com sprang to life. Tea Parties began popping up all across the United States, all centered on Washington's fiscal irresponsibility.[2]

Americans who were "fed up" responded to the rallying cry with protests against not only the bailouts and stimulus package but against government "tyranny" in general, including out-of-control spending. It was time to take back control of the country, the Tea Party movement claimed, and many Americans were more than ready to help with the cause. The media stoked the frenzy, covering the new Tea Party movement and also the backlash from the Obama administration and the political left, who called Santelli clownish and claimed he hadn't fully read the stimulus plan.[3]

Nearly every contemporary story or media account of the Tea Party movement in America describes it as a largely spontaneous, uncoordinated, populist movement that emerged in 2009 after Obama took office. Here's how *Encyclopaedia Britannica* chronicles the origins of the Tea Party, which is typical:

The Tea Party movement is a "conservative populist social and political movement that emerged in 2009 in the United States, generally opposing excessive taxation and government intervention in the private sector while supporting stronger immigration controls. Historically, populist movements in the United States have arisen in response to periods of economic hardship, beginning with the proto-populist Greenback and Granger movements in the 1860s and '70s and continuing with William Jennings Bryan's Populist Party in the 1890s and Louisiana politician Huey Long's Share Our Wealth program during the Great Depression of the 1930s.

"In the wake of the financial crisis that swept the globe in 2008, populist sentiment was once more on the rise. The catalyst for what would become known as the Tea Party movement came on February 19, 2009, when Rick Santelli, a commentator on the business-news network CNBC, referenced the Boston Tea Party (1773) in his response to President Barack Obama's mortgage relief plan. Speaking from the floor of the Chicago Mercantile Exchange, Santelli heatedly stated that the bailout would 'subsidize the losers' mortgages' and proposed a Chicago Tea Party to protest government intervention in the housing market.

"The five-minute clip became an Internet sensation, and the 'Tea Party' rallying cry struck a chord with those who had already seen billions of dollars flow toward sagging financial firms. Unlike previous populist movements, which were characterized by a distrust of business in general and bankers in particular, the Tea Party movement focused its ire at the federal government and extolled the virtues of free market principles."

It's a nice story. It's also a carefully crafted myth. The truth is that the funding mechanisms, central messages, and key pillars of the Tea Party movement were many years in the making. It is not a true grassroots movement but was strategically built to deflect anger away from corporations and redirect it at the government. A network had already been developed, funded by Koch and tobacco industry money, and only awaited a suitable opponent, which they found in Barack Obama. The willing public face was a brash-speaking CNBC editor known for his public railings against government spending.

Yet at each step along the way these same tobacco, oil, and other multinational corporations were quietly growing their own wealth by developing front groups to fight taxes of any kind—all under the guise of promoting personal freedom, pursuing the American dream, and moving America toward becoming a debt-free nation.

The mission statement on the Tea Party Patriots Web site in 2014 declares, "We envision a nation where personal freedom is cherished and where all Americans are treated equally, assuring our ability to pursue the American Dream." That means the right to speak out when the government is stepping into the areas of personal freedoms, such as picking doctors and insurance plans. It also includes living any way you wish, so long as your actions do not harm or hinder others.

The Tea Party Patriots—just one of many groups that have rallied around similar themes—states that it supports financial freedom (the opportunity to grow businesses with the reward of keeping the proceeds of hard work, therefore supporting more healthy competition among providers). The way to get out of our incurred debt as a nation? Through "a tax policy that is fair, flat, and fixed," instead of increasing the tax rate to support spending in Washington. Such a solution allows individual Americans to figure out how best to use their money, thus keeping their control over monies earned.

In a country that was solidified as a nation when colonists fought increasing British oppression, including the British Parliament's tax on tea imported from the East India Company to the shores of America, the allure of reduced taxes and individually keeping a bigger piece of the American pie is tantalizing indeed. What American wouldn't welcome retaining more dollars in his or her pocket on April 15?

An important bridge between the early formation of these Tea Party themes—and the "emergence" of those themes and movement after Obama was president—is former congressman Ron Paul. His son Senator Rand Paul (R-KY) is a beneficiary of years of careful work to build that movement. It's why Senator Paul was an early front-runner for the 2016 GOP presidential nomination and a darling of the Libertarian/Tea Party wing of the GOP.

When dozens of wealthy contributors to Charles and David Koch's donor network—which forms the backbone of the Freedom Partners network that contributed hundreds of millions of dollars in the last three federal elections—met in an annual meeting in the run-up to the 2014 midterm elections, nearly every potential GOP presidential aspirant made an appearance at the conference. But just two—Senator Paul and Indiana governor Mike Pence—were given a closed-door audience with the core donors of the Kochs' Freedom Partners network, *Politico* and other media organizations reported. That's because Senator Paul and his father, Ron Paul, helped build the modern Tea Party movement, and the Freedom Partners donors know it, so Paul is granted access to sit at the head of its considerable table.

Ron Paul, interestingly, likes to take credit for the creation of the Tea Party movement—not the "spontaneous" birth on the floor of the Chicago Mercantile Exchange in the spring of 2009 after Obama had already been elected president, but much earlier, during his quixotic but well-funded presidential campaign in 2007 and 2008. He's done so for years. There's some truth to his claims—perhaps more than even he knows.

In December 2007, a year and a half prior to Santelli's diatribe in Chicago, Ron Paul's presidential campaign supporters organized a donor drive, calling it a "tea party money bomb" around the 234th anniversary of the original Boston Tea Party. Paul's tea party money bomb was designed to raise campaign funds for his run in the GOP presidential primaries—and it was remarkably successful.

Paul's campaign articulated all of the now well-known themes and messages of the Tea Party movement that Paul had been trying out for a considerable time. Although Paul had been a Texas Republican congressman, he'd never been entirely comfortable inside the GOP. He ran for president in 1988 as the Libertarian Party's candidate—eight years removed from David Koch's run in 1980 as the vice presidential nominee on the Libertarian Party ticket.

A Web archive snapshot of a meet-up notice from December 19, 2007—synced with Ron Paul's "tea party money bomb" campaign fundraising efforts—makes the link between Ron Paul's network in Illinois and the Kochs' Americans for Prosperity network clear. "Are you tired of hearing about wasteful pork barrel spending in state government and at the national level?" read a "Meetup with Americans for Prosperity—Illinois" notice.

"Do you think that money could be put to better use? And do you think it's time someone did something about it? Come meet others who feel the same way, and learn what you can do about it. The Illinois chapter of Americans for Prosperity has been organizing people like yourself around the state, and helping them make their voices heard."

That same day, in the same forum, a Ron Paul supporter asked, "What happened 234 years ago yesterday? Well, if you're a Ron Paul fan, you know—but, if not, permit me to remind you of one of the most successful political stunts in American history: the Boston Tea Party."

By the spring of 2009—a year and a half later, after Obama was elected—it was largely the Paul Libertarian Party network in Illinois (through Ron Paul Meetup and his Campaign for Liberty groups) that created the propaganda surrounding Santelli's Chicago Mercantile Exchange outburst about a Chicago Tea Party. "We gave Rick Santelli the idea for the Tax Day Tea Parties," said one of Paul's colleagues, Dave Brady of the Libertarian Party of Illinois.

The truth is that Ron Paul, Citizens for a Sound Economy, and its successor, Americans for Prosperity, had carefully been constructing its populist, grassroots "freedom network" themes for many years. It became fully apparent in 2007, but it had been years in the making. The effort began in the mid-1980s, taking advantage of tobacco industry support and funding that began slowly after Ron Paul became CSE's chairman in 1984 and then accelerated as CSE fully integrated into prominent corporate front groups in Washington, DC, in the succeeding years.

In an unusual move for a sitting member of Congress, Ron Paul solicited the first donors to the fledgling Citizens for a Sound Economy. In a fundraising letter dated December 3, 1984—on stationery for "Congressman Ron Paul" as well as "Chairman, Citizens for a Sound Economy (incorporating Nat'l Taxpayers Legal Fund)"—before he had officially left political office (he would later return to politics), Paul asked donors to help support the new organization that he planned to direct:

"Your past support of the National Taxpayers Legal Fund (NTLF) has helped pave the way for the formation of what I feel will become the most effective citizens' group pushing for less government and lower taxes—Citizens for a Sound Economy (CSE)." (NTLF was a short-lived Washington-based nonprofit in the mid-1980s that claimed a modest grassroots tax reform membership.)

"As you know, I worked closely with NTLF in 1984 and am now Chairman at CSE which will absorb NTLF's efforts and do even more.

"Thanks to your past support we've created massive momentum across America and in Congress for passage of a 'Fair/Flat Tax.' I think you'll agree our new name—Citizens for a Sound Economy—says more clearly what our organization and goals are all about.

"With your continued support and with that of the millions of concerned Americans we hope to reach I feel confident 1985 will be the year Congress will pass a 'Fair/Flat Tax.' But we must be careful! Several of the so-called tax 'reform' plans being considered by Congress are really nothing more than huge tax increases in disguise. The only real 'Fair/Flat Tax' is one which significantly reduces the huge financial burden the federal government places on us taxpayers."

Paul was wrong about his predictions that Congress would take up the flat-tax concept, but he was right that both President Reagan and Congress would tackle the tax code. The Tax Reform Act of 1986, which simplified the tax code and removed a number of previous tax shelters, became a signature achievement of Reagan's second term in office. But it was no flat tax, as Paul would lament for years.

Yet Citizens for a Sound Economy—and its successor, Americans for Prosperity—would become the most prominent freedom and antigovernment movement in the country.

One other deep connection between Ron Paul and the freedom network has largely gone unreported over the years and is worth noting— their allegiance with and affinity for the John Birch Society, which is known for its far-right, anticommunist views. The Southern Poverty Law Center lists the John Birch Society as an extremist "Patriot group." Despite that their father, Fred, cofounded the group in the 1950s, Charles and David Koch have carefully separated themselves from the society. Paul did not.[4]

The John Birch Society was established in Indianapolis, Indiana, in 1958 to "promote less government, more responsibility, and a better world." Since its founding, the society, which claims it is "not a political organization but rather educational," has warned about "increased government spending, taxes, centrally planned inflation, the centralization of power in the government," among other topics. It is also "organized at the grass-roots level with paid coordinators and volunteer leaders who establish chapters in communities all across the country."[5]

The twelve founding members included Fred Koch. His staunch anticommunist views and support of the John Birch Society are well-known. But Ron Paul's support of the society and affinity with its "patriot movement" are not.

In early September 2008—as the Republican National Convention was taking place in Minneapolis, where Senator John McCain was introducing his vice-presidential nominee, Alaska governor Sarah Palin—a parallel Ron Paul convention at the Target Center took place that attracted several thousand followers. The "parallel" convention emcee, Tucker Carlson, didn't announce him, but a special guest—John McManus, president of the John Birch Society—spoke for ten minutes to a wildly cheering Ron Paul crowd.

One of the convention participants captured the McManus speech—which was largely ignored by media covering the RNC convention and the Sarah Palin media circus—and uploaded it to YouTube.[6] McManus concludes his usual angry diatribe against the evils of the US government with a fervent pitch. "If you like Ron Paul, you'll love the John Birch Society," McManus says to roars of approval from the thousands of convention participants.

The John Birch Society helped infuse its "patriot movement" efforts into the Tea Party movement. Ron Paul regularly headlined John Birch Society events around the country, including its fiftieth-anniversary celebration in 2008.

Today, it's hard to discern where the roots of the "patriot movement" promulgated by the John Birch Society begin and the Tea Party movement end.[7] But Ron Paul's clear affinity for its core beliefs, evidenced by his speeches to the society's members and his senior staff's migration from its headquarters over the years, makes the connections clear. Fred Koch's own views on the need for such a society in America are equally well-known. And in CSE, which Ron Paul helped form in 1985, those beliefs and movement principles found a home.

4

☆ ☆ ☆

Smedley Butler, a Fascist Coup, and the American Liberty League

In a fascinating, and largely unknown, story, Marine Corps general Smedley Butler may have uncovered the only known fascist plot to overthrow the presidency in America.

Butler, a popular soldier who fought in a number of America's foreign wars and also became famous while fighting for veterans' rights, testified before Congress in 1934 that a group backed by some of the wealthiest American businessmen of that era had approached him to lead veterans to revolt against President Franklin Roosevelt's New Deal reforms because they so disliked the regulatory actions. Before Butler died in 1940, he also penned a book called *War Is a Racket*, which has become a popular antiwar manifesto and has served as a blueprint to describe the military-industrial complex.

Smedley Butler's testimony in 1934 was before a special House committee formed to investigate fascist activities in America that might be connected to political activities in Nazi Germany and Italy in the 1930s. That committee, the House Special Committee on Un-American Activities, spent less than a year investigating fascist political activities before quickly turning toward its now-infamous efforts to identify Communist sympathizers in America.

Butler's testimony, which newspapers at the time dubbed the Business Plot, was the stunning focus of the first inquiries of the Special Committee on Un-American Activities. Butler described the Business Plot as a loose political conspiracy formed in 1933 to create a fascist organization built around the leading veterans' associations of the era. Butler, who was already well-known to hundreds of thousands of World War I veterans fighting for their rights in Washington—said that he was asked if he would lead such a group in an effort to overthrow FDR, and he refused.

The New York Times and other leading newspapers of that era dismissed Butler's tale as somewhat fanciful. Historians since then have questioned whether an actual coup was close to being put in motion, but those who have looked at Butler's testimony and other political activities at that time by FDR's opponents have concluded that some sort of a coordinated scheme was being contemplated to attack the New Deal reforms.

But while Butler's story has largely been forgotten, the central players in his tale—the founders and financial backers of the American Liberty League—most certainly have not. If anything, the American Liberty League's efforts to derail FDR's New Deal may well have created the political playbook that some of the corporate front groups have used the past twenty years.

The American Liberty League, made up primarily of conservative, pro-business Democrats and some Republicans, and backed by some of the biggest companies of that era, was formed in 1934, just a few weeks after Butler's appearance before the inaugural session of the Committee on Un-American Activities. The group's first chairman, Jouett Shouse, and other members of the league's executive committee were chosen to provide the appearance of bipartisanship. Shouse was a well-known Democrat and had helped lead the fight to end Prohibition. The American Liberty League's executive committee even included Al Smith and John Davis, who had both once been Democratic candidates for president.

But the real impetus—and financial backing—for the American Liberty

League came from the leadership of large companies such as DuPont, Sun Oil, and General Motors who were searching for effective ways to fight the New Deal.

The league's central goals echo many of the same central themes espoused today by groups such as AFP and others in the Koch donor network. The American Liberty League was formed to "teach the necessity of respect for the rights of persons and property as fundamental to every form of government . . . to teach the duty of government, to encourage and protect individual and group initiative and enterprise, to foster the right to work, earn, save and acquire property, and to preserve the ownership and lawful use of property when acquired."[1]

Almost from the moment of the American Liberty League's inception, FDR got the better of his opponents. He quickly labeled the American Liberty League as nothing more than a corporate front group built solely to protect the interests of big business.

The league gave it the old college try . . . literally. Its first attempts at grassroots recruitment were aimed at college students. It had signed up thousands of students at more than three hundred chapters in the run-up to the 1936 presidential election.

In the 1936 presidential campaign, FDR and his surrogates upped the ante. FDR's campaign manager said that the league was an "ally of the Republican National Committee [that would] squeeze the worker dry in his old age and cast him like an orange rind into the refuse pail."[2]

During the 1936 campaign, the league went to great, expensive lengths to disseminate its message. In its heyday, more than two hundred prominent American businessmen had signed on to the league's efforts.

The league created its own syndicated news service, a precursor to today's Franklin Center, built to organize political media efforts in state capitals. The league's syndication efforts reached as many as sixteen hundred newspapers. The league papered the landscape with pamphlets—most of them speeches or addresses by business leaders aligned with the league.

These went to newspapers, government agencies, libraries, members of Congress, and, of course, to aligned and funded political groups that, in turn, generated even more news stories.

The work of the American Liberty League was almost completely underwritten by only a handful of wealthy businessmen. The DuPont family alone was responsible for a third of its funding, prompting FDR's campaign to dub it the DuPont Liberty League.[3]

The league's close association with wealthy businessmen and the interests of large corporations such as DuPont, General Motors, and others made it an easy target for FDR, who needed a useful foil for his fiery public speeches to position himself in the 1936 campaign as someone aligned with the interests of ordinary Americans—as opposed to big business—who were still struggling in the Great Depression. Following FDR's landslide victory in 1936, the group began to fade from the political scene. It disbanded completely in 1940.

But the American Liberty League's spectacular failure to artificially create a popular political grassroots movement—built to oppose federal efforts to rein in big-business interests—served as a highly useful road map for those wishing to engage in later political fights in Washington, DC.

5

☆ ☆ ☆

What Drives Charles Koch?

The basic elements of Charles Koch's public story—the ones that have been meticulously refined by public-relations and government-affairs firms over the past two decades—are by now firmly established. It is, by any measure, an extraordinary story—one that is possible, perhaps, only in America.

How does the grandson of a Dutch immigrant and the son of a MIT-trained engineer become one of the wealthiest men in America? His father, Fred, was an innovator who didn't give up. He believed in free enterprise and in pursuing his dream, in spite of the naysayers. The same oil-industry titans who had made so many mistakes when they'd formed the American Liberty League to oppose FDR's New Deal didn't stop Fred Koch for long. He simply took his new technology elsewhere, including to Russia for the first few years. He also took advantage of opportunities that could potentially expand Koch Industries significantly, such as buying a minority stake in the Pine Bend refinery in Minnesota. He passed this relentless, forward-looking mind-set in business on to his sons.

When his father died in 1967, Charles took over the family business. He'd been groomed to lead it. One of his first acts was to double down on his father's smart move to purchase that small stake in the Pine Bend refinery. He rolled the dice and bought outright control of the refinery.

Charles has said for years that this acquisition largely made Koch Industries what it is today. He wrote in his 2007 book, *The Science of Success*,[1] that the Pine Bend acquisition was "one of the most significant events in the evolution of our company" because it "brought new capabilities to Koch Industries and led to many new opportunities." He also described how the Pine Bend purchase led to other new businesses in the chemical, fibers, polymers, and asphalt industries, then contributed to additional business opportunities in pulp and paper, petroleum coke, and gas liquids processing.

Over the years, thanks to the Pine Bend facility, about a quarter of all Canadian tar-sands oil has been refined by Koch Industries. Charles Koch owes a great deal of his fortune to the tar-sands oil of Canada[2] (a fact that has been obscured in the recent, very public dispute over the Keystone XL pipeline).[3] While it's true, as Koch Industries has said, that it has no direct financial interest in the Keystone pipeline, the business has historically made considerable sums from refining Canadian crude and would almost certainly benefit from cheaper transportation options such as Keystone. Today, Koch Industries is the second-largest privately held corporation in America. All of this business growth occurred under Charles Koch. He grew a $250 million annual business shortly after Fred Koch's death into the globe-straddling industrial colossus it is today.

The significant growth of Koch Industries under Charles's leadership is well-known. So is the very public dispute Charles and David waged with their brothers, Frederick and William, for control of Koch Industries.

William and Frederick sold their ownership stake in Koch Industries to Charles and David in 1983 for $800 million. That settlement nearly unraveled, though, when William sued Charles, alleging that he'd deliberately undervalued the company at the time of the settlement.

The Koch brothers' court battle lasted for more than a decade—and only came to trial in 1999. A Kansas jury ruled in favor of Charles, effectively ending the dispute and closing down the public fight between the four Koch brothers. Today, Charles and David Koch each own 42 percent of Koch Industries, making them the sixth and seventh wealthiest persons in America. Together, their net worths would likely make them the wealthiest individual in America.

Like his father, Charles seems to genuinely believe that government intervention is actually dangerous to American democracy. His guiding philosophy, market-based management, is built around "the principles that allow free societies to prosper . . . free speech, property rights, and progress," says the Charles Koch Institute Web site.

In short, he believes the market is a better enforcer of ethical behavior that leads to economic well-being than government intervention. His own governing concept, he told the *National Journal*, is "to minimize the role of government and to maximize the role of private economy and to maximize personal freedoms."[4]

He told *Forbes* in 2009 that he'd come to believe that America was threatened in much the same way that the American Liberty League believed FDR's New Deal threatened the nation's welfare. "We could be facing the greatest loss of liberty and prosperity since the 1930s," he said.[5]

He wrote in *The Wall Street Journal* in 2011 that government spending was fundamentally the root of all ills in American society. "Government spending on business only aggravates the problem. Too many businesses have successfully lobbied for special favors and treatment by seeking mandates for their products, subsidies (in the form of cash payments from the government), and regulations and tariffs to keep more efficient competitors at bay. Crony capitalism is much easier than competing in an open market. But it erodes our overall standard of living and stifles entrepreneurs by rewarding the politically favored rather than those who provide what consumers want."[6]

In 2014, Charles echoed the words of his father during the John Birch Society era, comparing President Obama's national health-care reforms to Communism. "This [Obamacare] is the essence of big government and collectivism," he wrote in *The Wall Street Journal*.[7]

What Charles Koch eventually mastered—in a way that none of the other business leaders who have aspired to control the American political process in a messy, combative democracy have—was the ability to apply a ruthless, focused business philosophy in politics. Rich Fink was the perfect partner in that effort.

"The plan he [Fink] and [Charles] Koch eventually set in motion involved a three-tiered model in which the production, packaging and marketing of ideas was akin to the manufacturing of Lycra (one of Koch Industries' signature products)," Daniel Schulman, author of *Sons of Wichita*, wrote in *Politico*.[8]

"Their plan for bringing about a free-market epoch and the business model of Koch Industries—gathering raw materials and refining them into more valuable products consumers desire—were basically one and the same."

Charles Koch—and Rich Fink, his consigliere in the nexus of business and politics—finally orchestrated a corporate approach to politics that worked in ways that previous efforts such as those by the American Liberty League had not. The American public did not see the business model behind the political efforts. That was by design.

"To facilitate the production of these raw materials, Koch pumped millions of dollars into hundreds of universities. These contributions—which totaled nearly $31 million from 2007 to 2011 alone—have gone to endow professorships, underwrite free-market economics programs and sponsor conferences for libertarian thinkers," Schulman wrote.

"Step two of the process, Fink once explained in *Philanthropy* magazine, entailed taking the intellectual output of these academic programs, ideas 'often unintelligible to the layperson and seemingly unrelated to real-world problems,' and refining them into a 'useable form.'

"This was the domain of the Cato Institute, Mercatus and the dozens of other free-market, antiregulatory policy shops that Charles, David and their foundations have supported. Organizations like these churned out reports, position papers and op-eds arguing for the privatization of Social Security; fingering public employee unions for causing state budget crises; attempting to debunk climate science; and making the case for slashing the welfare system and Medicaid.

"The third piece of the master plan was mobilizing citizen-activists—or at least creating the illusion of a grass-roots groundswell. These activists would agitate for the same policies the academics had conceptualized and the think tanks had refined into talking points and policy prescriptions. As David Koch once explained, 'What we needed was a sales force.'

"Again, Fink was the man with the plan. In 1984, he and the Koch brothers formed Citizens for a Sound Economy. It was in essence the bizarro-world version of Ralph Nader's Public Citizen. Where Nader fought to expand regulation, Citizens for a Sound Economy worked to eviscerate it. And where Nader battled corporate power, Citizens for a Sound Economy concentrated on harnessing it," said Schulman in *Politico*.

While few have attempted to connect the dots from Fred Koch's days in Stalin's Russia and then cofounding the John Birch Society in the 1950s to his son Charles's later efforts to create the business-political scaffolding to undergird the emergence of the Tea Party movement, Schulman says the pattern is there nevertheless.

"There is a direct throughline from Fred's beliefs to the Tea Party today," Schulman told *Vanity Fair* in 2014. "Most people do not know just how influential this family has been, affecting politics, business, and culture in both the twentieth and twenty-first centuries."[9]

While much has been written and said about Charles Koch, nearly all of it is based on speculation. He rarely gives interviews. The few pieces he's written were placed within the friendly confines of *The Wall Street Journal*'s editorial pages or other right-leaning newspapers or magazines sympathetic to his concept of market-based management, which has driven the nexus of his business-political network.

This, too, is almost certainly by design. The first rule of business is to leave as little as possible to chance. Take risks only when absolutely necessary and, even then, leave fallback positions. Leverage every conceivable asset and synergy to your advantage. Charles Koch has taken this relentless, always-efficient business model and applied it to the chaos of the political arena. Granting media interviews to those who can cause you harm doesn't make any sense at all in this model—because it is neither predictable nor advantageous to your overall strategies.

As a result, nearly everyone who wishes to understand what truly motivates Charles Koch—what has caused him to spend vast sums to achieve political synergies and success in ways that no other business leader before him has managed in America—is only guessing.

Only Charles himself can truly articulate why he's spent decades building on his father's political legacy even as he's turned the company his father founded into one of the largest privately held corporations in American history. Charles hasn't done so in a generation. That isn't likely to change.

6

☆ ☆ ☆

The Man Behind the Curtain

Rich Fink has held nearly every important Koch Industries and Koch donor network job imaginable since the mid-1980s. The Koch political network is as much his creation as it is Charles Koch's.

Fink clearly enjoys telling his simple, elegant story about how the Kochs decided in January 2009—on the eve of what the media reported as a spontaneous Tea Party movement a month later at the Chicago Mercantile Exchange—to pursue a grassroots political movement that would upset the White House. It's storytelling that works, on several levels, as all good narratives do.

It's also a story he doesn't tell much publicly because neither he nor the Koch brothers agree to many interviews with reporters. They prefer to use a Web site (www.KochFacts.com) to respond to media stories, or to release e-mail exchanges between reporters and senior communications officials at Koch Industries to highlight what they don't like in media coverage.

But Fink and the Koch brothers sat down for lengthy interviews with two reporters for their hometown paper, *The Wichita Eagle,* in the fall of 2012—after their outside public relations advisers and internal senior communications team told them that they needed to go on the offensive to counter White House and Democratic Party officials who were regularly calling them out in political media.

The two *Wichita Eagle* reporters did their best to draw Fink and the Kochs out, and many of their comments are illuminating descriptions of the vast donor cash machine that is rewriting the national political landscape in the wake of the Supreme Court's *Citizens United* case allowing unlimited corporate contributions as political free speech.

Fink tells this story (as he did to *The Wichita Eagle*) as the creation of a grassroots movement in response to events on the ground in 2009—not as a systematic, deliberate effort to remake one of the nation's two political parties. In Fink's story, he, Charles Koch, and David Koch met in the corporate headquarters of Koch Industries in January 2009, right after Barack Obama was inaugurated as president. They didn't like the direction the country was going, Fink said. They didn't like Obama, or what he was proposing to do to revive the moribund national economy.

Just as the American Liberty League in 1934 was funded largely by the DuPont family and their corporate allies to oppose FDR's New Deal reforms (the league formally dissolved in 1940), Fink said that they needed to use funding from corporate and donor networks to fuel a grassroots political opposition to Obama's presidency, and that it needed to start that spring of 2009.

"If we are going to do this, we should do it right or not at all," Fink told the two *Wichita Eagle* reporters. "But if we don't do it right or if we don't do it at all, we will be insignificant and we will just waste a lot of time and I would rather play golf. And if we do it right, then it is going to be very ugly."[1]

It's a nice story. It's also the best form of propaganda because it puts the Kochs' decades-long efforts to take control of the Republican Party in the best possible light with a story that everyone can instantly understand. The Kochs didn't like the direction Obama was taking the country, so they decided to climb into the arena and fight.

The truth is that the Koch donor network systematically constructed the scaffolding of the Tea Party movement as much as two years earlier than the spring of 2009—the elements of which only emerged years later as IRS tax forms became public. And that framework built on years of deliberate, systematic funding of corporate front groups in the states and Washington, DC, to oppose federal regulations from the Environmental Protection Agency that threatened Koch Industries' business practices, or to oppose the Food and Drug Administration's efforts to regulate the tobacco industry, which threatened the Koch network's longtime corporate front group partners at Philip Morris and the other major tobacco companies. The tobacco industry documents make clear that the Tea Party movement was, put quite simply, a step-by-step effort to protect the Kochs' own corporate interests and those of their partners.

"If we're wrong, we'd obviously be doing damage," Fink told *The Wichita Eagle.* "But we're absolutely convinced we're doing the right thing, based on the knowledge that we have. We realize we may be wrong. But you have to maximize the use of resources you have to achieve those results you want. That's what we're trying to do."

What's also true, and important to understand, is that Fink and the Kochs have worked hard to refine how corporate front group efforts—on behalf of big oil and tobacco companies—can influence the political and regulatory landscape.

What internal tobacco industry documents at the University of California, San Francisco's Legacy Tobacco Documents Library reveal, for instance, is how Fink created a political grassroots network to do corporate America's bidding—especially for the tobacco industry. This library is a digital archive of more than 14 million tobacco industry internal documents produced during litigation between forty-six US states and the seven major tobacco industry organizations.

In a letter to members of Congress on September 28, 1985, after the creation of Citizens for a Sound Economy and after Ron Paul had become its chairman, Fink weighed in on the federal tobacco program as CSE's first president. The big tobacco companies were just starting to engage in a protracted war with Congress over where and how they could buy tobacco.

At the time, all of the big tobacco companies were seeking to buy their tobacco much more cheaply from farming operations outside the United States—a move that the tobacco farming cooperatives in key presidential swing states such as Kentucky and South Carolina were fighting. Fink sided with the tobacco executives in favor of making it much easier for big tobacco companies to avoid tariffs and quotas that would drive up the price of tobacco imports.

"On behalf of the 220,000 members of Citizens for a Sound Economy, I urge you to consider the heavy costs of the U.S. tobacco program," Fink wrote to the members of Congress. "Any way you look at it, consumers and taxpayers ultimately foot the bill for this special-interest meddling in agriculture. The tobacco program is as protectionist as any tariff or quota directed at foreign producers. And its effects are the same. Consumers pay higher prices than they would have if the government had not intervened on behalf of a privileged few."

The "privileged few" Fink refers to are the handful of big tobacco-farming operations in several states that commanded high prices—propped up by the federal tobacco program price controls—and held considerable political power in those states. Fink made CSE stand with the executives of Philip Morris, RJR, and other big tobacco companies who wanted to buy tobacco from foreign producers more cheaply.

This tension would grow over time—and eventually separate the domestic US tobacco growers politically from the big-tobacco-industry executives. When the FDA declared jurisdiction over the tobacco industry a decade later, the tobacco growers in the United States generally sided with the public health community efforts to support FDA regulation because such regulation was in their best interest. Fink and CSE continued to use their growing grassroots political network to do the bidding of the big-tobacco-company executives and not the actual grassroots farmers—a framework established at CSE's inception for directing grassroots political efforts to do the direct bidding of corporate interests.

"The American people should be left free to, first, decide if they want to smoke, and, second, buy tobacco from whomever they choose at the market-set price," Fink wrote in 1985 on CSE's and the tobacco industry's behalf. Fink and CSE chose to ignore the growing public health and medical evidence that nicotine was addictive, and that young people were highly susceptible to the huge marketing campaigns waged by the big tobacco companies. Studies were starting to show, for instance, that nicotine addiction can begin in an adolescent brain after just ten or so cigarettes, which explains why tobacco companies had given away free ten-packs of cigarettes in places frequented by teenagers.

Several years later, Fink and CSE were still waging a steady campaign on behalf of the tobacco industry. By 1988, Dr. C. Everett Koop—the most prominent surgeon general in American history, who had courageously issued a landmark report on the harms posed by cigarette smoking, against the wishes of aides in President Reagan's White House—had elevated the public discourse around the tobacco industry's marketing and political practices to an unprecedented level in Washington, DC. Dr. Koop was then one of the most recognized people in the country by virtue of his very public stances on cigarette smoking. Fink and CSE took on Dr. Koop's efforts to use trade mechanisms to slow cigarette sales abroad.

On February 15, 1988, Fink, as president of CSE, which now claimed 250,000 grassroots members, wrote Dr. Koop, "I would like to express concern about the Interagency Committee on Smoking and Health's current inquiries into the subject of tobacco and U.S. trade policy. Government policies toward smoking are highly controversial, and they excite strong emotions among smokers and non-smokers alike."

As hundreds of internal tobacco industry documents would later show as they emerged in court documents now archived at UCSF, manufacturing doubt about the science of the harms of tobacco smoking and rallying strong emotions through media were key, central strategies of Philip Morris, RJR, and the other big companies. They used the Tobacco Institute to orchestrate and manufacture this doubt and emotion by funneling payments through law firms to scientists willing to publicly express doubt about the science of cigarette smoking and public health concerns.

In his letter to Dr. Koop, Fink also delivered another hammer blow about government intervention: "Precisely because of the divisiveness of the issue, both at home and abroad, we believe it would be a mistake to subordinate market-opening trade policy initiatives to a desire to export social policy to other countries." The CSE effort on behalf of the tobacco industry was part of a highly coordinated (and largely successful) effort to influence other senior Reagan administration officials to thwart Dr. Koop's effort to slow sales of cigarettes not only for foreign trade but also through educating American consumers about the risks of smoking. Two days after Fink's letter to Dr. Koop, the president of the Tobacco Institute, Samuel Chilcote Jr., praised the efforts of groups such as CSE to successfully blunt the efforts of Dr. Koop, according to an internal memo from Chilcote to the members of the institute's executive committee.

"As forecast at the Executive Committee meeting last week, the U.S. Trade Representative has successfully protested Dr. Koop's agenda for tomorrow's meeting of the Interagency Committee on Smoking and Health," Chilcote wrote in the internal memo. "We are encouraging pro-tobacco trade witnesses to attend the meeting and to be prepared to speak up." Chilcote included a list of key organizations, such as CSE, that were willing to stand with the tobacco industry in the effort.

Six days after this, on February 23, 1988, Chilcote wrote to Fink, "Please accept my thanks on behalf of the tobacco industry for your excellent letter . . . to Dr. Koop. We are grateful for [your support] on this issue and we especially appreciate the help rendered by you and members of your trade staff."

Later that year, on November 16, Fink testified before the National Economic Commission, which was considering a report on a number of economic, regulatory, and tax reforms. Fink had already started to refine the concept of fighting cigarette excise taxes on behalf of the tobacco industry by elevating the issue to a greater antitax fight that shielded the oil and tobacco industries from specific scrutiny. Fink also tweaked the story so that CSE wasn't funded by corporate donations from the tobacco industry or large donations from Charles and David Koch, but by small contributions from concerned citizens and taxpayers.

"Our members—250,000 individual Americans from every state and congressional district in the nation—contribute small amounts each year to fund CSE's activities," Fink testified. "In spite of their limited resources, our members are making sacrifices to promote sound economic policies in Washington. Their trust is something we take very seriously."

While there is a kernel of truth in this—there were certainly small contributions from individual Americans to CSE—the majority of its funds were from the Kochs and, later, the tobacco companies, as IRS and tobacco industry documents would show. But the creation of the grassroots myth was an important part of the corporate front group framework, and it was on full display in this testimony.

"CSE believes that the American citizen's voice has been little heard and much less heeded in the Washington debate over solutions to the deficit dilemma," Fink testified. "Inside the beltway, we hear continual talk about the necessity and inevitability of further tax increases. But outside the beltway, taxpayers are demanding that the federal government live within its means."

All of this dovetailed neatly with efforts being ginned up that year by RJR and Philip Morris in separate campaigns—and which would be fully realized by the spring of the following year—to organize smokers in grassroots campaigns to fight cigarette excise taxes by demanding smaller governments, fewer regulations, and spending restraints.

Fink and CSE were on the front end of those efforts and working hand in hand with the tobacco industry as it shaped the emerging strategies to fight taxes and regulatory burdens through grander-sounding freedom and citizen movements, internal tobacco industry documents show. But the corporate front group campaigns were just in their infancy at that time and would take shape in the next presidential administration.

7

☆ ☆ ☆

Why David Koch Never Loses

D avid Koch is competitive—maybe more so, even, than his older brother Charles, according to those who have worked with him over the years. He doesn't like to lose. This may stem, in part, from his earlier days as a basketball player at MIT, where he averaged 21 points a game (a school record) and held the single-game scoring record of 41 points until it was finally broken in 2009. He was so competitive that he told his twin, Bill—who sat on the bench at MIT while David starred on the court—never to compete with him . . . because Bill would lose. David Koch literally wore out his knees at MIT and "played basketball when you could be white and be good," he told *New York* magazine.[1]

But David Koch is also concerned, at least in part, about his public image. He learned from the public relations experts at Philip Morris, who mastered the highly nuanced practice of philanthropic funding to arts and medical centers to buy influence and credibility in places up and down the East Coast, say others who have watched his unexpected (and quite large) donations at iconic and well-known medical or cultural institutions ranging from Memorial Sloan Kettering, an integrative cancer center at MIT, and New York–Presbyterian Hospital to Lincoln Center, the American

Museum of Natural History, and the Smithsonian's National Museum of Natural History.

"A long-time philanthropist, Mr. Koch has given generously to a variety of organizations and programs," his philanthropic Web site reads. "In his lifetime, he and the David H. Koch Charitable Foundation have pledged or contributed more than $1 billion to cancer research, medical centers, educational institutions, arts and cultural institutions, and to assist public policy organizations."[2]

His Smithsonian gift of $35 million was the largest in the museum's century-old history. "I was just dazzled by the dinosaurs" after serving on the Smithsonian museum board for five years, he told the Associated Press.[3] Quite curiously, while much of the Koch-sponsored grassroots network bases its political activism on a rejection of established science, his philanthropic gift established the evolution and human-origins wing of the Smithsonian museum, while his gifts to leading medical institutions likewise help advance leading-edge medical science endeavors. "I have eclectic interests," he told the AP. "I give away a very large fraction of my income to support these worthy institutions, and I'm trying to help in the most important ways that I can to make the world a better place."

Friends and colleagues say he isn't all that focused on the political ma-chine that he and his older brother have built over the past two decades— that a near-death experience in an airplane crash has led him to look for meaningful philanthropic efforts instead. On February 1, 1991, USAir Flight 1349, while landing at LAX, collided with a SkyWest commuter plane that was taking off on the same runway, killing over thirty people. "This may sound odd, but I felt this experience was very spiritual," he said. "That I was saved when all those others died. I felt that the good Lord spared my life for a purpose. And, since then, I've been busy doing all the good works I can think of."[4]

His friends have described him in a handful of profiles as a modest, self-less, guileless philanthropist who is genuinely surprised when the spotlight swings in his direction and who was deeply troubled when White House aides criticized Koch Industries' central role in anti-Obamacare Tea Party rallies across the country. He has denied any role in Tea Party movement efforts, past or present. "I've never been to a Tea Party event. No one representing the Tea Party has ever even approached me," he said in the *New York* magazine profile. "The radical press is coming after me and Charles. They're using us as whipping boys."

Yet David Koch helped to found Americans for Prosperity Foundation, which organizes the Tea Party rallies. Also, David Koch told editor Brian Doherty of *Reason* that the Koch family has tight ideological control over the organizations they fund. "If we're going to give a lot of money, we'll make darn sure they spend it in a way that goes along with our intent. And if they make a wrong turn and start doing things we don't agree with, we withdraw funding."[5]

But while he may deny knowing much about how the Tea Party came to be—or even his own role in that effort—he strongly identifies with it. "It demonstrates a powerful visceral hostility in the body politic against the massive increase in government power, the massive efforts to socialize this country, which goes against the conservative grain of the average American," he's said.[6]

The closest he's ever come to publicly acknowledging his own, central role in the long rise of the Tea Party movement was during a speech in October 2009 to thousands of attendees at a convention hosted by the Americans for Prosperity Foundation he and his brother created and chaired. Independent filmmaker Taki Oldham filmed David Koch[7] as he presided over the convention, where the AFP California chapter described how they'd organized huge "tea parties" across the state, including ten thousand on the steps of the state capitol, and AFP chapter presidents in Michigan, Georgia, Oklahoma, and Maryland described how they'd organized dozens of other antitax and anti-government-control protests, including the largest single Tea Party Tax Day in the nation.

"This is remarkable—eight hundred thousand activists since we founded this organization five years ago [in 2004, five years before the so-called birth of the Tea Party movement]," David Koch said from the podium. "When we founded this organization five years ago, we envisioned a mass movement, a state-based one, but national in scope, of hundreds of thousands of American citizens from all walks of life, standing up and fighting for the economic freedoms that have made our nation the most prosperous society in history. Thankfully, the stirrings from California to Virginia, and from Texas to Michigan, show that more and more of our fellow citizens are beginning to see the same truths as we do."

8

☆ ☆ ☆

Tobacco Documents Trail

In 2013, a leading tobacco-control academic researcher, Stan Glantz from UCSF, and two postdocs, Amanda Fallin and Rachel Grana, produced a groundbreaking piece of scholarly work on the origins of the Tea Party movement and its deep roots in the tobacco industry's astroturf playbook. Using internal memos from the Legacy Tobacco Documents Library archive at UCSF, they traced the Tea Party themes from tobacco, oil, and corporate antitax groups to the present.[1]

"I was studying all of these Web sites for e-cigarettes, and I noticed that they all had this [Tea Party–styled] right-wing imagery behind it—don't take my guns away, for instance, behind a woman talking about e-cigarettes. She was a Tea Party advocate and a radio host, and I just thought it was quite interesting that they were promoting both the Tea Party and e-cigarettes," Grana told me.

"I saw another Tea Party leader . . . in another tobacco industry front group," she added. "And then I read that Philip Morris had given millions of dollars to Americans for Prosperity and FreedomWorks, and their predecessor, Citizens for a Sound Economy. So I put Citizens for a Sound Economy into the tobacco documents [in the Legacy archive at UCSF] and

I got thousands of hits. They'd gotten lots and lots of tobacco industry funding for years."

Fallin said she saw similar threads in her own tobacco work in the states. "I was doing work . . . in Kentucky on clean-air indoor-pollution laws, and there was always lots and lots of Tea Party opposition—lots of Tea Party groups coming in to oppose the clean-air laws. So I [wanted] to see if there was a link between tobacco funding and the Tea Party . . . which, it turned out, there was."

"The Tea Party did not come out of nowhere as a spontaneous reaction to Obamacare," Glantz told me. "These documents . . . explode the fundamental tenets of the Tea Party myth. You look at how the Tea Party is described in all of the mainstream media coverage, and it's still portrayed as this spontaneous grassroots uprising in 2009—and it's just not true."

Glantz, Fallin, and Grana published their work in a peer-reviewed, scholarly publication, *Tobacco Control,* and the research article didn't pull any punches, though it wasn't covered by the mainstream news media writing about Tea Party efforts to disrupt traditional GOP politics. In fact, the researchers said, it mostly reverberated inside the Tea Party ranks, threatened by its findings and conclusions. There it set off a firestorm—largely because they laid out in considerable detail how the tobacco industry's efforts to "quarterback behind the scenes" through fake citizen front groups over the years culminated in the Tea Party's supposed "virgin birth" in the spring of 2009.

"As of 2012, Americans for Prosperity [was] supporting the tobacco companies' political agenda by mobilizing local Tea Party opposition to tobacco taxes and smoke-free laws," wrote Fallin, Grana, and Glantz. "This support for the tobacco companies' agenda continues the tobacco industry use of AFP and [its] predecessor organization, Citizens for a Sound Economy, as a third-party ally since at least 1991.

"Starting in the 1980s, major US tobacco companies attempted to manufacture an astro-turf citizen smokers' rights movement to oppose local tobacco control policies. These . . . groups had grassroots membership in several localities, but were created, coordinated, and funded by the cigarette companies. Although the Tea Party is widely considered to have started in 2009, [this paper] presents a historical study of some of the tobacco companies' early activities and key players in the evolution of the Tea Party. Many people in the smokers' rights effort or the tobacco companies went on to Tea Party organizations."

Shortly after the research paper was published in 2013, factions of the Tea Party went ballistic in the blogosphere, while national groups in DC triggered a National Institutes of Health inspectors general's investigation of the study's funding from the National Cancer Institute, the researchers told me. The *Tobacco Control* paper was attacked by Tea Party movement leaders, who feared it would undermine their credibility as a populist, spontaneous, grassroots movement (rather than the clear result of long-standing corporate front group tactics shored up by tobacco and oil-industry interests).

"The Tea Party people went completely berserk right after our research paper came out . . . because we blew up their creation myth. That's what they were so upset about," Glantz told me. "The Tea Party people clearly saw the threat from our research paper and started beating up NIH. They forced an IG effort. In the end, the IG said there was no 'there' there. Nobody ever denied any of the facts in our paper. They were just trying to attack us, as sources of the information."

Rather than being a purely grassroots movement that spontaneously developed in 2009 after Barack Obama was elected, the researchers wrote, the Tea Party has, in fact, developed over time through decades of work and "boots on the ground"—a systematic and joint creation of the Kochs, the tobacco industry, and other corporate interests—by using antitax and antigovernment themes and front groups to do the bidding of their respective industries.

"The tobacco companies have refined their astro-turf tactics since at least the 1980s and leveraged their resources to support and sustain a network of organizations that have developed into some of the Tea Party organizations of 2012," they concluded in their paper. "In many ways, the Tea Party of the late 2000s has become the 'movement' envisioned by Tim Hyde, RJR director of national field operations in the 1990s, which was grounded in patriotic values of 'freedom' and 'choice' to change how people see the role of 'government' and 'big business' in their lives, particularly with regard to taxes and regulation."

The long-standing connection between the tobacco industry, the Tea Party movement, and corporate antitax front groups and associated organizations finally perfected the movement in 2009—a progression that few had chronicled, the paper concluded. Significant parts of academia, led by a hub at the Mercatus Center that has now spread to nearly three hundred American universities, had also been co-opted.

"We [found] that Koch Industries and its offshoots, the various related foundations, and Rich Fink did create various academic centers to propagate their theories," Grana told me. "You can see some of that funding and support in these documents."

By the end of their research efforts, they said, the roots of the Tea Party were obvious. The origins, methods, and principles behind the long rise of the Tea Party were hiding in plain sight.

"One of the most interesting things we found was that, every time we read another memo about CSE, we found another player who showed up later in the Tea Party movement," Grana told me. "We just started seeing so much overlap. So we just triangulated it with present day, and present-day searches. What we were able to do was find everything in those historical documents . . . and connect it to everything that you can find publicly available today for the Tea Party groups."

Glantz told me he hopes the public catches on to the truth behind the Tea Party efforts. "People [need to] see the broader patterns here. These connections really do transcend the tobacco story right up until today. There are just huge implications. People really need to see how all of these pieces fit together. You have to understand that this is the way the tobacco industry operates . . . to undermine effective government regulation of their activity.

And these models have been spread, basically, into just any sort of corporate interest—where science is related to public health or regulatory efforts—as a way to discredit the government.

"The Tea Party leadership's political agenda, and political positions, are actually discordant with what the people they're mobilizing actually think. That's cynical beyond words," he added. "You look at this and say, 'Oh my God, this is all too involved and too complicated,' which is of course something that was designed on purpose. It was designed to be obscure, and convoluted, and hard for people to penetrate. But you can also just look at a simple chart, and you see tobacco at the top, the Tea Party at the bottom, and CSE in the middle."

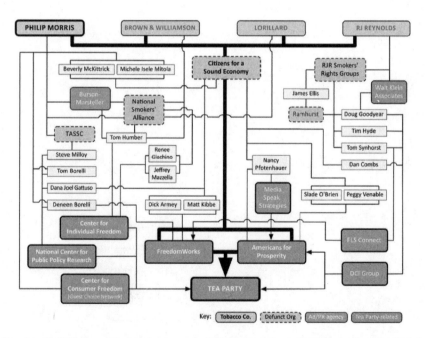

Graphic © 2013 from the academic study "'To Quarterback Behind the Scenes, Third-Party Efforts': The Tobacco Industry and the Tea Party," by Amanda Fallin, Rachel Grana, Stanton A. Glantz, *Tobacco Control*, TC Online First, February 20, 2013, doi:10.1136/tobaccocontrol-2012-050815, http://tobaccocontrol.bmj.com/content/early /2013/02/20/tobaccocontrol-2012-050815.full.pdf+html. Used by permission of Stanton A. Glantz.

9

☆ ☆ ☆

COFIRE

When Ronald Reagan submitted his final budget to Congress before leaving the White House in January 1989, he didn't travel to Capitol Hill for a series of high-level meetings with members of Congress. He presented it instead at a White House briefing to the alliance of manufacturing, trade, and antitax citizen groups called the Coalition for Fiscal Restraint (COFIRE), which had helped establish the baseline "no new taxes" pledge inside the Republican Party.

"You know, actually, I could tell this was a very supportive group when I walked into the room," Reagan said on January 9, 1989, according to papers from his presidential library. "Someone in the back of the room began to chant, 'Two more weeks! Two more weeks!' But it's not over yet, and there's still work to be done. And I figure if I'm going to do some, it's now or never.

"Today I submit to Congress my final budget. And I want to thank all of you for your support, both on this budget, as members and friends of Coalition for Fiscal Restraint, and so many of you for your help over the years. By taking the pledge against any tax hike and fighting to control spending, you put the national interest first, and you put the 'iron triangle' in its place. The country needs more people like you in Washington."

Reagan's days in the political sun of Washington, DC, were ending. George H. W. Bush, his vice president, had been elected president, and all of the political media attention was focused on Bush's rise to power. No one paid much attention to Reagan's final budget address to COFIRE at the White House, which is hardly surprising. After all, few national political reporters in those days paid much attention to the ways in which big corporations handled coalition and grassroots political lobbying. The workings of such coalitions—alliances of political groups formed to pursue a common goal or oppose a common foe—were, by and large, a mystery to the media.

But they should have paid closer attention. To track where the Kochs have placed their considerable financial resources in their long, deliberate journey to remake the Republican Party in their image, all any observer needs to do is simply follow the arc of Rich Fink's career. As Reagan was ending his career and Bush starting his presidency, Fink left his position as president of the Citizens for a Sound Economy. He quietly moved over to run Koch Industries' government relations office in Washington as its executive vice president, lending behind-the-scenes assistance to anything that was of top-tier importance to the Kochs. Rich Fink has repeated this pattern his entire career as Charles and David Koch's principal government-relations, public-affairs, and political adviser.

In Reagan's second term, COFIRE, as the architect of the GOP's anti-tax center, rose to brief prominence. However, it faded quickly in the first two years of Bush's administration. It was one of two coalitions that Koch Industries and Charles and David Koch funded and supported during the Reagan and Bush years—but is the only political coalition that Koch Industries has ever publically put its name to. COFIRE's chairman, Mike Monroney—the son of a former Democratic US senator from Oklahoma—was also a senior adviser to CSE at the time he chaired COFIRE. And one of the key financial and named corporate partners of COFIRE during the Reagan years was Philip Morris.

The outline of how and why Rich Fink, head of the Koch political network, worked with Philip Morris on COFIRE is on display in a May 6, 1987, letter from Roger Ream at Citizens for a Sound Economy to Fred Panzer at the Tobacco Institute. In the letter, which was a follow-up to a meeting between another longtime Koch network operative, Wayne Gable (who chairs the Kochs' Freedom Partners today), and the Tobacco Institute, Ream outlined the logical ways in which Philip Morris and CSE could work together through COFIRE:

"CSE chaired several important coalitions in 1986 and held leadership positions in many others. CSE will press ahead with legislative programs to help improve American competitiveness and reduce the burden of taxes, government spending, and regulation of the U.S. economy." Ream concluded with a pitch for tobacco industry support because Fink had recently been appointed to two presidential commissions and advisory councils.

In January of 1989, though Reagan was leaving the White House within weeks, his senior staff had nevertheless submitted a final budget to Congress that hewed closely to the philosophical and political centerpiece of his presidency—a commitment to cutting taxes as a way to spur a growing economy.

"The reason no new taxes are needed is because our strong and growing economy will in the next fiscal year produce an additional eighty-four billion dollars in tax revenues without any increase in tax rates," Reagan told COFIRE in his address at the White House. "Thanks to our record expansion, the money is literally rolling in. Those who want to tax away even more hard-earned dollars from working people ought to be ashamed of themselves.

"The bottom line is that our budget protects the working families of America, provides adequate support for those who depend on government, maintains our national defense, reduces the deficit by nearly seventy billion dollars, and does not raise taxes.

"Moreover, it places America on track to a balanced budget and even a modest surplus by fiscal year 1993. With America now in its seventh-fourth month of economic growth, I am proud to say this budget will help assure our nation's prosperity in the years to come. It's been a long and hard fight, but it sure has been a rewarding one—until you read what others say about it."

Reagan also took dead aim at his critics who had battled him for years over taxes and regulation. "The usual crowd is calling for higher taxes. Never mind that federal revenues are higher than ever before. Never mind that they're growing at a healthy clip. Never mind that raising taxes would be the surest way to kill the economic goose that lays the golden eggs. Never mind the sorry record of new revenues being used not for deficit reduction but for even higher spending. Never mind the facts: the big-government crowd wants more taxes.

"They also want more spending and more federal regulation. Basically what they really want is to repeal the last eight years and repudiate last November's presidential election. They want to deny the economic triumph the American people have achieved, ignore the will of the people clearly expressed at the polls, and tax away even more of the people's money.

"And their plan for doing this is to give the American people a fiscal sob story: that revenue is scarce here in Washington and there isn't enough money to go around. Well, if people buy that story, it will be the greatest flimflam job I've seen since the movie *The Sting*."

It was vintage Reagan. It hardly mattered at this stage of his presidency whether any of it was even remotely true—his principal legacy of cutting taxes for the largest corporations in America so that their wealth could be transferred to the people was, by now, firmly established. It was a bedrock principle of the Republican Party and created and managed behind the scenes by Koch Industries and Philip Morris through COFIRE.

Before COFIRE faded in the middle of President Bush's only term in office, the coalition did its best to hold the line against any new taxes—a pledge that worked perfectly to cover all political fights against any form of tax, whether a tax on crude oil exports or imports at the heart of Koch Industries' business or excise taxes on a pack of cigarettes at the heart of Philip Morris's business.

In a signed opinion piece to the *Christian Science Monitor* in December 1990,[1] Monroney (identified as both a senior adviser to CSE and as chairman of COFIRE) railed against a new federal budget deal agreed to by Congress and President Bush that would raise taxes, violating the "read my lips" pledge that Bush had made during his presidential campaign.

Earlier that year, acting as COFIRE's chairman, Monroney had tried with no success to convince the White House not to sign on to a massive tax increase plan circulating in Congress.

"We have strongly supported your pledge not to raise taxes on grounds that, like you, we are concerned that increasing taxes would have an adverse [effect] on continued economic growth," Monroney wrote to President Bush on behalf of COFIRE. "We are equally concerned about the burden which continuing large federal deficits [place] on future generations, and we are convinced that revenues generated by increased taxation will not be used to reduce these deficits. We urge you to stand firm in the current budget negotiations for deficit reduction through restraints on the growth of federal spending and, for reasons stated above, to resist all pressures for new or increased taxation."

But Bush didn't heed the warning from COFIRE and other corporate groups in Washington and signed on to the tax deal.

Monroney sent up the distress signal in his *Christian Science Monitor* piece: "It is one thing to hope fervently that the recent federal budget agreement will reduce the deficit and spur our sluggish economy. It is quite another to expect this to happen. Within a year or two, when it becomes apparent that federal deficits have continued to spiral upward, it will also be apparent that this agreement is only yet another example of Washington's appalling inability to manage the nation's fiscal affairs.

"This agreement includes a tax increase of $164 billion, the biggest in American history, and at a time when the economy is already wavering on the brink of a recession. This package will not reduce the deficit. Deficits will continue to mushroom unchecked, and to label the agreement a 'deficit reduction' package is to perpetrate yet another hoax on the American public."

The shot across the bow from Monroney, as COFIRE's chairman and chief spokesman for the coalition created by Koch Industries and Philip Morris to hold the line on taxes, should have been heeded by Bush's political advisers. It wasn't. The Bush White House was consumed with successfully prosecuting the Gulf War and wasn't paying much attention to domestic affairs. It badly miscalculated how political coalitions such as COFIRE would react to Bush's decision to renege on his no-new-taxes pledge. Monroney said as much in his piece:

"The most important obligation for decision-makers in Washington is to retain public confidence in their ability to govern responsibly and to report honestly on their decisions. Sadly, that confidence can only be further eroded when the consequences of the recent budget agreement are realized.

"The truth is that it represents another flagrant example of false hopes, the result of which should cause sleepless nights for every young American who will bear the ultimate burden of interest payments on the growing national debt.

"Want to know who is to blame? Quite simply, apart from a confused electorate which has difficulty in singling out who's at fault, it's those in Congress who can't resist the temptation to tax and spend, and a president, preoccupied with Saddam Hussein, who missed a golden opportunity to set them straight."

COFIRE would fade from the scene shortly after this. Philip Morris pulled its financial support when it became obvious that Bush wasn't responding to COFIRE the way that Reagan had. Philip Morris then quietly moved its financial backing to a second corporate coalition that the Kochs' CSE was likewise moving toward.

But COFIRE's brief moment in the political sun is an important footnote in history. It is the first, and only, time that Koch Industries came out from behind its usual bewildering array of corporate front groups to publically support a coalition. It also defined a political line in the sand that Bush stepped across—and paid the price for when his reneging on his no-new-taxes pledge contributed to his defeat when seeking reelection.

10

☆ ☆ ☆

Enough Is Enough

In the spring of 1987, Waterford Township in Minnesota banned smoking on public property. It was part of a growing trend in America against secondhand smoke, with dozens and eventually hundreds of towns similarly voting to ban smoking in public spaces.

Waterford Township was small, with less than five hundred residents at the time. Thirty of its citizens voted for the outdoor-smoking ban. No-smoking signs were put up in the park near city hall, as well as the parking lot and a roadside park nearby.

The next day, tipped off by antismoking activist groups, national news media started to show up to cover the story about the outdoor-smoking ban in Waterford Township. All of the big tobacco companies noticed as well, and a new campaign concept emerged.

The Tobacco Institute used the fight in the small Minnesota town to develop a new media and grassroots model to stem the growing awareness of the harms of smoking and secondhand smoke. In a lengthy campaign document in the Legacy Tobacco Documents Library, the Tobacco Institute and the two major tobacco companies funding it, Philip Morris and RJR, began to create an elaborate, national campaign that would be waged in every state in the country around the theme Enough is Enough.

The new Enough is Enough campaign found one citizen in Waterford Township who was willing to publicly protest the public smoking ban in front of the assembled TV crews. "That's when people started to get fed up and the supervisors started to hear from people who didn't attend the annual meeting," said one news report, quoted at the start of the Tobacco Institute's elaborate campaign document. "Two dozen residents told the supervisors that the ban was an unwarranted invasion of privacy."

The tobacco companies searched for and found sympathetic voices. A town board chairman complained about this "unwarranted invasion of privacy." A sympathetic TV crew filmed the Waterford Township board's reversal of its earlier ban on public smoking two months later, which the Tobacco Institute campaign then magnified as the beginning of a revolution against government regulation of essential freedoms.

"Just another episode of small-town democracy?" the Tobacco Institute asked in its internal industry-campaign document. "Perhaps. But the episode also is symptomatic of where the nation has come with a growing national obsession against smoking—a pastime that is chosen by one-third of American adults and that predates America itself. A ban on smoking out of doors?"

The tobacco industry had clearly decided that its survival was at stake with the public smoking bans and launched a highly orchestrated campaign to invoke the right to freedom and antigovernment themes everywhere the antismoking slogans appeared.

The Enough is Enough campaign also was created to identify those who would fight taxes and regulation of the industry under the banner of personal freedom. An internal Tobacco Institute document reveals that the tobacco industry was interested in "breeding a nation of informers" who would take on anyone challenging the right to smoke. "Most threatening of all in the excesses of the anti-smoking movement is the erosion of personal freedoms," the document said.

When the city of San Diego began to debate whether smoking should be banned throughout Jack Murphy Stadium during San Diego Padres baseball games and San Diego Chargers football games, the tobacco companies' campaign held it up as an example that those who opposed secondhand smoking had gone too far.

"Today smokers are forced to deal with harassment and other excesses from a vocal minority. In their adamant refusal to accept even reasonable accommodation, anti-smoking extremists are leading society down dangerous paths. Smokers and fair-minded nonsmokers alike are saying 'Enough is enough!' We've reached the limit."

The genius of the Tobacco Institute campaign was that it draped the effort to shield the tobacco industry from taxes and regulation under freedom and flag banners. "The single-minded focus on smoking has come at the expense of addressing important public issues and threatens key Constitutional and other rights," the Tobacco Institute said. Regressive taxes were being imposed. First Amendment rights were being abridged. Unions were not being allowed to negotiate the right to smoke in the workplace. Cities weren't regulating "dirty office air" because they were focused instead on getting rid of secondhand smoking. It was propaganda at its very best.

The Enough is Enough campaign became the defining effort of the tobacco industry for the next five years, culminating in a massive national effort in 1993 to block the efforts of President Bill Clinton and First Lady Hillary Clinton to use a national cigarette excise tax as the centerpiece of a huge public health-care reform effort.

The tobacco industry tested its campaign themes time and again during those years. The first big push after Waterford was in California in 1988—to defeat antismoking Prop 99. Philip Morris and RJR created Californians Against Unfair Tax Increases (CAUTI), which combined orchestrated citizen protests with a massive TV advertising blitz against the ballot proposition, for instance. The themes of those California TV ads would become the propaganda centerpiece of the Enough is Enough citizen protest and media campaign for years to come.

So who were the architects of the Tobacco Institute's and tobacco giants' Enough is Enough campaign, which began in 1987 and continued to grow until taking full prominence during the 1988 presidential campaign and into the early Clinton years? The Tobacco Institute's campaign document doesn't name any authors, but other tobacco industry documents provide the clues needed to solve the equation.

According to the documents, the media architect of the tobacco industry's Enough is Enough campaign was future Fox News Channel chairman Roger Ailes, who made millions from the campaign in those years.

The themes are evident in the 1988 CAUTI TV ads created by Ailes Communications. Prop 99, an initiative by the Coalition for a Healthy America, proposed a cigarette tax of twenty-five cents a pack to pay for increased health care benefits. In an ad simply called "America," produced by Ailes's firm, the camera scrolls across pristine outdoor vistas and closes on the Statue of Liberty while an orchestra sound track plays "America the Beautiful" in the background. "In America, we are free to be ourselves," intones the somber voice of the narrator. "We don't punish people for things we don't like, or beliefs we don't share. In America, we believe in freedom and fairness."

A second CAUTI ad from Ailes's firm is even more direct, using the political construct of the conservative, angry white man objecting to infringement on his personal freedoms that Bush campaign operatives used effectively in key swing states. The ad, called "Fighting Words," uses a white, older man sitting at a crowded bar, railing against infringements on his freedoms.

"Do you think for yourself, or do you like people telling you what to do?" asks the man. "I know I have the right to make my own decisions. Have you heard about Proposition Ninety-Nine? That's the one that's going to triple the tax on cigarettes. I don't even smoke. This is a freedom issue." The man jabs the bar counter forcefully. "Proposition Ninety-Nine was designed by one group to punish others and keep the money for themselves. In America, we just don't do that. And when they start fooling around with my freedom, well, those are fighting words."

Another unexpected voice rose to prominence at this time. While he wasn't directly involved in the tobacco-tax fights alongside Ailes and CSE, Rush Limbaugh also rode the coattails of this campaign. While Ailes Communications was creating the Enough is Enough campaign for the tobacco giants and CSE was helping execute it with orchestrated citizen protests, Limbaugh was coming into his own as a media personality. Using millions of dollars of promotional money from tobacco companies, Ailes converted Limbaugh into a TV performer and became executive producer of his late-night show while the Enough is Enough campaign was spreading across the country.[1] By 1993, according to the tobacco industry campaign documents, Enough is Enough had become the centerpiece of the tobacco industry efforts to stop taxes and regulations through a freedom campaign fought in citizen and TV media efforts in states.

As Hillary Clinton's efforts to implement public health care reform became the biggest issue in the first term of her husband's presidency, the Enough is Enough campaign became perhaps the most prominent effort to thwart it in state after state.

In 1992, Roger Ailes very publicly said that he was done with politics. He has maintained this stance for years. In 2001, he submitted biographical materials (under oath) as part of a House hearing into election-night coverage and said unequivocally that he had retired from anything political in 1992. A profile of Ailes in *Rolling Stone* also repeated this claim: "In 1992, Ailes retired completely from political and corporate consulting to return full-time to television."[2]

This inconsistency only became apparent once the tobacco industry documents emerged years later. In 1993, Ailes, in fact, ran the entire Enough is Enough media and grassroots citizen campaign being waged against Mrs. Clinton's health care reform effort, according to a lengthy internal memo in the tobacco archives. Documents in the archives also name the Kochs' Citizens for a Sound Economy as the lead grassroots group orchestrating the citizen protests in the states against "Hillarycare," as it was dubbed by her opponents in the media.

Ailes and CSE worked side by side with Philip Morris and RJR senior officials to orchestrate the appearance of a grassroots uprising against Hillarycare, the campaign document shows. In a September 1993 internal memo from Scott Ehrlich to senior communications officials at Philip Morris, called "Enough is Enough Campaign Update," the Ailes communications firm lays out its efforts to fight Hillarycare:

"The mailing to the 1,500+ state level taxpayer groups is just being completed and will go out in Thursday's mail. It includes reprints of the ad and other ammunition for the upcoming fight." Ailes was also coordinating between Philip Morris and RJR. "My understanding is that RJR will be going out with a direct mail piece following the Clinton speech."

Another internal tobacco industry memo from the spring of 1993 contains a "PM/RJR contact sheet," which lists Roger Ailes as the head of the Enough is Enough campaign along with top officials from the two tobacco giants. In fact, the strategy document lists the senior-most communications officials from Philip Morris and RJR working closely with Ailes on the campaign at the heart of their joint Tobacco Task Force. The memo also lists the central groups waging the Enough is Enough campaign on behalf of the tobacco industry. It includes the internal industry employees, the Tobacco Institute, and CSE.

Roger Ailes's efforts on behalf of the tobacco giants are largely unreported in biographical media coverage of the controversial and combative Fox News chief. But a few have picked up on the threads. "In a precursor to the modern Tea Party, Ailes conspired with the tobacco companies to unleash angry phone calls on Congress—cold-calling smokers and patching them through to the switchboards on Capitol Hill—and to gin up the appearance of a grassroots uprising, busing 17,000 tobacco employees to the White House for a mass demonstration," said the *Rolling Stone* profile.

"But Ailes' most important contribution to the covert campaign involved his new specialty: right-wing media. The tobacco giants hired Ailes, in part, because he had just brought Rush Limbaugh to the small screen, serving as executive producer of Rush's syndicated, late-night TV show. Now they wanted Ailes to get Limbaugh onboard to crush health care reform. 'RJR has trained 200 people to call in to shows,' a March 1993 memo revealed. 'A packet has gone to Limbaugh. We need to brief Ailes,'" the piece said.

What the 1993 internal tobacco industry documents show quite clearly is that Ailes and CSE developed their media themes and citizen-protest structure during the period they successfully derailed Hillarycare in President Clinton's first term. Ailes' "Fighting Words" and "America" media buys in California led up to the presidential election. Enough is Enough, begun in 1988 as a protest against bans on public smoking, morphed into a larger campaign during the early Clinton years, designed to shield efforts to fight cigarette taxes behind a flag-waving freedom campaign.

11

☆ ☆ ☆

Allied Forces

Midway through President George H. W. Bush's only term in the White House—with the "morning in America" glory years of the Reagan presidency fading with each passing day—R.J. Reynolds Tobacco Company's Tommy Griscom and Tim Hyde began to look for a grand, unifying theme capable of creating a mass political movement that could serve their rather unique corporate needs.

Money wasn't an obstacle. RJR had more than enough money to pay for multiple, expensive public relations campaigns and grassroots mobilization efforts. Government-affairs, public-relations, and top-tier law firms on K Street in Washington, DC, were always lined up, willing to take the considerable sums of money that both RJR and Philip Morris consistently showered on the city to protect the tax, regulatory, and legal interests of the tobacco industry.

Passion, focus, and unifying themes were the problem. The Bush presidency had largely ignored every single important domestic issue as it prosecuted the Gulf War. Bush, a former CIA director and foreign policy expert, had virtually no interest or even stomach for the political blood sport of domestic politics in America.

While Bush surrounded himself with holdovers from the Reagan era, the best architects of the grand themes of the Reagan White House—such as Tommy Griscom, who had been Reagan's communications director—had cashed in for K Street partnerships and firms or lucrative senior positions with Fortune 500 corporate firms with deep, vested interests in DC politics.

Griscom, who had also once worked for Rupert Murdoch's News Ltd., was known in political circles for his willingness to cut against the grain and go against conventional political wisdom. As Reagan's communications director in 1987, for instance, Griscom had fought the State Department and the White House diplomatic corps for perhaps the most famous speech of Reagan's presidency—his speech at the Berlin Wall, where he demanded that Soviet leader Mikhail Gorbachev "tear down this wall."

I got to know Griscom (and came to greatly admire and appreciate his considerable talents) during my own years of fighting for FDA jurisdiction over the tobacco industry and for the marketing and regulatory victories that the public health community was able to win over the years. Griscom is a shrewd, brilliant political communications strategist who chose, for whatever reasons, to use those talents to protect the beleaguered tobacco industry after leaving the White House.

In the fall of 1990 Griscom was RJR's executive vice president for external relations and was charged with forging a new grassroots media and political campaign that could defend RJR and the tobacco industry from the growing number of legal, public relations, and regulatory challenges it was facing.

During this time, for instance, I first proposed to my boss, FDA commissioner David Kessler, the novel idea that the federal agency declare jurisdiction over cigarettes and join the public health fight. Secondhand-smoke campaigns were starting to take root in cities and offices. Scientists were becoming better at exposing the merchants of doubt who'd long confused the American public about the addictiveness and dangers of smoking.

In this charged atmosphere Griscom asked his senior team to come up with a plan to turn the political winds. Griscom wanted a new way to rally people around the flag, freedom, and patriotism—as Reagan had often done during his presidency—that simultaneously defended the core corporate interests of the biggest oil, tobacco, automotive, and chemical industries, which were constantly under siege from consumer and public health advocates.

Tim Hyde—who served as Griscom's top lieutenant as the senior director of public issues at RJR and would later manage political field operations for the Dole/Kemp presidential campaign in 1996 and cofound the DCI Group in Washington—delivered to Griscom one of the great, tour-de-force campaign memos about a new political paradigm that would come to define the state of the art for corporate front groups for years to come.

The single-spaced, seven-page memo to Griscom was titled "Coalitions" and became public more than a decade later in the wake of the tobacco industry's Master Settlement Agreement. This agreement, reached in November 1998 between the state attorneys of forty-six states, five US territories, the District of Columbia, and the largest tobacco companies in America, set standards for the advertising, marketing, and promotion of tobacco products. It also required the tobacco industry to pay the settling states approximately $206 billion over the first twenty-five years.[1] Hyde's memo would ultimately encompass nearly every aspect of the RJR effort to change the way in which politics operated at both the grassroots level and top tier in America and Washington.

"You asked for my thoughts on how we might build broad coalitions around the issue-cluster of freedom, choice, and privacy; and what organizations, interests and groups might be engaged in such coalitions," Hyde wrote. "First of all, I think coalition-building should proceed along two tracks: a) a grassroots, organizational and largely local track; b) and a national, intellectual track within the DC-New York corridor. Ultimately, we are talking about a 'movement,' a national effort to change the way people think about government's (and big business') role in our lives. Any such effort requires an intellectual foundation—a set of theoretical and ideological arguments on its behalf."

Both Griscom and Hyde (who had also once run the Republican Party in Iowa, the most important primary state in presidential politics) knew what the political system in Washington responded to, what prompted it to react when it was threatened or prodded. What they needed was a new, carefully orchestrated movement that would challenge Washington institutions on behalf of the tobacco industry, under the guise of defending freedom and bemoaning big-government solutions.

"The Reagan revolution didn't happen on election night in 1980, but began in 1960 with Reagan's Republican Convention speech," Hyde wrote. "This movement slowly gained credibility in the 60s and 70s as think tanks and journals in DC began to argue and persuade the rest of us of the perniciousness of high taxes, etc. They provided the intellectual underpinnings for what was happening politically out in America. Simultaneously, these ideas were fermenting at the grassroots level as groups, organizations, and individuals struggled on behalf of candidates who embodied them."

But the Reagan Revolution—twenty years in the making—was no longer the defining political infrastructure of the Bush era. The Republican Party had lost its direction, after clawing its way back from the political wilderness, Griscom and Hyde both felt. Simply fighting for tax cuts was no longer enough. They needed something more, something different, that would be the start of a new political movement, while also serving RJR's and the tobacco industry's needs. And this new movement, like the Reagan Revolution, might take every bit as long to bring to power—but it had to start, they felt, and RJR, with its considerable financial resources, was a natural engine of that change.

"There is, I believe, considerable sentiment in the conservative community to redefine or at least broaden the word 'choice,'" Hyde wrote. "Many conservatives believe that 'choice' is the fundamental concept—the core—of their cause, and thus feel outfoxed that it has been taken over by the abortion rights folks. I think there is already a strong predisposition on the part of many conservatives to agree with us on our issues, though one that hasn't been very well articulated yet."

Hyde believed that the tobacco industry's core ideas that needed defending, along with those of aligned corporate interests such as Koch Industries and the oil, chemical, and automotive industry giants, could dovetail nearly perfectly with this new concept of freedom and choice.

"In terms of grassroots coalitions, there are a plethora of groups, clubs organizations and interests across America . . . that have the following similarities: they are local or state-based; they are small and generally disorganized; they rarely agree with or work with each other across issues or time (indeed, they frequently spend as much time fighting each other as they do their common enemy); [and] when they rarely coalesce, it is around a particular candidate in a particular campaign."

In this chaos, Hyde and Griscom both saw, was the possibility of a new movement that could organize these disparate groups, centered around a new concept of freedom and "choice" that would serve the right corporate interests.

"Coalition-building in political campaigns, if done right, is a rigorous but straight-forward process," Hyde wrote. RJR should set about building a new coalition around this concept of a new movement. At its center would be groups such as the Kochs' Citizens for a Sound Economy and others that were already formed and willing to work with them. Hyde then proposed that they inventory the entire grassroots political landscape and identify the most likely allies and partners.

Hyde started his inventory list with the "gun guys" who could be swung to the new movement with the right incentives. "We always think of the NRA as the lone source of pressure on gun control issues," he wrote. "The NRA is effective, national, and monolithic, but there are a multitude of other groups in this category, some of them statewide and some of them local. Most localities are rich in rod and gun clubs, shooting ranges, '1789' groups, and so on. Though many of them are not overtly political, they are allied with the NRA on specific issues and candidates, and they all hate government telling them what to do."

Hyde then ticked off other potential allies—the "Evangelicals," union-busting groups, existing PACs (political-action committees) such as Newt

Gingrich's GOPAC, and think tanks such as the Manhattan Institute that could create the necessary intellectual framework behind the movement. But he wrapped up his inventory wish list with the most important target— "taxpayers' organizations," such as the Kochs' CSE and Grover Norquist's Americans for Tax Reform, that were already somewhat engaged on the state level and could be co-opted easily for the fights against state excise taxes on packs of cigarettes. "Most states have some sort of . . . ideological anti-tax group, and they should be [an important] part of our allies' kit," Hyde wrote.

RJR's existing field operations and smokers' alliances, Hyde concluded, could dovetail nicely with a new effort to organize other like-minded groups around patriotic, freedom, and personal-choice themes. "All of this, in my view, should be part of an 'Allied Forces' program, a program that includes not only our traditional allies—employees, growers, suppliers, and the like— but the broad range of economic and ideological confederates." Hyde's RJR field operations staff had already begun to plan how to use its grassroots muscle to "execute Allied Forces" objectives. "Now it is time to add details and timelines to the plan, communicate it to the field, and begin executing," Hyde told his boss.

Hyde and Griscom got their wish and began to implement their plan for an Allied Forces campaign successor to the twenty-year Reagan Revolution. According to other internal tobacco industry memos, they were quickly joined by their fiercest industry rival, Philip Morris, which was coming to nearly identical conclusions about the need for such a new political movement that rallied disparate groups and organizations to their cause.

12

CART

Burson-Marsteller is a global public relations company with more than a hundred wholly owned and affiliate offices in ninety-eight countries. It was the largest public relations firm in the world throughout the 1990s. By the end of that decade, its annual fees were just shy of $300 million a year.

Its Washington, DC, office was a curious place in the 1990s. While all of its corporate public relations accounts were run from one floor, a second office one floor below managed the business, actually driving a significant portion of its revenue. That floor managed the National Smokers Alliance for Philip Morris—an unprecedented effort to mobilize millions of smokers behind the various political and grassroots campaigns that the tobacco giant deployed against state excise taxes, public-smoking bans, Hillarycare, and the FDA's push to regulate cigarettes.

Philip Morris and the leadership of the National Smokers Alliance knew perfectly well that its grassroots network was manipulated for corporate ends. It was not, in any sense, a real grassroots campaign. This highly orchestrated network could be called upon to deliver phone calls, visits, letters, and people with specific agendas to events as needed.

Even the internal memos among their senior leadership (all made public more than a decade later as part of the tobacco industry's Master Settlement Agreement and revealing what went on behind the scenes) describing the activities and reach of the National Smokers Alliance always put the word *activists* in quotes. A good portion of the "activists" were, in fact, their own employees or contractors. The rest tended to be smokers who received discounts and free paraphernalia as a reward for joining NSA.

The National Smokers Alliance was a bit of a shell game, but it was also highly lucrative for Burson-Marsteller—a key account that contributed to its position as the largest PR firm in the world. Those who worked in the DC office didn't speak of it much, according to those who worked in the Burson offices during the 1990s. They tended to refer to it as "the other floor." The NSA operated independently of the rest of the business.

But while its "activists" may not have been real grassroots activists in the usual sense of the word that most people understand, it was nevertheless highly effective. At any given time, the National Smokers Alliance was capable of delivering up to 2 million live people to various political efforts. And, in the early years of the Clinton presidency, Philip Morris needed every single one of those "activists" in their effort to fight a war on multiple fronts in Washington, DC.

"It is certainly no understatement to say that it is open season on the tobacco industry in Washington," the head of Philip Morris's DC office, Kathleen Linehan, told Philip Morris's board of directors in the spring of 1994, when a variety of challenges to the tobacco industry were all presenting themselves, according to an internal memo on her presentation. "For the industry to be so seriously challenged, on so many fronts, is unprecedented. We must contend with an overtly hostile Administration, a frenetic media, powerful Congressional opponents, and a highly sophisticated anti-tobacco lobby. And, there is no question that the legislative, regulatory and media piling on is well orchestrated. It is within this atmosphere that we must also deal with the tobacco excise tax as a financing source for [President Clinton's] health care plan."

What Philip Morris needed desperately in the early years of the Clinton presidency was allies who could defend its interests—without seeming to be tobacco activists. RJR was searching for much the same thing, and the two tobacco giants eventually joined forces under a Tobacco Task Force umbrella that worked together to defeat Hillarycare by coordinating their activities through the firms and groups they funded in DC. Enough is Enough had proved so successful in the fight against Hillarycare that it jumped over to become the centerpiece of the DC-based Coalition Against Regressive Taxation (CART), which was beginning to wake from its humble beginnings to become a force to be reckoned with in Washington.

CART was "formed in March 1986 to oppose excise tax and tariff increases proposed as part of tax reform" and had among its "participating firms" the American Petroleum Institute, Philip Morris, RJR, and the Tobacco Institute, says the Legacy archive. It was heavily funded by the tobacco industry and partially managed by the Kochs' Citizens for a Sound Economy, but it included a broad array of other ideological groups and businesses.

CART was a nearly perfect corporate front group for Koch Industries and the tobacco industry at the time. It could mobilize letters, phone calls, and people from a variety of businesses—as well as sponsor expensive paid media—without ever appearing to be serving just Koch Industries or the tobacco industry. Nevertheless, that was mostly what CART did, and had done, since its creation during Reagan's second term.

A letter from the president of the Tobacco Institute, Samuel Chilcote, to his executive committee in the spring of 1986, for instance, describes the phenomenal success of a full-page ad in *The Washington Post, The New York Times,* and fifty of the largest newspapers in nearly every state in the United States that delivered a sharp and direct message to members of Congress thinking about voting for an excise tax on cigarettes: "Act Now or Pay Later." It was a massive, expensive advertising campaign, and somewhat unprecedented at the time. It was also effective.

The president of CART was a largely unknown executive from a small trade group. Thomas Donohue was both the president of CART and the CEO of the American Trucking Associations during the Reagan, Bush, and Clinton administrations. Donohue learned how to perfect the art of successful corporate grassroots campaigning through CART before leaving both organizations to become the CEO of the US Chamber of Commerce, which he now runs.

Donohue, as the head of CART, could always be relied upon to weigh in against virtually any sort of tax or regulation threatening a prominent industry—though CART most often worked on behalf of the tobacco industry or those issues that a company such as Koch Industries had chosen to oppose. CART, in fact, represented nearly all of the businesses in the United States (such as tobacco, oil, and beer companies) that paid the bulk of federal excise taxes. What CART became quite good at doing was blocking cigarette and fuel taxes under a much broader antitax agenda.

"On behalf of [CART], I am writing to ask that you oppose any amendments to the Omnibus drug bill which would increase excise taxes on tobacco, alcoholic beverages or fuels," Donohue wrote to Senator John Danforth (R-MO) in the fall of 1988. "There is no justification or precedent for making one group of taxpayers finance government activity that affects everyone."

Earlier that year, Donohue had also successfully mobilized the CART members to oppose any tax revenue increases that were under consideration by a prominent blue-ribbon commission considering ways to reduce the federal budget deficit. "We are united in our opposition to increases in excise taxes as a means to reduce the deficit, whether these taxes go into general revenue, existing trust funds, or some type of 'deficit reduction trust fund,'" Donohue testified before the National Economic Commission. "Opposition to excise tax increases is broadly and soundly based."

Against this backdrop in the spring of 1992 Gary Auxier—the talented executive vice president and chief operating officer of the DC office of Burson-Marsteller—proposed a visionary new campaign to deal with myriad challenges facing the tobacco industry at the end of the Bush administration. Auxier would eventually create the National Smokers Alliance and run it from Burson-Marsteller's DC office, before "leaving" the public relations firm to become NSA's vice president.

"Thank you for inviting Burson-Marsteller to submit a strategic proposal to the Coalition Against Regressive Taxation (CART)," Auxier wrote on April 6, 1992, to John Doyle, who was at the time the media relations director for Tom Donohue at the American Trucking Associations while also managing outreach coordination for CART. "We welcome the opportunity to bring our resources to bear against the growing charade among lawmakers who would cast themselves in the popular 'no new taxes' vein while supporting or even initiating 'hidden' taxes that erode consumer spending power and business profitability."

Auxier proposed to CART a first-ever media and grassroots campaign to combine efforts—similar to the Allied Forces concept that was under review by Tommy Griscom and Tim Hyde at RJR—and use groups such as CSE to take a much harder ideological position on taxes and government regulations than corporate America was used to taking.

"One area we would like to explore with CART, as a program evolves from the strategic proposal, is the idea of a much stronger, much harder-edged approach to accountability for individual lawmakers who attempt to subvert the tax issue," Auxier wrote to CART's leadership. "Our experience with broad-based coalitions has been that a consensus for such direct action is difficult to achieve."

What Auxier was saying politely was that corporate America had never been good at threatening politicians, of either party. Corporate lobbyists tended to play both sides of the street, while more ideological groups could work much more aggressively on just one political party. CART, Auxier suggested, could use ideological groups like CSE to do its bidding—without corporate fingerprints.

What Auxier then laid out in his proposal to CART was the framework for what, in today's world, would look remarkably and undeniably like the Tea Party movement:

"Rather than fight a particular tax or group of taxes, the central concern of [CART] is the growing trend of shifting taxes from traditional and straightforward sources of revenue to hidden sources, initiated by lawmakers who want to claim they won't raise taxes. While CART's existing resources are formidable, there is opportunity to identify and mobilize previously unused or unrecognized allies to build these resources into an even more effective political machine."

CART could take advantage of both the presidential election cycle and efforts to manufacture anger over taxes and government that would directly benefit CART's members, Auxier said. "Current anti-tax, anti-government anger can be tapped to support anti-excise tax efforts. The national election cycle provides the best opportunity to educate candidates and the electorate and to begin the process of holding candidates accountable for their positions and records on excise taxes."

What Auxier proposed was new to the political landscape. First, he said, they needed to exploit that the American public was oblivious of the "impact of hidden taxes on their lives" by convening new polls identifying this threat and widely publicizing them through both paid and earned media (publicity gained through promotional and media relations efforts other than paid advertising). Once properly educated by what would essentially be a propaganda blitz, he said, they would react in anger over the hidden taxes. "Burson-Marsteller would then create a turnkey campaign manual for CART members, arming them with a combination of a 'Regressivity Bible' and tactical actions that would help them mount awareness/accountability campaigns in targeted districts."

The next phase of the campaign was what would permanently alter the political landscape in a way that had never before been tested.

Auxier recommended "mounting a guerilla campaign . . . focused on the presidential candidates. Using the resources provided by state and local member affiliates and their employees, we would use our expertise in grassroots mobilization and experience in campaigning to create highly visible activity at three key campaign appearances for each of the two major party candidates."

But the campaign needed a grand theme, Auxier believed. Propaganda was only good and useful if it motivated lots of people around universal themes that were not immediately identified as a means to protect oil, tobacco, or manufacturing interests.

"Grounded in the theme of 'The New American Tax Revolution' or 'The New Boston Tea Party,' the campaign activity should take the form of citizens representing the widest constituency base mobilized with signage and other attention-drawing accoutrements such as lapel buttons, handouts, petitions and even costumes," he wrote. "Events would be selected for maximum leverage [on Congress]. Our media relations specialists would provide support before, during and after the events to extend message delivery."

CART would, in effect, unify a new Tea Party movement around anger at taxes and government, drawing in the widest possible array of groups. It would "recruit allies from among such interest group categories as aging, competitiveness, consumer, local and state government, minority, recreation and tourism and women's business," Auxier wrote. "The independence of these allies is their greatest strength, but building the relationship now creates the option of later recruitment."

Auxier knew that this concept of a "New Boston Tea Party" already resonated with senior officials at Philip Morris, one of the key financial backers of CART—a theme that would continue to grow over the next several years.

Philip Morris Magazine, the nation's first major magazine for smokers, debuted in July 1985 and had been mailed free to about 150,000 people interested in the company's views. One magazine issue Philip Morris added to its tobacco document archive in 1999 featured the concept of a "Tea Party–Boston Style." A special "PM Notebook" section pulled together various Tea Party–styled themes and messages such as "The most famous excise tax protest in American history took place on the chilly night of December 16, 1773" and included an original graphic of protesters quietly dumping tea overboard. "To avoid identification, some disguised themselves as Indians; others blackened their faces with coal dust, or shadowed their features with wide-brimmed hats. Many had pistols stuck in their belts. Almost all of them carried hatchets."

All of the themes that Auxier laid out in his Tea Party memo to CART were deployed within the year—first against the BTU tax in President Clinton's initial budget submission to Congress (the campaign was almost exclusively driven and funded by Koch Industries through Citizens for a Sound Economy), and then in a broad-based effort to attack the cigarette excise tax increase initially at the heart of the Clinton health care reform effort.

A snapshot of the *Freedom Trail* newsletter from the spring of 1993 of the smokers' rights coalition that Philip Morris funded and Burson-Marsteller managed for them featured a similar theme as a way to fight excise taxes. "New Englanders don't like unfair taxes—remember the Boston Tea Party?—and they're fighting mad over proposals in Washington to raise the federal tax on cigarettes. In Maine, Rhode Island, New Hampshire, and Vermont, smokers and others concerned about tax fairness have taken up the gauntlet thrown down by those in Congress and the administration who think that smokers ought to be forced to pay for public programs benefiting everyone."

The newsletter included dozens of examples of ways in which the National Smokers Alliance, managed by Burson-Marsteller (and a concurrent smokers alliance run by RJR), were working closely with antitax groups such as CSE to fight Washington, DC.

The lead item in an internal memo from David Nicoli, who ran Philip Morris's government relations efforts in Washington, DC, to CEO Michael Miles, detailing the tobacco giant's political and grassroots campaign priorities that year, makes it clear exactly who was now leading the effort to whip up popular antitax sentiment against Hillarycare:

"To fight Clinton's proposed 75 cents per pack excise tax increase, we are also working behind the scenes to oppose the Clinton package as a whole. The House Energy and Commerce Committee will be a key battleground over the Clinton health care plan, and we are giving $400,000 to Citizens for a Sound Economy—a free market based grassroots organization—to run a grassroots program aimed at 'swing' Democrats on the Committee. We also will be supporting efforts of anti-tax groups in selected districts of Energy and Commerce 'swing' Democrats to carry the message to the grassroots that a vote for the Clinton health plan is a vote for massive tax increases."

A sweeping plan in an internal memo at Philip Morris called simply "Tobacco Strategy" also explains CSE's important role in that strategy. "We are funding a major . . . grassroots initiative (through CSE) in the districts of House Energy and Commerce members to educate and mobilize consumers, through town hall meetings, radio and print ads, direct mail, patch-through calls to the Capitol switchboard, editorial board visits, polling data, meetings with Members and staff and the release of studies and educational pieces.

"The goal of this effort is to show the Clinton plan as a government-run health care system replete with higher taxes and government spending, massive job losses, less choice, rationing of care and extensive bureaucracies. CSE is taking aim at the heart of the plan—employer mandates, new entitlements, price controls, mandatory health alliances, heavy load of new taxes and global budgets—and, with the program well underway, is by all accounts getting rave reviews in the respective districts."

As a number of internal memos from that year show, Philip Morris had a difficult balancing act with certain members of that committee, where the Clinton health care reform plan would likely rise or fall in a contest of wills between Representatives John Dingell (D-MI) and Henry Waxman (D-CA). Philip Morris supported a number of the "swing" Democrats on the committee through financial campaign donations, and it needed a surrogate to attack them without PM's fingerprints. The Kochs' CSE provided the perfect cover for that effort—a ploy that proved immensely successful and helped stall and eventually kill the entire health care reform effort as CSE and a second surrogate, Grover Norquist's Americans for Tax Reform, launched a series of grassroots attacks in these congressional districts.

A second internal memo from David Nicoli to senior Philip Morris officials on August 2, 1993, also ties the CSE efforts to Roger Ailes's Enough is Enough campaign: "Due to significant political changes since the Presidential election, Roger Ailes' original strategy of targeting an anti-excise tax campaign in 'marginal' Clinton states from last year's election should be modified."

Nicoli added that Ailes had orchestrated the Enough is Enough campaign against Clinton during the presidential campaign, and that work had largely succeeded in making it nearly impossible for even moderate Democrats to keep voting for tax increases.

"We believe that these difficult votes could portend a true reluctance by members to vote for another tax increase," Nicoli wrote. "The expected passage of the President's budget package, with its heavy reliance on taxes has put moderate and conservative Senate and House Democrats in a precarious political situation. Although a significant number of Democrats have bucked the White House, some of those who have not are in real trouble back home. As a result, we see opportunities to expand our base of tobacco state members. Executing an anti-excise tax ad campaign in states and districts . . . would keep the 'anti-tax' pressure on those who have already responded to such pressures in the budget and would intensify pressure on those under scrutiny back home."

Nicoli was prescient, and right. The 1994 midterm elections would sweep Democrats out of power in the House of Representatives for the first time in a generation, ushering in Newt Gingrich as Speaker of the House.

But it would be years before the true nature of the opposition—its Tea Party–styled efforts funded by Koch Industries, Philip Morris, and the tobacco industry—were known. An abstract from Laura Tesler, PhD, and Ruth Malone, PhD, RN, in the *American Journal of Public Health* in July 2010, as the debate over Obamacare was just beginning, is a good example.[1] The public health journal study—"'Our Reach Is Wide by Any Corporate Standard': How the Tobacco Industry Helped Defeat the Clinton Health Plan and Why It Matters Now"—explores the way in which the tobacco industry's Tea Party–styled campaign derailed the Clinton health care plan, and how it could happen again with the Obama plan.

"We explore how the two biggest U.S. tobacco companies, Philip Morris and RJ Reynolds, and their now-defunct trade association, the Tobacco Institute, worked together to mobilize right-leaning think tanks and smokers' rights, labor, and left-leaning public policy groups to help defeat the Clinton plan," the abstract said.

"Through a coordinated, nationwide initiative, the industry helped persuade policy makers that considerable public opposition existed to both a funding mechanism—a tobacco excise tax increase—and the plan as a whole. This case [study] offers lessons for the current health care debate, highlighting the importance of funding transparency for interpreting activities of think tanks, advocacy groups, and 'grassroots' movements and the need for advocacy organizations to consider how accepting corporate donations may compromise their agendas."

The public health researchers drew a straight-line parallel from the successful efforts to kill Hillarycare to the tactics being used against Obamacare more than a decade later.

"As occurred with the Clinton plan, numerous opposing coalitions and 'grassroots' groups have appeared" to attack the Obama health care reform effort, the public health researchers wrote. "Patients United Now and Patients First were created by Americans for Prosperity, formerly Citizens for a Sound Economy, the single largest recipient of Philip Morris funding to generate opposition to the Clinton plan. These and other groups have deployed similar tactics, including organizing protests at town hall meetings and hanging a Congress member in effigy, just as an SRG[2] burned an effigy of Hillary Clinton."

Toward the end of President Clinton's first term, CART began to fade just as COFIRE had outlived its usefulness at the end of Reagan's time in office. The CART juggernaut, though, made Donohue a star in Washington political circles. Donohue used CART's opposition to the Clinton health care plan to team up with a then relatively unknown member of the House of Representatives, John Boehner, to organize the big-business community in DC. When the US Chamber of Commerce publicly supported Hillarycare, Boehner used that action to rally a coalition of House GOP members in opposition. It was his first big step on the way to becoming Speaker of the House years later.

Donohue, meanwhile, used CART's efforts to become the US Chamber of Commerce's president and CEO midway through Clinton's term in office. The Chamber's annual budget was just $3 million a year when Donohue became its CEO. Donohue used CART's tobacco/oil political coalition model to grow the Chamber. As a result, by 2000 the Chamber's annual budget had grown to $55 million a year—a nearly twentyfold increase that included $35 million for its core operations and another $20 million a year for "special projects," according to *The Wall Street Journal*. Donohue, and his House ally, John Boehner, had perfected the path of the corporate front group that CART had pioneered.

And Philip Morris was now all-in with its new grassroots political paradigm and willing to spend a vast sum of money each year on the National Smokers Alliance at the center of it. "Tom Humber [NSA's president, and a former senior vice president of Burson-Marsteller] tells me that the organization [now] has 1.3 million valid members," a Philip Morris executive wrote in a 1994 internal memo describing the rapid growth of the effort. "The organization's budget for 1994 is about $18 million, most of which is spent on administration associated with start-up. PM is paying the lion's share, with $1 million from B&W and about $500,000 in membership dues. Tom is seeking to take NSA's budget to $20 million in 1995 to continue building membership and counter increased taxes and smoking restrictions. Tom said he expects the budget to level at $15 million beginning in 1996."

Philip Morris was also now clearly enamored of the Boston Tea Party construct and its effectiveness as a campaign theme to characterize citizen protests against taxes. *The New York Times* reported in June 1994 that three thousand tobacco farmers mounted a "modern day Tea Party" by throwing bales of tobacco into the Kentucky River to protest the cigarette tax proposal in the Clinton health care plan.[3] The story made national news as a spontaneous outpouring of citizen anger at the Clinton health care proposal. *The Times,* as well as every other media story on the event, didn't mention who had organized the event or why.

But internal tobacco documents (which were not made available in a searchable database at UCSF's Legacy archive until late 2002 as a result of the Master Settlement Agreement) showed that one of Philip Morris's public relations' firms, a subsidiary of the Worldcom Group, had orchestrated the Boston Tea Party reenactment in Kentucky—and had big plans to keep using the Tea Party theme in future efforts.

In a memo to senior officials at Philip Morris in late 1995, the PR firm took credit for the Kentucky Tea Party protest against the Clinton health care plan and proposed that a sweeping Tea Party movement could be orchestrated to block the FDA's effort to regulate cigarettes. It proposed a Tea Party–styled campaign in six states that were considered key to President Clinton's reelection and where Philip Morris could similarly mobilize thousands of tobacco farmers to protest government taxes and regulation.

The Tea Party movement concept had also taken root at the highest levels of Philip Morris as well by then. "The government's plan to influence personal behavior through higher taxes is reminiscent of colonial times," Philip Morris CEO Miles wrote to shareholders at the time. The American people had responded in anger over unjust taxes back then, he concluded in his note, suggesting that such an uprising might again be justified in America.

The power of orchestrated anger against taxes and government regulation, within the framework of a Tea Party movement, clearly had staying

power. It worked. The real question was whether this new political paradigm, which had worked so well to derail the BTU tax and the cigarette
excise tax at the heart of Hillarycare and helped sweep the Democrats out
of power in the House of Representatives, could be extended and developed
further and essentially institutionalized within the Republican Party.

13

☆ ☆ ☆

Get Government off Our Back

When the Food and Drug Administration signaled its intent in February 1994 to regulate the tobacco industry by classifying nicotine as a drug—the idea that I had first proposed and then pursued relentlessly with my boss, FDA commissioner David Kessler—Tommy Griscom and Tim Hyde got busy with their plan inside RJR. It would become a key part of the Tobacco Strategy that merged the grassroots goals and political financing aims for both RJR and Philip Morris throughout the nineties.

"In a major policy reversal, the Food and Drug Administration Friday asserted its authority to classify nicotine as a drug—a move that could lead to regulating or even banning virtually all cigarettes. But the agency urged Congress to provide clear direction on what it should do," Ed Chen reported in the *Los Angeles Times* on February 26, 1994.[1]

"In a letter to anti-smoking advocates, FDA Commissioner David A. Kessler all but accused the tobacco industry of stoking a public addiction, citing 'accumulating' evidence that nicotine content in cigarettes is being manipulated for that very end—thus making cigarettes, in effect, a drug that falls under FDA jurisdiction," wrote Chen, who is now the director of federal communications for the Natural Resources Defense Council in Washington.

"If the agency eventually reached such a formal finding," Kessler noted, "it could have dramatic effects on our society. A strict application of these provisions could mean, ultimately, removal from the market of tobacco products containing nicotine at levels that cause or satisfy addiction." An FDA spokesman added, 'The real bottom line is: We and the Congress need to address this issue and determine whether or not we are to regulate cigarettes. Is this in fact what the public will is?' "

Internal memos released more than a decade later clearly show that senior officials at RJR, Philip Morris, and other major tobacco companies viewed Dr. Kessler's move—officially signaled in a letter to Scott Ballin, who coordinated a major public-health antismoking coalition from the DC offices of the American Heart Association—as a declaration of war against their industry. They began to pull out everything in their political grassroots, financial, and lobbying tool chest to block the move from the spring of 1994 onward, the documents show.

While Philip Morris was preoccupied with CART, the Kochs' Citizens for a Sound Economy, and Tom Donohue's efforts to rope other industries into the Tobacco Strategy in opposition to first the Clinton health care reform plan and then FDA jurisdiction over the tobacco industry, RJR deployed its own nationwide political grassroots strategy mapped out by Hyde and Griscom.

It was called Get Government Off Our Back, and it was a massive success by nearly every conceivable measure, two researchers at the University of California, San Francisco, Dorie Apollonio and Lisa Bero, reported in a detailed assessment of the effort in the *American Journal of Public Health* in the spring of 2007.[2]

That sort of careful assessment of the RJR political grassroots effort was only possible after the internal tobacco documents became available publicly a decade after the fact so that researchers could connect the dots among the various front groups that RJR funded and deployed as part of the effort. It had been too difficult to piece the puzzle together without the release of those 14 million internal tobacco industry documents.

"We investigate[d] how industries use front groups to combat public health measures by analyzing tobacco industry documents, contemporaneous media reports, journal articles, and press releases regarding 'Get Government Off Our Back,'" wrote Apollonio and Bero.

"RJ Reynolds created Get Government Off Our Back in 1994 to fight federal regulation of tobacco. By keeping its involvement secret, RJ Reynolds was able to draw public and legislative support and to avoid the tobacco industry reputation for misrepresenting evidence. The tobacco industry is not unique in its creation of such groups. Research on organizational background and funding could identify other industry front groups. Those who seek to establish measures to protect public health should be prepared to counter the argument that government should not regulate private behavior."

RJR's ability to defend itself was slowly being eroded in the face of widespread reporting of the harms of smoking, as well as revelations that the Tobacco Institute had used a half dozen major law firms to funnel funding to scientific researchers willing to confuse the public about the dangers of smoking. While RJR and Philip Morris would continue to coordinate fake science efforts through the Tobacco Institute (and with Steve Milloy's PR effort out of APCO Worldwide, the Advancement of Sound Science Coalition) to peddle doubt about the science of smoking, in truth they needed nontobacco allies—and a much bigger political platform built around freedom of choice and patriotic themes.

Because the tobacco industry had a history of intentionally misrepresenting scientific evidence as it tried to influence government regulation, while being linked to tens of thousands of smoking-related lung cancer deaths each year, its reputation had suffered.

"These factors have compromised the tobacco industry's reputation with the general public and made political association with its interests a liability," Apollonio and Bero wrote. "The creation of a seemingly independent organization advantaged the tobacco industry by presenting its anti-regulation agenda as an expression of popular will, and allowed industry lobbyists access to policymakers who were otherwise unwilling to work with them."

RJR's secretive, extensive political grassroots effort to build a network of angry people willing to yell about government tracked precisely along the strategies outlined in Tim Hyde's memo—including reach into seemingly disconnected communities ranging from homeless shelters to gay and lesbian activist groups upset about the national government's reaction to the AIDS epidemic.

"The tobacco industry recruits potential allies from all ideological backgrounds," the researchers wrote. "Frequently, these organizations are financially compensated in exchange for advocating on behalf of tobacco industry political goals."

A February 22, 1995, letter to a state legislator from the head of the Kansas chapter of Get Government Off Our Back is a good example of its reach. Its letterhead lists no less than twenty-nine separate organizations, from family values and justice groups to business and antitax nonprofits. It included the NRA's "CrimeStrike" unit, Traditional Values Coalition, Home School Legal Defense Association, U.S. Term Limits, American Legislative Exchange Council,[3] Competitive Enterprise Institute, and a host of others. RJ Reynolds' name was nowhere to be found on it though the company solely financed the coalition.

"For too long in American government, regulation has been a way of life," the letter read. "At the federal level alone, an average day last year saw over 200 pages of new regulations added to the Federal Register, and thousands more created at the state and local levels. Home and business owners have had to fight to use their property as they see fit, and the cost of unfunded federal mandates has nearly bankrupted many cities, counties and states. In short, government has grown out of control."

The letter then described the GGOOB effort as a "newly formed ad hoc coalition of individuals, businesses and grass roots organizations throughout America dedicated to bringing a fundamental shift to the priorities of government at all levels" and asked the state senator to join them on a rally on the steps of the capitol in Kansas.

Another campaign document, a backgrounder designed to answer questions about the nature of the coalition, reiterated GGOOB's goal of rolling back regulations at all levels—but did not mention that it was funded by just RJ Reynolds or that it had been formed for the narrow purpose of defending the tobacco industry. Instead, it said that citizens, small businesses, and civic groups had grown weary of "unwarranted government interference" and had spontaneously risen up to fight back. They were furious at Washington and wanted to send a message, it said. "If we don't stop this growth now, the American system could be in danger of collapsing under the weight of big government," it concluded.

Bear in mind that RJ Reynolds formed the political coalition and funded it in its entirety for the *primary* purpose of attacking the FDA tobacco rule (and, secondarily, an OSHA investigation around secondhand smoke). That was its real target. RJR created an entire antiregulation coalition, across dozens of groups in nearly every state in the country, to mask its true intent in attacking this one regulation that threatened its industry.

RJ Reynolds's extensive political grassroots effort was vastly different from other tobacco industry efforts. "Unlike the goals of other front groups exposed by tobacco industry document research, the goals of the front group created by RJ Reynolds in 1994, Get Government Off Our Back, were not overtly tobacco-related," Apollonio and Bero reported.

Broadening the focus to fighting governmental interference in general, rather than only on behalf of the tobacco industry, explained the GGOOB's enormous success in driving the early victories of Newt Gingrich's GOP takeover of the House and the anger against the national government in DC surrounding taxes, regulation, and spending.

RJR also benefited from the earlier successes of the Kochs' Citizens for a Sound Economy, COFIRE, and CART to successfully defeat the BTU tax and Clinton health care reform, it said. "Organizations learn from each other in part because they sometimes use the same legal or public relations firms to organize political activities, and RJ Reynolds's success with Get Government Off Our Back is consistent with the activities of other(s)."

Apollonio and Bero found more than three thousand internal tobacco industry documents detailing the activities of Get Government Off Our Back that related to efforts to attack FDA jurisdiction over the industry as well as the efforts of the federal Occupational Safety and Health Administration to define the harms of secondhand smoking in the workplace.

RJR started its campaign simply enough in the summer of 1994—as the midterm elections loomed and political analysts began to speculate whether the Republican Party might be able to take control of the House of Representatives—with a full-page advertisement in newspapers around the country that depicted a man standing in front of a pickup, looking out at the reader. "I'm one of America's forty-five million smokers. I'm not a moaner or whiner. But I'm getting fed up. I'd like to get government off my back."

The initial RJR newspaper ad said that the federal government meant to take away all of our personal liberties and freedoms. It wanted to take away cigarettes first. Guns, beer, fast food, and even buttermilk would be next.

That fall, the public relations firm Mongoven, Biscoe, and Duchin, which RJR had used to advocate pro-tobacco efforts around the country (including an effort to organize veterans groups to oppose the OSHA secondhand smoke rules), submitted a proposal called "Get Government Off Our Back" that was designed to further amplify the campaign. The PR firm (which subsequently merged with the corporate PR firm Stratfor of WikiLeaks infamy) launched the campaign but never identified RJR as the funder in any of its materials.

The Get Government Off Our Back political effort grew quickly as groups joined the coalition. Materials circulated by the PR firm said that the growing number of groups joining the coalition were part of a "grass roots movement responding to the belief of many Americans that our government, at all levels, is growing out of control."

The political coalition began to make demands of Washington, DC, many of which were incorporated into the Contract with America that Representatives Newt Gingrich (R-GA) and Richard Armey (R-TX) created that fall as a promise of reforms to come if the Republican Party took control of the House of Representatives. The Get Government Off Our Back coalition's central resolution demanded that elected officials "reduce the size of government and the number of needless regulations at all levels of government."

Initially, in 1994, the coalition was made up largely of tobacco growers and distributors. That changed in 1995, after the GOP seized control of the House. "The new 'sponsors' appeared to consist only of ideologically motivated groups who sought to limit government regulations, and the roster no longer mentioned organizations that had obvious tobacco connections," Apollonio and Bero wrote. "[It now] included groups such as the U.S. Chamber of Commerce and Citizens for a Sound Economy, as well as a range of property rights groups."

The researchers dissected some of the funding from the internal tobacco industry documents. "Citizens for a Sound Economy . . . received millions of dollars in contributions from the tobacco industry in the 1990s . . . which it used to fight FDA regulation independently as well as in concert with Get Government Off Our Back." The Kochs' CSE also used the tobacco funds in other ways, including for a CSE spin-off group called U.S. Term Limits.

The researchers never found any mention of the tobacco funding in any of the available public literature about the political coalition. How did GGOOB get started, according to its own Web site in 1995? The movement was portrayed as a spontaneous uprising of anger at government actions in Washington—much the way the later Tea Party movement appeared without seeming to be prompted or organized in 2009.

"Because of the growing number of cases of government waste and abuse nationwide, civic groups and other organizations have already been forming all over the country to respond to the problem," the PR firm wrote on behalf of the coalition on its Web site in a March 8, 1995, document now in the Legacy archive. "So the strength of this movement is, and will remain, at the grass roots level. It's only because the problem is becoming so prevalent that it is pushing its way into the national spotlight."

The effort to mask the tobacco industry's interests behind a broader ideological framing worked. "Get Government Off Our Back claimed that government should leave individuals and businesses to make their own accommodation, a position that drew extensive public support," Apollonio and Bero wrote. "Its apparent focus on a broad ideological issue deflected attention from its underlying tobacco industry agenda."

The coalition hit its stride in 1995, organizing antiregulation rallies in twelve states. State and federal lawmakers began to show up to speak at the rallies, never knowing that RJR was solely funding the effort or behind it. A groundswell of antiregulation petitions started to circulate. The central Get Government Off Our Back resolution demanding a moratorium on all federal regulations in Washington became the central focus of these efforts. The Contract with America from Gingrich and Armey incorporated the coalition's resolution into their work in DC.

In 1995, at the height of the Gingrich-Armey revolution, the House of Representatives passed a bill that froze new federal regulations and demanded that in the future no "unnecessary" federal regulations be allowed—an unprecedented action in the history of Congress. The legislative text of the ban on all federal regulations "matched the Get Government Off Our Back resolution nearly verbatim," Apollonio and Bero found. The antiregulatory provisions of the Contract with America were written by lobbyists from regulated industries, led by the tobacco industry and based on the political grassroots efforts by CSE and others.

The PR firm and RJR then accelerated their plans to organize "action corps" and "truth squad" media tours in the states through the coalition. Whenever possible, the internal tobacco industry documents showed, RJR chose to deploy allies from the coalition to do its bidding rather than its own lobbyists on issue after issue.

By the fall of 1995, the transformation was complete. Individuals affiliated with ideological organizations in the coalition signed op-eds written by RJR; forwarded RJR position papers widely under the coalition's name; and advocated against the FDA and OSHA regulations independent of the tobacco industry.

Like COFIRE and CART, the RJR political coalition eventually ran its course after several years once the threat of the FDA and OSHA regulations subsided and the agencies had been forced by Congress to scale back their ambitions somewhat in the face of political realities. The FDA tobacco rule, for instance, would lose 5–4 in the Supreme Court and only return years later to finally be put in place in the first year of President Obama's administration. But the legacy, impact, and implications are clear.

"Get Government Off Our Back was clearly a pure industry front group throughout its history; RJ Reynolds and a public relations firm were entirely responsible for its creation, organization, activities and maintenance," Apollonio and Bero concluded. "And although some individuals appear to have volunteered to join the group, many of the organizations involved were financially compensated for their participation."

Without question, the RJR effort had changed the political landscape. "RJ Reynolds's decision to create Get Government Off Our Back appears to have been an unqualified success. [It] drew popular support from the public and from legislators" and shielded the tobacco industry at a critical juncture in DC. "The history [of this coalition] suggests that policymakers, advocates, and the media should be cautious in accepting the claims of groups that purport to reflect popular disaffection, whether or not they appear to have an industry connection," the researchers concluded.

GGOOB succeeded because it promoted the tobacco industry's interests as part of a greater ideological fight—just as Tommy Griscom and Tim Hyde had intended—without anyone in the national media or elsewhere ever asking how an unknown organization could appear as if from nowhere to fund multiple rallies and events, widely publicize them, and make its agenda a top priority both for national advocacy groups and political Washington.

14

☆ ☆ ☆

The Tobacco Strategy

By the middle of the Clinton presidency, the Kochs' Citizens for a Sound Economy had consolidated its position as Philip Morris's preferred antitax front group willing to do the industry's bidding in every key state excise tax fight. According to dozens of internal tobacco documents, CSE would remain Philip Morris's principal ally in those antitax fights until its dissolution during 2003–4, when it became Americans for Prosperity.

CSE had consolidated its position as the tobacco industry's go-to group for a number of reasons. Rich Fink—Charles and David Koch's closest government and political adviser since the mid-1980s—had courted the industry and its funding for a decade alongside several of the other groups that the Kochs funded, with CSE foremost. CSE had committed both its organizational operations as well as partial funding from the Kochs in several key fights, including the BTU tax and the Clinton health care plan. And it had shown a willingness to lead broad-based industry coalitions, such as CO-FIRE, that allowed the tobacco industry to hide behind ideological fights.

And CSE was able to secure favored nation status with Philip Morris for a fourth reason. Two of its own senior staff migrated from CSE midway through the Clinton presidency to positions within Philip Morris.

Michele Isele Mitola was CSE's vice president for development and raised funding for its antitax, antiregulatory efforts in the states from Philip Morris and the tobacco industry overall. For instance, a July 1, 1996, memo from her to Pat Donoho, the senior vice president of the Tobacco Institute, thanked the tobacco company for providing funding to CSE so it could run a campaign in New Jersey. "Thank you for the good news" about the funding "for our work to promote market-based solutions to economic policy problems," she wrote.

What did Philip Morris secure with that CSE funding? "New Jersey CSE helped beat back another effort to raise cigarette taxes in 1996," according to a Web archive snapshot of New Jersey CSE's webpage. "Pitched as a solution to the very real woes of New Jersey's public school system, the cigarette tax would have been the wrong solution. We launched a campaign to defeat it, including an educational mailing, patch-thru phone calls and paid radio advertising." In other words, precisely the sort of antitax, antiregulatory campaign fieldwork that the Koch's Americans for Prosperity has deployed for years.

Isele Mitola left CSE to become Philip Morris's senior manager for issues management and public affairs, where she was responsible for managing the tobacco company's network of public affairs professionals and public relations firms in all fifty states. Part of her job was to deploy Philip Morris's Tobacco Strategy, with CSE as the preferred third-party ally of choice.

A second official, who had worked on telecommunications and legal reform issues at CSE, Beverly McKittrick, left to become the director of federal policy for Philip Morris, where she helped coordinate strategies around the complicated legal and regulatory issues facing the company and the industry overall. McKittrick, who has a law degree from Stanford, had previously worked for Senator Paul Laxalt (R-NV) and the Senate campaigns for political strategist Haley Barbour.

McKittrick led many of the internal discussions at Philip Morris about ways to respond to the threat of FDA and OSHA regulation, as well as looming legal challenges from states and the Department of Justice, according to internal tobacco industry documents. In an internal memo around a plan to deal with FDA dated October 2, 1995, for instance, McKittrick led the discussion inside Philip Morris that laid out their strategies and allies.

The long-term objective of their strategies was "to create [a] political environment where 'moderates' of both parties on the Hill can vote for legislation that divests FDA of any power to regulate tobacco because they are convinced that FDA is already [performing] miserably in accomplishing its 'core mission,'" she wrote. Philip Morris's long-term strategy, which they ultimately deployed, was to attack FDA relentlessly for failing to focus on drug approval—a theme that provided common cause with major pharmaceutical companies—as it pursued efforts to block the agency's regulatory jurisdiction over nicotine and cigarettes.

Meanwhile, McKittrick wrote, the company's short-term objective was to "quarterback, behind the scenes, third-party efforts to launch, publicize and execute a broad non-tobacco-based attack on the many failings of the FDA with respect to its currently authorized statutory activities."

Leading that charge under the heading of Third-Party Groups acting on their behalf was the Kochs' Citizens for a Sound Economy, she wrote, which would "monitor and help direct [the] multi-front action plan."

The strategy was to use seemingly disconnected third parties to attack the FDA, led by CSE, by working with two House oversight subcommittees—one chaired by former CSE adviser Representative David McIntosh (R-IN) and a second chaired by Representative Joe Barton (R-TX)—that were consistently convening hearings to question senior FDA officials about their mission.

"Both Barton efforts and McIntosh/Shays [Representative Chris Shays, R-CT] efforts are ongoing in [the] House," she wrote, according to the internal memo now housed in the Legacy archive. "[We] need media, lobbying and policy support from third-party groups in support of these efforts."

Philip Morris also wanted third-party groups, led by CSE, to work with House Appropriations Committee staff to gut the FDA's budget. CSE had already been successful in convincing the House to cut the federal agency's budget the previous year, following its announcement that it would regulate the tobacco industry. "Preparations [are] needed for FY97 appropriations for [the] House and Senate," she wrote. "CSE should lead here, as they did on [the] FY96 efforts. [We] need to work with CSE to develop [an] appropriations strategy with teeth."

But, thanks to earlier work through Tom Donohue's CART coalition, which had done the tobacco industry's bidding for years, CSE also now had direct access to Representative John Boehner—who'd moved into a House leadership role as the head of the House Republican Conference, which determined the major legislative actions under consideration by the GOP-controlled House.

"CSE sits at [the House Republican Conference] table with Boehner concerning Republican priorities," McKittrick wrote. Philip Morris should "look for opportunities here for CSE in moving other groups to FDA."

What McKittrick meant by this strategy is that the Kochs' group, CSE, would use its "seat at the table" with Boehner to bring other ideological third-party groups into the political fight, and that they would make the fight about regulatory overreach—not jurisdiction over the tobacco industry.

McKittrick closed her strategy session by describing the range of paid advertisements that Philip Morris would be funding through third-party groups in publications such as *Roll Call,* the *Hill,* and *Congressional Monitor,* as well as national newspapers such as *The Washington Post* and *The New York Times*—all of which would be "critical at raising the temperature level" around antiregulation attacks centered on agencies that included the FDA, EPA, and OSHA.

Even earned media—the ability to convince reporters that regulations were a bad thing and that the federal regulatory agencies weren't doing their jobs—wasn't out of the question if CSE was able to work with other Koch-funded groups to coordinate an overall attack on government regulations. "CSE has [some] creative ideas for earned media," she said. "This needs to be encouraged with other appropriate groups."

McKittrick had other allies within Philip Morris for her plan. According to a memo in the same time frame laying out notes for a presentation by Steve Parrish, who was the senior-most official at Philip Morris responsible for all of its government and public affairs activities, CSE and two additional third-party groups had launched a broad attack on the FDA "as an agency out of control and one failing to live up to its congressional mandate regarding regulation of drugs and medical devices."

The memo stated that CSE and the two other groups had "conducted an aggressive media campaign toward these goals, incorporating the issuance of policy papers, conducting symposia, filing petitions with FDA and taking other steps to keep the public and media focus on the agency."

Meanwhile, the legislative strategy through the McIntosh and Barton hearings—combined with CSE and third-party group access to Boehner's conference and a focus on "soft" Democrats on various committees who'd received tobacco industry donations over the years—was starting to pay dividends. "On the legislative front, a group of southern Democrats [began] negotiating with the White House early this year on behalf of the industry seeking to eliminate any role for the FDA in the regulation of tobacco."

The industry had proposed a compromise where it would voluntarily ban marketing and advertising of cigarettes to youth and restrict youth access to cigarettes in return for the White House's agreement to drop the plan to regulate cigarettes.

The Clinton White House ultimately rejected the offer, which prompted CSE to move into action more broadly. "Members of Congress—at the urging of several outside groups, including Citizens for a Sound Economy—began taking a much closer look at the FDA appropriations request," the Parrish presentation notes said. "That scrutiny led to the successful efforts to eliminate $300 million sought by FDA to consolidate its offices in a new federal campus, by any measure a major setback for Kessler."

The FDA had asked Congress to colocate all of its different centers that regulated drugs, food, and medical devices on one campus—much the way the National Institutes of Health are consolidated on one campus in Washington. CSE had, by this time, developed enough expertise and access to convince Congress to block the campus consolidation.

The third-party allies were also able to convince Congress to freeze the agency's budget; order Dr. Kessler to restrict where his own employees could work and on what issues; and to curtail the scope of his tobacco investigation (though not kill it). CSE and Philip Morris also planned on bringing Dr. Kessler up on charges of "obstruction of Congress" over his answers related to the tobacco rule.

CSE and the other third-party allies had been able to convince Congress to consider a bill designed to "reform" the agency and its mission. "As a result of the growing focus on FDA from inside and outside Congress and the groundwork laid through the oversight and investigations committee work [hearings convened by Representative McIntosh, the former CSE adviser, and Representative Barton], legislation to reform the FDA . . . is expected to be formally introduced [soon]. A key provision in the reform legislation will be to restrict FDA's regulatory authority," the Parrish presentation notes said.

The third-party outreach efforts by CSE and others blanketed the Hill, the memo added. "In recognition that Kessler ultimately would play some regulatory role regarding tobacco, an aggressive campaign was conducted over the past six months to educate members of Congress and their staffs regarding the issue of regulation."

CSE and Philip Morris had even orchestrated a last-ditch effort, urging the White House to block the FDA's plan to issue the tobacco rule. At the prompting of CSE and other third-party groups, "participants circulated Dear Colleague letters throughout Congress and submitted op ed pieces to their hometown newspapers challenging the need for FDA regulation," the memo said. A congressional delegation prompted by all of this lobbying activity took another run at the White House in an attempt to convince it to block Dr. Kessler's efforts, but it fell short as well, the Parrish notes said.

Nevertheless, "the groundwork that has been laid legislatively has been designed to create a receptive atmosphere in Congress for legislation that will be introduced to eliminate FDA's role in tobacco regulation."

Surprisingly, the efforts even prompted more progressive Democrats who regularly worked with organized labor to attack Dr. Kessler's efforts. "Efforts in Congress also were made to identify unlikely allies—those who generally are more concerned with the politics of regulation rather than the substance—and resulted in meetings with [White House officials] Sen. Chris Dodd (D-CT) and Rep. Dick Gephardt (D-MO). Labor also presented opposition to Kessler's role in regulation," said the Parrish notes.

Because Philip Morris was pulling out all the stops to block the FDA's regulatory activities, they also hired political advisers who had worked for Clinton at the White House or in his first presidential campaign to lobby on the issue. And they mobilized tobacco growers to lobby Senator Mitch McConnell (R-KY) and others who listened closely to the growers in their states.

But Philip Morris was also focused on winning the public relations battle it was now engaged in with the FDA and Dr. Kessler, who had successfully convinced the American public that the tobacco companies had preyed on children for years through their marketing tactics. As a result of the FDA investigation internal documents were even then emerging that showed the tobacco companies knew nicotine was highly addictive, and that giving away cigarettes to minors would create "customers for life" once they were addicted.

So, again largely using third-party allies such as CSE, Philip Morris had begun to try to win the public relations battle by defining youth smoking on their own terms. Their principal strategy, according to the Parrish notes, was to define it as an issue for the states to deal with, not FDA.

"Efforts focused primarily on defining youth smoking as one that properly should be addressed at the state and local level, rather than having FDA intervene with any regulatory scheme," the notes said. "Third-party

spokespeople were identified in each state to address the issue of FDA regulation with local media." CSE and other Koch-funded groups served that
function in many of the states, as they had in New Jersey and California on
cigarette excise tax efforts.

Philip Morris also proposed to use third-party allies, including CSE, to
head the FDA off at the pass with a voluntary, fifty-state marketing ban on
materials aimed at children—such as the infamous "Joe Camel" ads that
RJR's marketing teams had created so effectively in an advertising campaign
clearly aimed at teenagers.

"In all 50 states, the stated goal [is] to endorse or pass reasonable marketing laws which stop minors from purchasing cigarettes, with a minimum
of government interference in the marketing of the cigarette to adult smokers," the notes said. Philip Morris enlisted the American Legislative Exchange Council to do its bidding in the states. ALEC successfully convinced
a number of state officials to contact the White House to object to the FDA
rule—arguing that it was rightfully a states' rights issue. The Tobacco
Institute worked with retail trade groups on a parallel voluntary effort that
was supposed to increase education about sales of cigarettes to minors in
the fifty states.

Finally, the internal campaign document for Parrish shows that Philip
Morris coordinated a comprehensive public relations effort primarily aimed
at bringing third-party allies on board. "[Philip Morris] representatives with
scientific credentials were assigned the task of meeting with various 'think
tanks' to discuss the issue of FDA regulation and generate guest editorials
and comments to the media. Those team members who were identified as
taking a public role in [the company's] response were given media/commu-
nications training, focusing on the effective delivery of company messages"
to the third-party groups.

Once this was in place, Philip Morris then launched its own youth access program called Action Against Access, which incorporated "voluntary
and proposed legislative steps to address the issue of youth smoking." The
company launched an aggressive paid and earned media campaign behind

the voluntary youth access program, all of it coordinated through its network of third-party allies.

Philip Morris was so wired into the political process that it filed a federal lawsuit against the "FDA rule"—the FDA's claim for jurisdiction over tobacco products and its intention to prevent and reduce tobacco use by minors—literally the moment the agency officially filed its "notice of intent" in the *Federal Register*—well before President Clinton even had a chance to announce it at a press briefing at the White House that afternoon. In fact, Philip Morris had materials in the hands of its third-party allies led by CSE before Clinton had announced the FDA rule and had already booked speakers for TV news appearances across the country with the help of Burson-Marsteller, its public relations firm.

While it is difficult to assess the full extent to which Philip Morris was able to blanket the political process through its third-party allies such as CSE, an internal memo stamped "Attorney-Client Communication, Privileged and Confidential" from David Nicoli (Philip Morris's vice president for government affairs in Washington) to Kathleen Linehan (Philip Morris's chief lobbyist) on their extensive political activity in DC makes the potential scope of such efforts clear.

Summing up just one month of its "greatest hits," Nicoli said that the company and their third-party allies had convinced both Senator Nancy Kassebaum (R-KA) and Representative Thomas Bliley (R-VA), chairman of the House Energy and Commerce Committee, to meet with Dr. Kessler's boss, Secretary of Health and Human Services Donna Shalala.

They'd generated a letter from southern Democratic senators to President Clinton's chief of staff, former representative Leon Panetta. They'd convinced a dozen House members to meet with the president's chief of staff and political director on the FDA rule. They'd convinced southern Democratic governors to weigh in with senior White House officials. They'd convinced Representative Bliley to "call CEOs re: (the) need to move fast" and in "secrecy" to weigh in with Congress and White House officials.

They even managed to convince Panetta to come to the Hill solely on this issue to meet with Bliley. "Panetta says 'by all means, let's do it,'" Nicoli wrote. "Panetta will come meet Bliley in his office."

Nicoli also laid out in great detail how Philip Morris was orchestrating the third-party attacks on the FDA. "Rep. Barton/CSE [held a] press conference on FDA poll/FDA findings," he wrote. Anti-FDA paid ads under CSE's name began running in Beltway media outlets. They also paid for full-page third-party ads in *The New York Times* and *The Wall Street Journal*.

CSE also began work with Representative McIntosh on the sweeping regulatory moratorium bill that was simultaneously being promoted by RJR's Get Government Off Our Back coalition. "McIntosh [will hold] hearings on [the] regulatory moratorium focus on FDA/EPA," Nicoli wrote. "Prospects look good in [the] House, dicey in [the] Senate." Nicoli proved correct. The moratorium passed the House but ultimately failed in the Senate.

Nicoli also said that CSE had successfully organized an appropriations subcommittee hearing on cutting FDA's budget. "CSE [is] preparing questions . . . [and] working up, distributing opposition materials to [the] FDA campus, which [the] GOP is focusing on."

Their third-party allies even outflanked the major public health coalition, the Coalition on Smoking and Health, run by the American Heart Association, Nicoli said. The Tobacco Institute held a press conference to release 1.1 million signatures against FDA regulation. The public health coalition released its own list of 250,000 signatures the next day.

By this time, CSE was now being funded handsomely by Philip Morris for its work. An internal Philip Morris budget shows CSE as the top recipient of its third-party ally contributions. A letter from CSE president Paul Beckner to Philip Morris's Steve Parrish in 1996 asked him to renew an annual, ongoing general operations grant of $500,000.

"It is clear from the legislative events of the past year that public policy is most effectively formulated through the support of grassroots citizens," Beckner wrote. "With [more than a decade] of experience educating and mobilizing grassroots citizens, CSE [is] uniquely positioned to take leadership roles in educating citizens to support policies that reduce government spending, cut taxes, and eliminate unnecessary government regulations."

As evidenced by all of this activity, the FDA tobacco rule was an important issue not only to members of Congress. Concern was growing within the Clinton White House that the issue of FDA regulation of tobacco would become the key issue that would tip a handful of swing states such as Kentucky, North Carolina, and South Carolina into the GOP column in the 1996 elections—a strategy that Tim Hyde took with him when he left RJ Reynolds to run coalition field operations for the Dole/Kemp presidential campaign in 1996. In fact, Dr. Kessler told me, President Clinton almost decided not to allow the FDA rule declaring jurisdiction over the tobacco industry to go forward over concerns that it might jeopardize his reelection. An internal memo from Hyde to Tommy Griscom before he left RJR to head up field operations for Dole's presidential campaign makes the scope of their third-party work in states equally clear—and illustrates how closely they were coordinating their Tobacco Strategy with third-party groups such as CSE. RJR had significant third-party efforts under way in Georgia, Florida, Iowa, Tennessee, Indiana, New Jersey, Ohio, Wisconsin, New Hampshire, Texas, Missouri, North Dakota, Minnesota, Massachusetts, and Rhode Island. Every third-party effort was designed to block the FDA, Hyde wrote.

In the end, President Clinton chose to allow the FDA tobacco rule to go forward and risk his reelection prospects in a number of key, swing states where the industry's third-party Allied Forces concept was in full motion. Despite a full-court press, waged through its network of third-party allies, the tobacco industry was unable to block the political action, either in Congress or at the White House.

But it had achieved something through the fight—it had refined and honed its antiregulatory, antigovernment messages, and third-party coalition strategies in ways that had never before been seen or tried.

15

☆ ☆ ☆

A Road Map for
Antigovernment Anger

The Clinton White House tried again to bring back a national cigarette excise tax toward the end of its second term in office and also to get a share of the profits from a previous lawsuit. In 1998, forty-six states had received portions of a windfall from their state attorney general suits against tobacco companies for Medicaid costs associated with people who smoked. In its 1999 budget submission to Congress, the White House proposed a fifty-five-cents-a-pack tax on cigarettes and that roughly $19 billion of those Medicaid reimbursements from the tobacco companies should go to the federal government, which had funded part of those Medicaid costs. Citizens for a Sound Economy was now fully prepared to take this on for the tobacco industry and to lead a broad state-by-state charge to demonize it.

Early on in its growing partnership with the tobacco companies, according to internal tobacco documents, CSE had nurtured the relationship in order to use the industry's Allied Forces network of employees and smokers for CSE's own political grassroots strategies. Now, in 1999, according to an extraordinarily detailed proposal submitted to the tobacco companies as part of the Tobacco Strategy, CSE had reached the apex of the tobacco industry's list of third-party allies.

The CSE proposal, called "Stopping new tax increases by presenting a positive alternative to the president's tobacco plan," dated March 5, 1999, asked for nearly $2 million from the tobacco companies to do their bidding. The funds would be divided between CSE's 501(c)(3) and 501(c)(4) arms.

"President Clinton's State of the Union address and 1999 proposed budget left no doubt that the era of big government is far from over," said the proposal. "Repeating a theme from last year, the president once again plans to pay for his 66 new spending programs (which would cost taxpayers more than $100 billion during the next five years) largely on the back of the tobacco companies and smokers."

The CSE proposal also addressed the potential for even more ominous attacks on the tobacco industry, which they were prepared to defend against. "The president also has proposed suing the tobacco industry, making an end-run around Congress and the Constitution to raise more revenue and fuel the growth of government."

Echoing many of the same themes that the Tea Party movement uses today to decry President Obama's "end run" around Congress through the use of executive authority—complete with veiled threats of impeachment proceedings—CSE laid out the case for why Clinton could do as he wanted unless he was stopped.

"Given that Republicans control Congress, one might think that such a tax-and-spend scheme would be dead on arrival," the proposal said. "However, the president does not need legislation to obtain much of this revenue. The federal Health Care Financing Administration can begin collecting the Medicaid reimbursements from the states immediately."

CSE then turned to the looming threat of legal action against the industry as a whole, under RICO racketeering authority. The Racketeer Influenced and Corrupt Organizations (RICO) Act had historically been used by the FBI and federal authorities to pursue the mob, but now President Clinton's Justice Department had decided to pursue legal action against the industry under the RICO statute because federal funds had paid a percentage of the Medicaid expenses of smokers. This effort at the federal level was similar to the one by the states to recover expenses from the tobacco companies that had led to the Master Settlement Agreement with forty-six states.

"The president's proposed tobacco lawsuit is a legal shakedown aimed at either a settlement or legislation that provides the excise tax revenue and regulatory concessions the administration failed to achieve last year through legislative channels," the CSE proposal said. "To bring the suit, the administration could employ or enter into a contingency-fee agreement with the same trial lawyers who brought the state tobacco lawsuits, providing them with yet another windfall should the administration win or settle the case."

CSE proposed a full, nationwide attack to derail everything all at once—the national cigarette tax, the RICO lawsuit, and the Medicaid reimbursement plan. To do so, they laid out a line-by-line budget plan for both the key states and Washington.

It included funding for message testing, mailings, tax club forums, leadership training seminars, legal analysis, a speakers bureau, a call center, coalition building, lobbying, a "congressional staff education event," thought leader "activation," opinion piece ghostwriting, "personal activist alert calls," an online campaign that included digital advertising, guerilla field activity, federal agency report cards, polling, a consumer booklet, brochures, policy education outreach, and earned media public relations campaigns.

It was, by every conceivable measure, a full-blown, national political campaign designed to attack taxes, regulation, and the executive authority of a Democratic president—funded completely by the tobacco industry through the Kochs' third-party group. It would be easy to assume this was a Republican Party campaign—after all, it was against a Democrat in power. However, such an assumption is far from the truth. Instead, this effort was funded by the tobacco industry and managed by the Kochs' most prominent 501(c)(3) and 501(c)(4) at that time.

"To stop the administration's federal tax, spending and regulatory growth scheme, their litigation bargaining chip must be removed," the CSE proposal said. "The best way to do this is to create a grassroots backlash against the administration's entire proposal, calling it what it is—another tax-and-spend plan that increases the role of government and benefits only the trial lawyers."

It was, in short, a blueprint for orchestrating populist anger against a sitting president, built around the tobacco industry's priorities and field operation and managed by a network created by the owners of the largest private oil company on earth. But there would be additional benefits, CSE promised:

"[We] will work to stop the lawsuit, while at the same time creating an atmosphere in Congress that makes it difficult for the budget or any possible lawsuit settlement to include a tax increase or increased Food and Drug Administration regulations. We will build the grassroots support needed on the ground to ignite a protest on any front that can help to stop the administration's revenue grab. Throughout the effort, [we] also will work to ensure that the message resonating from Congress and our coalition allies is 'pro-taxpayer.'"

While CSE was orchestrating big tax, regulatory, and antigovernment fights through the states for a national audience, it was also doing hand-to-hand combat for the tobacco companies in the states with entirely separate budget line items.

It waged the tobacco industry's war in California in 1998, for instance, in an effort to block Prop 10, which proposed an excise tax of fifty cents a pack to fund the Children and Families First Initiative.

"Well, it seems as if tax and spend politics has taken a bit of an unusual twist in California," CSE president Paul Beckner wrote on October 19, 1998, as part of a letter campaign that blanketed the state in advance of the Prop 10 vote. "Proposition 10 would raise cigarette taxes by 50 cents a pack and is designed to pay for a laundry list of programs supposedly targeted at kids. A larger government would seem to be the actual target, however."

Beckner promised Prop 10 would be a massive, scary plan to hire thousands of bureaucrats who would control people's lives. "The $700 million annually collected through this new tax would be used to create a mammoth 59 new government commissions, staffed with 8,000 bureaucrats and almost no accountability on how they spend your money. We cannot stand on the sidelines and let this happen."

The Prop 10 proponents didn't care about children, Beckner said. No, they were "attempting to institute a power grab in the name of children. When one looks closely at [the] Proposition, it becomes apparent that it is harmful to California's schools and actually takes money away from the citizens of California."

Beckner said, "Let there be no misunderstanding. Proposition 10 amounts to nothing more than a breathtaking expansion of government at the expense of your freedoms. This proposal would put more money from the citizens of California into the hands of unaccountable political appointees and their bureaucracies."

During these years, in the second half of the Clinton presidency, House majority leader Richard Armey—who would become chairman of the Kochs' Citizens for a Sound Economy when he retired from Congress several years later—began to experiment with rallies and events built expressly around Boston Tea Party themes. He worked with CSE on these staged Tea Party events, according to documents and published reports.

Armey wanted to eliminate the federal income tax—another longtime target of free-market libertarians—and replace it with a national sales tax. He felt that this could be accomplished by a populist tax revolt based on the Boston Tea Party. He roped other House members into his Tea Party efforts. He directed third-party allies to take out national ads in *Parade* magazine for a "second Boston Tea Party" and urged them to mail tea bags to members of Congress. He and three other GOP House members stood on the steps of the Capitol next to volunteers dressed in colonial-era costumes who dumped tea on the steps. He worked with two members of Congress to toss the federal tax code into Boston Harbor.

But not until CSE started sponsoring Tea Party rallies in support of the flat tax in North Carolina and other tobacco-growing states on Armey's behalf—almost a full decade before the "spontaneous" creation of the Tea Party movement—did Armey's ideas start to take hold at least somewhat at a real grassroots level.

It's nearly impossible to tell precisely how much total funding the Kochs' CSE received from Philip Morris, RJR, and the Tobacco Strategy group. While budgets for some years are available and specifically list CSE's efforts as their top third-party ally, other years aren't accessible. But at the start of the Clinton years, CSE was receiving at least $500,000 a year.

By the midpoint of Clinton's presidency, that annual support had likely moved to $2 million a year for national efforts and additional funding on a state-by-state basis for excise tax or smoking ban fights. That probably lasted until at least 2003 due to the ongoing nature of the FDA regulatory threat, continued excise tax fights, the global tobacco settlement litigation, and the Department of Justice's RICO suit. So, in CSE's efforts to spearhead the tobacco industry's third-party ally efforts for more than a decade, it may have received up to $20 million while it perfected the industry's Allied Forces strategies. But this is a guess, because the funding and its purposes are only revealed in places where the tobacco companies discussed budgets in the documents available in the Legacy archive.

What is certainly true, and well-defined in the documents that are available, is that the tobacco companies began the Clinton years with a broad antitax, antiregulatory strategy intended to mask their corporate aims . . , and the Kochs' CSE became their most trusted third-party ally in that Tobacco Strategy effort as they collectively learned what worked (and what didn't) in federal budget, regulatory, and legal fights in Washington.

16

☆ ☆ ☆

Mobilization Universe

The Department of Justice sued several major tobacco companies in 1999 for fraudulent and unlawful conduct, asking for reimbursement of federal tobacco-related medical expenses. The federal circuit judge who heard the case initially dismissed the Department of Justice claims for reimbursement but allowed DOJ to bring the case back under the Racketeer Influenced and Corrupt Organizations (RICO) Act, which had historically been used by the FBI and federal authorities to pursue the mob.

Reluctant at first—and subjected to a heavy lobbying blitz orchestrated by Philip Morris and RJR through third-part allies such as CSE—Clinton's DOJ did eventually sue on RICO grounds that the tobacco industry had engaged in a decades-long conspiracy to mislead the public about smoking risks, secondhand smoke, and nicotine addiction. The RICO suit also accused the industry of deliberately manipulating the nicotine delivery of cigarettes to enhance their addictiveness and deliberately misleading the public in its advertising and marketing practices.

The DOJ lawsuit under RICO was a double-edged sword for the tobacco industry. It clearly made them nervous, according to scores of internal documents. The tobacco industry had hoped to escape the Clinton years without further entanglement with the White House over tax, regulatory, or legal issues, but career DOJ prosecutors could theoretically keep the lawsuit going beyond the Clinton presidency. However, the lawsuit was also an opportunity. It could easily be made to appear as if using the RICO statute, which seemed ill suited to the tobacco industry, was a massive political overreach by Clinton's DOJ. The companies weren't the Mafia, and they hadn't conspired together to defraud Americans . . . at least as far as the public knew. Their PR teams, both inside and outside the industry, were prepared to demonize the Clinton administration for adopting what seemed, on its surface, a significantly overstated claim—that the tobacco industry and its third-party allies had essentially lied and defrauded the American public for decades.

But, as the tobacco documents showed, they had, in fact, jointly created and run a Tobacco Strategy and an Allied Forces plan over the years to fight tax, regulatory, and legal challenges. Third-party groups such as the Tobacco Institute and CSE had been central to that strategy throughout those years, and this is where the industry was most vulnerable.

The industry had orchestrated and coordinated attacks on studies and scientists that revealed the dangers of smoking by presenting fraudulent research through the Tobacco Institute (along with the Council for Tobacco Research). This is a principal reason that the institute eventually disappeared as a result of court settlements. The tobacco industry likely assumed their conspiracy to confuse the public—by financially supporting the research of scientists who would say anything big tobacco asked them to—would emerge through the DOJ lawsuit. They may also have known, according to the memos and documents later released, that their political and legal efforts through third-party groups would make them vulnerable to charges of industrywide collusion.

In short, it was obvious—and they knew it internally, the documents showed—that the DOJ lawsuit would eventually prove to have merit. That worried them no end. They only had one potential play—a blatantly political one that could kill the RICO lawsuit in the cradle before Clinton left office. They had to mobilize their universe of third-party allies and throw everything in their arsenal at the lawsuit to force the political system in Washington to halt the suit before it could take on a life of its own with federal prosecutors.

That was precisely the action they took, internal documents and memos show. And the Kochs' Citizens for a Sound Economy was at the top of their tightly coordinated group of third-party allies mobilized to do their bidding by bringing withering pressure on Congress and the White House through state-based action and direct lobbying in DC. By the end of the Clinton era no other group was even close to the top of the tobacco industry's list of third-party allies in coordinating the response. There was CSE—and then everyone else.

Philip Morris called this all-out attack on the Department of Justice's RICO lawsuit the Mobilization Universe, according to an internal Philip Morris memo detailing the specifics of the third-party allies and their respective budgets for its implementation. The PM external affairs team created a game plan to make the RICO lawsuit politically unpalatable and put together a budget with its allies to carry it out. The strategy was to position the move to expose the industry's decades-long effort to lie about the dangers of smoking as a deluded political conspiracy by Clinton political operatives.

They also intended to hang the RICO suit as an albatross around the neck of Clinton's vice president, Al Gore, who they assumed would become the Democratic Party's presidential standard-bearer in the 2000 election.

One of the Mobilization Universe memo's key points was that the DOJ lawsuit was "bad for Gore and Senate and House Democrats in 2000." The document described it as "politically-motivated litigation"; said it revealed a political alliance between Clinton's DOJ and trial lawyers who constantly bedeviled big companies; and termed it nothing more than a "money grab" by DC.

The Mobilization Universe plan was crafted to bring in the widest variety of political allies possible. It would show other corporate CEOs the "slippery slope/ramifications for U.S. business" and that the DOJ suit was really a "massive increase in government involvement in the private sector." Mobilization Universe would claim that the suit was the first in a series of actions by Democrats to attack big business across the board.

The Philip Morris budget request for the launch of the Mobilization Universe reflected those political priorities. The US Chamber of Commerce—which had, by this time, seen its annual budget grow from just $3 million a year in 1996 when Tom Donohue became its CEO to more than $50 million a year, including $20 million for "special projects"—was given $500,000 by Philip Morris for the part it would play in the Mobilization Universe. Grover Norquist's Americans for Tax Reform would be given $750,000. Groups called Coalitions for America, Frontiers for Freedom, and the Small Business Survival Committee would be given smaller amounts, ranging from $50,000 to $200,000.

But at the top of the list, with a budget more than double that of any other line item in the "business and third-party allies" section, was the Kochs' Citizens for a Sound Economy at $2 million. The only other budget items that rivaled CSE's were those for public relations and lobbying support for firms represented by DC insiders such as Carter Eskew (who would later run the message and advertising team for Gore's 2000 presidential campaign) and GOP political campaign consultant Alex Castellanos.

The Mobilization Universe was built to win a political war over the RICO lawsuit both in the air and on the ground. It had just one simple goal—to "avert White House filing of [the] federal suit." To achieve this end, it would "leverage third-party relationships" to "oppose [the] DOJ appropriations request for [the] federal suit task force"; "oppose federal legislation enabling [a] cause of action against the industry"; and "persuade the administration and Senate and House Democrats of the political liability in a federal suit."

John Scruggs—Philip Morris's chief in-house lobbyist at the time—explained the three central goals of the Mobilization Universe strategy in a February 26, 1999, internal memo to senior leadership inside Philip Morris: to strip the federal lawsuit task-force funds from DOJ's appropriations budget in Congress, defeat legislation that expanded the DOJ lawsuit to other areas, and "bring political pressure to bear on [the] administration, particularly Vice President Al Gore, sufficient to stop the filing of a federal suit prior to the November 2000 elections."

Scruggs was even more explicit later in his memo: "Vice President Gore must be convinced that pursuing an unwarranted suit against the industry will negatively impact his presidential ambitions. House Democrats must be convinced that such a suit will make it more difficult to secure the requisite seats to take the House majority back from the GOP. Senate Democrats must be convinced of the same. The objectives . . . can only be achieved through a massive grassroots, grass tops and media campaign directed at [these] entities." Scruggs then explained that the effort would be split into two paths—one aimed at Republicans and the other aimed at Democrats. CSE would lead the political efforts aimed at Republicans to "solidify our base in opposition."

In a later private memo to Tom Collamore at Philip Morris, Scruggs described the pivotal role that CSE played throughout that year to explain why they were paid more than twice as much money as any other organization (including the US Chamber of Commerce) in the political fight. He claimed that CSE added a "level of value" because of their "significant grassroots assistance," including "direct lobbying on the lawsuit." They had also implemented a communications plan that "very creatively mixed work on the lawsuit, FET [a proposed federal excise tax] and Medicare prescription drugs."

The Mobilization Universe that CSE was essentially running on Philip Morris's behalf had a long list of key targets that it would bring into the political effort—national business organizations, national tax-policy organizations, broad-based national policy organizations, state policy organizations, public interest legal foundations, media organizations, business and professional trade groups, and political advocacy organizations. The full range of potential third-party activities CSE would coordinate included op-eds, editorials, letters to the editors of newspapers, media appearances, spokesperson training, policy resolutions, speeches, forums, congressional testimony, lobbying, coalition-building, membership education, and rapid response.

The portfolio of national and state business, legal, tax, and media policy organizations listed inside the Mobilization Universe—about half of them funded by Koch philanthropies at one level or another over the years—was a who's who of groups that consistently promoted free-market, liberty, patriot, and freedom themes. In a third internal tobacco memo outlining Philip Morris's "core allies" that would lead the political fight, CSE was at the heart of it alongside the National Association of Manufacturers, the US Chamber of Commerce, the National Restaurant Association, and others. It looked a lot like a national political campaign—and was funded at the level of a national political campaign—with key messages that resembled those of the Tea Party movement a decade later.

The Mobilization Universe strategy ultimately failed to deliver its central political aim, which was to force Gore and the Democrats to end the RICO lawsuit in order to win the presidency and take back the House. CSE and the GOP third-party allies did their part, but the Democrats balked, later documents show. The RICO lawsuit survived the Clinton years and extended into President George W. Bush's presidency. CSE remained a central player in efforts to block the lawsuit as it worked its way through the system. The industry continued to employ the Mobilization Universe strategy in Bush's first term, this time targeting the GOP specifically, instead of both Democrats and Republicans.

CSE president Paul Beckner wrote a letter to President Bush on January 31, 2002, with an explicit plea to intervene and force DOJ to drop the lawsuit:[1] "I want to write and offer what I believe are some helpful suggestions on how the Department of Justice can better focus its resources and mission in light of the enormous challenge it faces after September 11." Beckner described how Bush's predecessor, Bill Clinton, had conducted "egregious" witch hunts of "productive and legal U.S. businesses" like Microsoft and Philip Morris through an abuse of DOJ's antitrust and RICO authorities. He hoped that Bush would place much greater emphasis on counter-terrorism activities at DOJ in the wake of 9/11, which would mean dropping the tobacco lawsuit.

"If priorities for the DOJ are to be determined by FY 2001 budgetary requests, the previous administration believed antitrust and RICO enforcement to be 20 times more important than the department's counter-terrorism fund," Beckner wrote. "While the past administration's unrelenting pursuit of American business was wrong before September 11th, today it is not only misguided policy, but also an unwise use of scarce resources and focus."

He then made as direct a political appeal as possible to Bush: "As we now find ourselves in the middle of an attack within our borders, a war abroad, and an economic recession, I believe that the Department of Justice should reallocate the precious resources it has to protect our homeland and prosecute the war against terrorism, rather than pursuing this costly lawsuit."

Beckner's letter to President Bush on the RICO lawsuit is one of the last entries in the massive tobacco industry archives at UCSF, which include more than 14 million documents. After years of blocking efforts under the global tobacco settlement to release its memos and documents, the industry agreed to stop doing so shortly after this last effort to convince the Bush White House to drop the DOJ suit. The Legacy Tobacco Documents Library began to accept the cache of documents and assemble the database that year.

The Mobilization Universe strategy failed to convince Bush to drop the lawsuit—largely because senior White House aides couldn't afford to so blatantly bail out the tobacco industry by then and drop the suit. Still, it would be another four years before the Department of Justice's RICO lawsuit would reach its conclusion.

On August 17, 2006, federal judge Gladys Kessler issued a historic 1,683-page opinion holding the tobacco companies liable for RICO violations by fraudulently hiding the health risks associated with smoking and for marketing cigarettes to children. "Substantial evidence establishes that [the tobacco companies] have engaged in and executed—and continue to engage in and execute—a massive 50-year scheme to defraud the public, including consumers of cigarettes, in violation of RICO," Kessler wrote.

The tobacco companies appealed to the US Court of Appeals. Almost three years later on May 22, 2009, a three-judge panel (including both Democratic and Republican appointees) unanimously upheld Judge Kessler's RICO findings. While it dismissed some of the remedies that had been sought by public health advocates, most of them remained intact.

The federal appeals court also ruled that the First Amendment does not protect corporations when they make fraudulent statements. This was a stunning defeat for the tobacco companies, who had staked their defense on their First Amendment rights to free speech (including political speech). However, the federal court said that their deliberate efforts to deceive the public superseded that right.

"[The tobacco companies] knew of their falsity at the time and made the statements with the intent to deceive," the bipartisan three-judge panel wrote in their opinion. "Thus, we are not dealing with accidental falsehoods, or sincere attempts to persuade."

The tobacco companies ultimately decided not to appeal the decision that their statements were not protected by the First Amendment, though they continued to object to many of the remedies outlined in the initial Kessler decision.

Thus the Mobilization Universe strategy failed to achieve its political ends, either with the Democrats in the Clinton White House or with Republicans during the Bush administration. But it succeeded in other ways.

Like the Tobacco Strategy and Allied Forces that preceded it, Mobilization Universe taught all of the critical players how to coordinate their work through a complicated web of third parties. They learned how to use key messaging and campaign themes for broad political purposes, and then how to adapt the terms to challenge specific issues affecting corporate business practices in Washington and the states.

But the Mobilization Universe strategy and the tobacco companies' failed attempt to use the First Amendment to shield their efforts as protected political speech has a postscript. Constitutional scholars will now look at it closely in the wake of the *Citizens United* decision in 2010 and attempts to deal with the ruling in subsequent federal elections. In *Citizens United v. Federal Election Commission*, which allowed corporations to direct essentially unlimited contributions into the political system, the Supreme Court transformed the political landscape, unleashing unprecedented spending in election cycles by tax-exempt organizations, who don't have to disclose their donors.

Judge Kessler's ruling (as part of the Department of Justice's RICO suit) makes it illegal—and, perhaps, even criminal—for large corporations to collude with each other if they deliberately lie to or deceive the public as part of their political grassroots mobilization efforts. Those efforts are not protected as political speech under the First Amendment, and that lack of protection applies to their third-party allies as well.

Whether the public likes it or not, American democracy is now seeing an unprecedented amount of corporate-directed funding—in the hundreds of millions of dollars during each national election cycle every two years—spent directly for or against candidates under the *Citizens United* decision.

But the RICO finding against the tobacco companies (and their third-party allies such as the Tobacco Institute) that their work—if built on fraud or deception—was not protected as political speech under the First Amendment is almost certainly a counterbalance against corporate-led coalitions that engage in similar efforts.

The *Citizens United* decision was brought before the Supreme Court by a third-party group that wanted to allow corporations to spend whatever they wished in federal elections. The Kessler ruling was upheld by a three-judge federal panel. The Supreme Court refused to hear any further appeals, so Judge Kessler's ruling was final—and may offer a counterargument when corporate-led coalitions engage in fraud to wage their campaigns. No one has yet used this counterargument against the torrent of nearly unlimited corporate spending under *Citizens United*—but it is available nevertheless.

The Kochs' donor-driven political network has benefited immensely from the *Citizens United* decision. After all, free, unhampered speech is an important part of the Kochs' DNA. It was their own corporate front group that led the tobacco industry's third-party fight against the DOJ RICO lawsuit for years. Ironically, that same lawsuit is the one area in which big tobacco's massive network is perhaps vulnerable—because of a single ruling by a federal judge—and may be tested significantly in the future.

17

☆ ☆ ☆

The Quarterback

When the national media have reported on the corporate front groups or coalitions created, run, or managed by Rich Fink, Charles Koch, or Koch Industries, they tend to dismiss their ability to either mobilize actual armies of grassroots volunteers or that the Kochs were really quarterbacking efforts with funding and organizational muscle.

Both are serious mistakes and fail to recognize what has only become apparent after the posting of the Legacy archive and tax records for groups like CSE, Americans for Prosperity, Freedom Partners, and others.

The effort to create and direct a national political grassroots network behind myriad corporate front groups was always hiding in plain sight. It only became apparent more than a decade after the fact as public health researchers looking through millions of tobacco industry documents pieced together parts of the puzzle.

In truth, political grassroots campaigns need actual volunteers to do such things as knock on doors, make phone calls, or send letters and throw tea— or bales of tobacco—into harbors and rivers. Rich Fink seemed to be concerned with putting "boots on the ground" because it was the only way to move beyond corporate astroturfing and deliver actual people to political

fights. It appears that was why he chased the tobacco companies so assiduously for years and cultivated a deep relationship with them through
both funding and campaigns in the states. It appears that he learned early
on, starting in the 1980s and more fully through big political fights in the
Clinton presidency, that the tobacco companies offered the quickest, most
effective route to recruiting actual boots on the ground.

The tobacco companies could mobilize tens of thousands of employees,
growers, and service providers, all of whom would work side by side with a
much broader (and loosely connected) network of millions of smokers that
Philip Morris and RJ Reynolds had assiduously organized into alliances in
the 1990s.

The National Smokers Alliance, with its initial annual budget of $18 mil-
lion from Philip Morris in 1993, had created an army of 2 million smokers
almost overnight. That army could be made available to its principal third-
party ally, CSE. All that CSE, and then Americans for Prosperity, had to
do was establish a common cause to fight for. The Tea Party movement
paradigm—with broad themes against taxes, regulation, and a government
that denied personal freedoms—was clearly, and somewhat obviously for
anyone paying careful attention, that fertile common ground.

The Tobacco Strategy or Allied Forces network of volunteers provided
all the grassroots muscle that the Kochs and Rich Fink required to achieve
their growing political aims. But for it to be effective—for Koch Industries,
Philip Morris, and RJR to be able to quarterback and direct the action behind the scenes for various political fights such as the Clinton health care
reform effort and, years later, the Obamacare debate—both the funding
sources and the true nature of the campaign goals needed to remain secret.

That was true of RJR's Get Government Off Our Back effort that dovetailed so perfectly with the Contract with America efforts led by Newt Gingrich and Richard Armey, and which brought its central resolution—a
government-wide moratorium on all regulations—to the floor of the House
of Representatives, where it passed. And it was true of Philip Morris's highly
successful coalition efforts to use its Allied Forces concept to ultimately de-

rail Hillary Clinton's health care reform efforts because a cigarette tax hike had been proposed as part of it.

The third serious mistake is to simply assume that entities such as CSE and then Americans for Prosperity could somehow rise to national, organizational prominence without significant underwriting from the Kochs' various philanthropies. Yes, CSE did receive significant funding from Philip Morris and the tobacco companies throughout the 1990s. CSE was, after all, Philip Morris's principal third-party ally. Its successor, Americans for Prosperity, likewise sought tobacco industry funding for cigarette tax campaigns in the states.

But the core is Koch philanthropic funding, derived from the wealth of two brothers whose combined net worth would make them arguably the wealthiest person on the planet. In good times and bad, this promise of significant funding allows them to do their work in ways that are simply not available to any other third-party group.

When Citizens for a Sound Economy suddenly disappeared as an entity during 2003-4—its 501(c)(3) and 501(c)(4) entities became Americans for Prosperity and FreedomWorks—every national media story on the dissolution focused obsessively on the fact that its leader, former House majority leader Richard Armey, left to run FreedomWorks.

No one even bothered to report that, while publicly distancing themselves from FreedomWorks, the Kochs quietly stepped in to solely fund the creation of Americans for Prosperity. Nor did the media report that Rich Fink came back to briefly direct Americans for Prosperity before handing it off to Nancy Pfotenhauer, then the head of Koch Industries' Washington office, who ran it precisely according to the wishes of Fink and Charles Koch. And they certainly didn't report that Americans for Prosperity was able to take on all of the functions and work of its predecessor, CSE, including its antitax campaigns in state capitals on behalf of the tobacco industry.

The Kochs have never discussed why CSE was dissolved into various entities throughout 2003–4. Even KochFacts.com is largely silent on the issue, simply describing the dissolution as a disagreement among principals (without further elaboration). Thus an organization that had for more than a decade been carefully and deliberately cultivated to quarterback Allied Forces political coalitions (with significant help from the tobacco industry) quietly, somewhat ignominiously ended. So why was CSE really dissolved?

While there may have been disagreements among principals, such as Armey and the Kochs, over the ultimate political aims of the organization, the timing of the dissolution raises a more likely answer. When the tobacco companies signed the Master Settlement Agreement in November 1998 with forty-six of fifty state attorneys general, they agreed to dissolve the Tobacco Institute and make two decades' worth of internal tobacco documents that had been secret largely under attorney-client privilege available publicly through the American Legacy Foundation.

The tobacco industry did abolish the Tobacco Institute in early 1999 as a result of the settlement, but it continued to fight the release of its internal documents for years. CSE dissolved within months of the internal tobacco documents' becoming available—and searchable online by public health scholars and law firms alike seeking to explore connections that had, until then, been hidden. The Kochs' CSE emerged as the quarterback of much of the tobacco industry efforts in literally thousands of these documents. Though the tangled roots required careful extrapolation and years of work—the most recent article was published only a year or so ago—at least three major public health scholarly articles in the *American Journal of Public Health* and *Tobacco Journal* eventually traced much of the path.

The more likely reason CSE ended and Americans for Prosperity took its place was that information about CSE being the tobacco industry's principal and most important third-party ally in so many big political fights was now publicly available. Such revelation substantially dimmed its effectiveness as a behind-the-scenes quarterback.

Much as with the research conducted by public health scholars surrounding RJR's Get Government Off Our Back political coalition work that had dovetailed with the Gingrich-Armey Contract with America in Washington, not until 2013 were three UCSF researchers able to work their way through thousands of documents in the Legacy archive to run down the myriad ways in which CSE had worked closely with Philip Morris on its aims, and with its funding.

Stan Glantz, Amanda Fallin, and Rachel Grana (the UCSF public health researchers) told me it took them months to put the pieces together before publishing a lengthy analysis of the ways in which the tobacco industry efforts created and refined the paradigm of using third-party allies to wage fights built around the tax, regulation, and antigovernment themes of the Tea Party movement. CSE was at the center of nearly all of it, they found. Fallin and Grana told me that when they plugged CSE into the Legacy database at UCSF, they were shocked at how many hits came up. They numbered in the thousands.

Glantz also told me that he'd tried to get science and environmental groups and publications outside the tobacco-control movement interested in the study and what it said about the way in which the Kochs' groups had worked so closely with the tobacco companies on their key political issues. He got no takers. It's why they ultimately published the article in *Tobacco Control*, he told me.

What he hadn't expected was the way in which the various Tea Party groups in the states and nationally noticed immediately. "They went ballistic," he told me. That's when GOP congressional staff demanded the National Institutes of Health inspector general investigation of Glantz's work for the *Tobacco Control* article, which ultimately found nothing other than their rigorous, academic review of hundreds of tobacco documents in the Legacy archive. But the reaction of the Tea Party groups in the past year to the *Tobacco Control* article speaks volumes about the sensitivity of the Koch donor network and Tea Party groups to the notion that they are an orchestrated and manufactured movement for corporate aims, Glantz believes.

What did Glantz, Fallin, and Grana discover in their study published in *Tobacco Control*? They essentially proved the tobacco industry's Allied Forces concept of using third-party groups to do their bidding in big political fights under the banner of populist anger at taxes, regulation, and the national government in Washington. The Tea Party movement, with the Kochs' Citizens for a Sound Economy, was at the center of much of it.

"CSE supported the agendas of the tobacco and other industries, including oil, chemical, pharmaceutical and telecommunications, and was funded by them," the researchers wrote in *Tobacco Journal*. "In 2002, before Tea Party politics were widely discussed in the mainstream media, CSE started its US Tea Party (http://www.usteaparty.com) project, the website of which stated 'our US Tea Party is a national event, hosted continuously online and open to all Americans who feel our taxes are too high and the tax code is too complicated.' Between 1991 and 2002 the tobacco companies, mainly Philip Morris, provided CSE with at least $5.3 million. Philip Morris gave CSE $250,000 annually in the early 1990s to start six state chapters."

They found that CSE had risen through the ranks to become Philip Morris's most trusted third-party ally. "Philip Morris designated CSE a 'Category A' public policy organization for funding," they found. " 'Category A' organizations were 'the largest and most important/sustained relationships' that were assigned a 'PM senior relationship manager' to put them at the 'center of a network of information-sharing among PM people involved with the organization' and '[assure] systematic and ongoing relationship activities.' "

Because CSE and Philip Morris were closely aligned and two CSE advisers were now running both federal policy and field operations, Philip Morris also kept ratcheting up their support.

"In response to an internal 1999 email asking whether CSE was worth its current level of funding, Philip Morris' vice president of federal government affairs replied: They are adding this level of value. They have provided significant grassroots assistance, in the nature of several thousand calls to the Hill on direct lobbying on the [Justice Department RICO] lawsuit, some media as well as continuing a very useful level of activity on FET [a federal excise tax]/prescription drugs [a proposal to expand Medicare and fund prescription drugs with a tobacco tax]. Throughout the August [congressional] recess they have been very active on our behalf in the field in key states with key Members."

Glantz, Fallin, and Grana also found document after document illustrating how the tobacco industry had turned to CSE in every major political fight—with a willingness to turn the event into a broader war on taxes, regulation, and big government.

"During the 1990s, the tobacco industry was facing a multitude of threats. CSE helped the industry oppose these challenges, including the Environmental Protection Agency's (EPA) second-hand smoke risk assessment (1992), the Clinton healthcare reform plan which included a tobacco tax (1993–1994), the Occupational Safety and Health Administration's (OSHA) proposal to regulate workplace smoking (1994–2001), FDA regulation of tobacco products (1994–1996) and the DOJ RICO case against the tobacco industry (filed in 1999), as well as tobacco taxes (throughout the 1990s)," they wrote.

In the Allied Forces fight against the Clinton healthcare concept, CSE was at the center. "The tobacco industry waged a major campaign between 1993 and 1994 to oppose President Bill Clinton's healthcare reform efforts, particularly the $0.75 cigarette tax to help finance it. The tobacco industry worked with a broad coalition against the proposed reform, which included CSE and RJR's smokers' rights groups and others."

CSE was also driving RJR's Get Government Off Our Back. "In the mid-1990s, RJR hired the public relations firm Mongoven, Biscoe & Duchin to run the 'Get Government Off Our Back' coalition primarily to oppose OSHA regulation of workplace second-hand smoke (as well as FDA regulation of tobacco products). CSE was one of 39 GGOOB members, 18 of which were tobacco industry–funded and three more that had split off from tobacco industry–funded groups. The third-party coalition promoted an October 1994 resolution calling for smaller government and fewer regulations and fought smoke-free laws," the three researchers wrote.

In addition, they uncovered the deliberate effort by CSE to lead the attack in Congress and at the White House on Dr. Kessler's effort at the FDA to regulate cigarettes. "In February 1994, the FDA started investigating regulating nicotine as a drug and cigarettes and smokeless tobacco as drug-delivery devices. In March 1994, Philip Morris CEO [Michael] Miles recognized that 'The Administration has emerged as clearly anti-tobacco . . . [based on] Kessler's recent trial balloon on FDA regulation on the industry. This will also get worse. . . . It seems to me that we need to seriously reconsider whether our current passive defense strategy is the right strategy, or whether we have 'less to lose' by being more ferocious.'"

The researchers also found that CSE attempted to use the GOP takeover of the House as a much larger opportunity. "The political landscape changed after the November 1994 mid-term elections, when Republicans took control of Congress. A Philip Morris October 1995 draft action plan established the long-term goal of '[creating a] political environment where "moderates" of both parties on the Hill can vote for legislation that divests FDA of any power to regulate tobacco because they are convinced that FDA is already failing miserably in accomplishing its "core mission."' They partnered with CSE 'to quarterback behind the scenes, third-party efforts to launch, publicize and execute a broad non-tobacco-based attack on the many failings of the FDA with respect to its currently authorized statutory activities.'" CSE directed the action on all fronts.

A year later, CSE had upped the ante. "Throughout 1995, CSE worked to discredit the FDA and push for major limitations on its authority. CSE published critical commentary about the FDA, and ran full page ads in *Congressional Monitor* and the *Washington Times*. Their 'Death by Regulation' radio ads accused the FDA of being slow to approve drugs, thus leading to unnecessary death. CSE also opposed funding a modernized FDA building, one of Kessler's priorities." CSE chairman C. Boyden Gray (an heir to the RJ Reynolds tobacco fortune) testified against the building in Congress, citing the FDA's "overregulation" and "growing bureaucracy," and attacked FDA's slow approval of drugs. CSE also tried to reallocate FDA resources to "product approval process" by partnering with former CSE fellow Representative David McIntosh (R-IN) to freeze the Office of the Commissioner's budget.

In the last year of the Clinton presidency, the researchers found the document trail showing how CSE quickly became the third-party ally quarterbacking the efforts to halt the Department of Justice's RICO lawsuit against the tobacco industry. President Bush chose not to halt the effort. CSE stepped in—again—to lead the political efforts to roll back the effort on behalf of the tobacco industry.

"President Clinton announced in his 1999 State of the Union address that the DOJ was planning a case against the tobacco industry to recover smoking-induced Medicare funds under the RICO Act. In February 1999, Philip Morris's vice president of federal government affairs outlined three strategic goals for fighting the lawsuit: (1) to fight the $20 million dollar appropriation for the lawsuit; (2) 'bar consideration or defeat any legislation that enhances the ability of the DOJ to successfully bring a cause of action against the tobacco industry'; (3) exert 'political pressure' to block filing of the lawsuit. CSE supported these goals during 1999. CSE president Paul Beckner wrote to Senate majority leader Trent Lott (R-MS) and House Speaker Dennis Hastert (R-IL), 'On behalf of our 250,000 grassroots members, I urge you to oppose the federal government's proposed lawsuit as well as any legislation to facilitate this unprecedented action. CSE members and staff contacted policymakers, drafted commentaries, aired ads and sent out action alerts against the case.'"

The CSE efforts got some traction in Congress. "On July 22, 1999, Congress rejected DOJ's appropriation request. [The lawsuit was then funded by the Departments of Defense, Health and Human Services, and Veterans Affairs.] The industry and its third-party allies failed to stop the lawsuit, which the DOJ filed on September 22, 1999. The next day, CSE's Michele Isele Mitola was quoted in the *Washington Times:* 'We see this as a political ploy to find ways to raise more revenue to fund their [the government's] tax-and-spend agenda.' CSE continued opposition until at least 2002, encouraging supporters to ask newly elected President George W. Bush to end the lawsuit. These efforts failed, with federal judge Gladys Kessler ruling in 2006 that the major cigarette companies and their affiliated organizations constituted a continuing racketeering enterprise to defraud the public."

Outside Washington, the public health researchers also revealed the trail of tobacco industry support for CSE's antitax groups in the states.

"CSE opposed state tobacco taxes. For example, in 1996, the Tobacco Institute (then the tobacco companies' political and lobbying arm) provided New Jersey CSE with [funding] to fight a tobacco tax increase using mailings, radio advertisements and patch-through calls."

In short, Glantz, Fallin, and Grana found that the seemingly disparate pieces of "grassroots" movements were far from spontaneous or random. They were a clear, consistent, long-range game plan by the Kochs to create allied partnerships that work as closely as possible on the tobacco industry's central political efforts. The resulting partnerships greatly benefited the aims of both the Koch donor network allies and the tobacco industry, and directly formed the themes that would eventually be revealed as the Tea Party movement.

18

☆ ☆ ☆

Seamless Transition

For more than a decade, Citizens for a Sound Economy carefully and deliberately implemented the Kochs' master plan. A quick overview of that organization's work reveals astounding accomplishments.

CSE managed and directed three separate national political grassroots campaigns for the tobacco industry—the Tobacco Strategy, Allied Forces, and Mobilization Universe campaigns. It led and (through the Kochs' philanthropic arms) funded two powerful antitax and antiregulation business coalitions that were also partially funded by the tobacco companies—COFIRE and CART—all in concert with congressmen such as John Boehner, who later became Speaker of the House. It perfected two highly successful political-messaging campaigns that masked the tobacco industry's aims behind antigovernment rhetoric—Enough is Enough and Get Government Off Our Back—with Roger Ailes, now chairman of the Fox News Channel, Tommy Griscom, formerly President Reagan's communications director, and other talented communications pros.

CSE quarterbacked behind the scenes for multiple powerful coalitions—all with common goals.

COFIRE, the powerful Washington business coalition, had been instrumental in building the "no new taxes" centerpiece of the Reagan Revolution by learning how to oppose industry-specific excise taxes on cigarettes and other commodities.

COFIRE then faded away, to be replaced by yet another broad-based antitax coalition, CART, which had been systematically built in part to kill a national cigarette excise tax by attacking and ultimately defeating Hillarycare.

Allied Forces attacked mounting numbers of state-based cigarette excise tax threats to the tobacco industry by directing third-party ideology groups to do their bidding more broadly on antitax efforts.

Philip Morris–RJR's Tobacco Strategy blocked FDA regulation over the tobacco industry for years by organizing a broad array of groups to attack regulations at nearly every federal agency in DC.

Philip Morris's Mobilization Universe put political pressure on Washington over Clinton's last budget proposal and a looming Department of Justice RICO lawsuit aimed at tobacco companies.

CSE spent millions to defeat the BTU tax in President Clinton's first budget to Congress by working closely with the American Petroleum Institute on paid media campaigns in the states that isolated moderate Democrats up for reelection.

Ailes's Enough is Enough political rhetoric was effectively tested against the Clinton presidential campaign and then against Hillarycare.

The propaganda power behind Get Government Off Our Back was sufficient to convince the House of Representatives to pass a moratorium on all federal regulations in the wake of Newt Gingrich's Contract with America.

Then, with virtually no explanation, no acknowledgment of CSE's history, Rich Fink and Charles Koch simply disbanded the organization during 2003–4. After creating the form and function of what looks remarkably like the Tea Party movement with the might and nationwide resources of the tobacco companies at its political center, CSE became the ghost of political campaigns past.

Why? A careful look at the career and moves of former House majority leader Dick Armey gives some solid clues.

CSE and Dick Armey worked together for years on rallies in tobacco states such as North Carolina—and on the steps of the US Capitol—to bring about a "new Boston Tea Party" antitax revolution. When Armey retired in 2002, the group he chose to lead was the Kochs' Citizens for a Sound Economy. That same year, CSE created the U.S. Tea Party Web site.

"Today, the American tax burden is larger than ever, and the tax code grows ever more complex," CSE said on the U.S. Tea Party Web site. "Like those patriots in 1773, Citizens for a Sound Economy feels it is time for another symbolic protest in the best tradition of our Founding Fathers.

"In 2002, our U.S. Tea Party is a national event, hosted continuously online, and open to all Americans who feel our taxes are too high and the tax code is too complicated." The Web site described the U.S. Tea Party as a project of Citizens for a Sound Economy. "Dump some tea!"

Like Ron Paul before him—who left Congress to lead CSE and start a new antitax revolution—Dick Armey was leaving to join what he knew was the premier third-party ideological group in the country that matched his political framework.

"For 18 years in the House of Representatives, Dick Armey fought tirelessly for lower taxes, less government, and more freedom. Now, he's joining CSE to lead the same political revolution," the organization said in announcing that Armey was going to lead it.

Armey was equally as enthusiastic. "During my time as Majority Leader on Capitol Hill, I came to recognize that grassroots action is the most important factor in winning at politics," Armey said in the same press release. "That's what CSE is all about. I know CSE and its members well from past campaigns on the Flat Tax, Social Security reform, and school choice. In every issue that matters to the U.S. economy, CSE is right there in the fight. I am very excited to be a part of this great organization."

A year later, that same powerful organization disappeared, replaced by two new groups—Americans for Prosperity and FreedomWorks.

KochFacts.com, the Koch Industries Web site that answers questions directed at Charles Koch and his philanthropic and political efforts, describes CSE's end in just one bland paragraph:

"In 1984, Dr. Richard Fink, Charles Koch, David Koch and Jay Humphreys co-founded Citizens for a Sound Economy and Citizens for a Sound Economy Foundation. Over time the participants in CSE and the CSE Foundation developed different visions. In 2004, due to philosophical differences, CSE Foundation and CSE discontinued their affiliation. The CSE Foundation was renamed Americans for Prosperity Foundation and AFP Foundation created a 501(c)(4) organization, Americans for Prosperity. CSE merged with FreedomWorks. Koch has no ties to and has never given money to FreedomWorks."

According to FreedomWorks' own Web site, the organization didn't exist before that "merger": "FreedomWorks was originally founded as Citizens for a Sound Economy in 1984," their "About Us" section says.[1] The truth is that Empower America, cofounded in 1993 by Reagan administration education secretary William Bennett and former congressman Jack Kemp, and CSE joined forces to form a new organization, FreedomWorks.

But why allow CSE, an organization with such firepower and history, to simply vanish into the night? There are several potential reasons. Armey may, in fact, have wanted to take the organization in one direction, while Charles Koch and Rich Fink preferred a different path. Other donors may have wanted to direct a slightly different political campaign model, and FreedomWorks met that need. Or it might have been time to sunset CSE after years of working closely with the tobacco industry on multiple national political and messaging campaigns that created a highly successful paradigm for creating populist anger aimed at Washington over taxes, regulations, and government programs. Ending CSE would effectively bury any record of the organization's solely doing the tobacco industry's bidding for more than a decade just as thousands of internal tobacco industry documents were becoming public that would describe those activities.

What is curious is that CSE merged with another organization (Empower

America) to form FreedomWorks, while the Kochs supposedly walked away from everything they'd built with CSE in order to create a brand-new organization, Americans for Prosperity, seemingly from nothing. It was as if they wanted CSE to simply fade away, while they took their carefully constructed, highly effective grassroots political campaign network to a new place with no trace of any earlier trailblazing. In fact, KochFacts.com goes out of its way to state that Koch Industries has never financially supported FreedomWorks, which merged with CSE.

The Kochs and Fink allowed the big names associated with the split—Armey, former Bush White House counsel C. Boyden Gray, and former vice-presidential candidate Jack Kemp—to gather up all of the media attention at the time. The public eye was on where Armey and Kemp had gone—on FreedomWorks. CSE became merely a name of the past, with no one to care what had happened to it and nothing that could connect it to anything that the Kochs might build going forward.

Regardless of the reason for the split, though, the media's focus on FreedomWorks allowed Americans for Prosperity to go about its business quietly. Fink came back to run AFP briefly, just as he had every other Koch political or policy venture, before turning it over to Nancy Pfotenhauer. Nearly every aspect of the grassroots political campaign model that Fink and the Kochs had created through CSE over the years transferred in near totality to Americans for Prosperity. The Kochs and Rich Fink made certain that there was no slippage in the transfer of knowledge and relationships that they'd created and nurtured carefully over more than a decade's worth of campaign work.

In the last year of CSE's existence, according to IRS tax records, the various philanthropies run by Charles and David Koch (along with Koch Industries) had provided the bulk of its funding—a total of more than $7 million. When Americans for Prosperity launched, David Koch provided the bulk of its first-year funding—more than ten times that of any other donor, according to its IRS Form 990 filing that year. Americans for Prosperity picked up its tobacco industry antitax campaign work in a variety of states immediately as well—almost as if nothing had changed from the CSE days. It was a nearly seamless transition.

In its first full year as the new entity (in 2005), Americans for Prosperity's state director in Texas, Peggy Venable, led efforts to kill off a proposed smoking ban under consideration by the Texas legislature—precisely in the same way that CSE had once fought the tobacco industry's war on secondhand smoke and state excise taxes. "I think the [smoking ban] bill is dead," Venable told the *Fort Worth Star-Telegram* that year after the Kochs' Americans for Prosperity had led the political campaign to defeat the bill.

Venable described the group's opposition to the Texas smoking ban in the time-tested and successful political framework that CSE and the tobacco companies had deployed for more than a decade through the Tobacco Strategy, Allied Forces, and Mobilization Universe—as an intrusion on private-property rights and an overreach by government bureaucrats. It wasn't until a full two years later that the *Houston Chronicle* reported that the Americans for Prosperity in Texas political campaign against the smoking ban had been underwritten by the tobacco industry.

Americans for Prosperity took credit for defeating a smoke-free bill in North Carolina in 2007. In 2008, Americans for Prosperity opposed a cigarette excise tax in Illinois. This time, as in earlier CSE/tobacco coalition campaigns, they argued that the tax would cost jobs. In 2009, Americans for Prosperity opposed an indoor-air-pollution law directed at secondhand smoke in Missouri. The campaign was financed by tobacco companies. This time, the central argument was that the secondhand smoke regulation infringed on personal liberty and jobs.

The Tea Party movement is also alleged to have started spontaneously in 2009, with Americans for Prosperity rising up to serve as the backbone of the various groups and splinters across the country.

In April that same year, Melissa Cohlmia, a company spokesperson for Americans for Prosperity, "denied that the Kochs had direct links to the Tea Party, saying that Americans for Prosperity is 'an independent organization and Koch companies do not in any way direct their activities.' Later, she issued a statement: 'No funding has been provided by Koch companies, the Koch foundations, or Charles Koch or David Koch specifically to support the tea parties,'" Jane Mayer reported in *The New Yorker*.[2]

David Koch denied being at any Tea Party event and said he'd never been approached by a Tea Party representative, yet he was the chairman of the board of AFP, Mayer added.

She also noted that Peggy Venable, "who draws a salary from Americans for Prosperity, and who has worked for Koch-funded political groups since 1994," declared, "We love what the Tea Parties are doing, because that's how we're going to take back America!" In a later interview, she "described herself as an early member of the movement, joking, 'I was part of the Tea Party before it was cool!'"

Peggy Venable was also the organizer of the "Texas Defending the American Dream" summit, which took place over the July Fourth weekend, 2010, and was held by the advocacy wing of the Americans for Prosperity Foundation. Venable warned that administration officials "have a socialist vision for this country," Mayer reported. The event was advertised as a call to average Americans, whose "voices . . . are being drowned out by lobbyists and special interests." And then came the promise: "But you can do something about it." Intriguingly, no mention was made of the corporate funders of the event. "David Axelrod, Obama's senior adviser, said, 'What they don't say is that, in part, this is a grassroots citizens' movement brought to you by a bunch of oil billionaires.'"

Big tobacco had also learned an important lesson from watching the Kochs. To distance itself from its previous history, Philip Morris had created a brand-new company—Altria. In 2009, Americans for Prosperity went to work in Virginia on behalf of Altria to block a smoking ban. AFP hired a company to make thousands of calls to the offices of Virginia legislators who were considering such a ban. It was, in every sense, just like the good old days. But it wasn't CSE working for Philip Morris this time. Now it was Americans for Prosperity working against government intrusion on behalf of Altria.

19

☆ ☆ ☆

Sleight of Hand

L ittle has been written about why CSE—after considerable success in
DC and the states to build a Tea Party–styled, antitax network in partnership with the tobacco industry's aims—underwent a split into Americans
for Prosperity and FreedomWorks during 2003–4. KochFacts.com describes the split cryptically, as if somehow the two parts of the same
organization—its 501(c)(3) and 501(c)(4) entities—were somehow at odds
with each other. "Over time the participants in CSE and the CSE Foundation developed different visions," KochFacts.com said.

The description doesn't make sense. CSE and CSE Foundation were part
of the same network. It wasn't as if one did something without the other's
knowledge. Charles Koch and Rich Fink have given only a handful of
interviews—with friendly journalists at *The Weekly Standard, The Wall Street
Journal,* the Philosophy Roundtable's magazine, and two respected reporters for the local newspaper, *The Wichita Eagle,* who had covered Koch Industries favorably—but they always repeat the same litany about CSE's
funding.

CSE, they argue, was a "true" grassroots movement with thousands of
small donors that added up to a budget. But the truth—which reasserted

itself with the inadvertent public release of AFP donors in 2003 (and an earlier release of CSE donors in 2001)—is that both AFP and CSE relied heavily on various Koch entities for the majority of their financial backing, *National Journal* reported in 2013.

CSE was eventually able to attract significant tobacco funding for its work throughout the 1990s. But more than 80 percent of its budget over the years, by published accounts, was from various Charles and David Koch foundations, directed by Rich Fink. It was that way in the 1990s when I briefly consulted to it, and it was true a decade later as CSE became Americans for Prosperity.

In 2001, the IRS Schedule A forms showed, CSE received four large donations of $1 million or more that made up the lion's share of its funding—$2.3 million from the David H. Koch Charitable Foundation; $1.65 million from another Koch foundation, the Claude Lambe Charitable Foundation; more than $1 million from Koch Industries; and $1 million from David Koch. It also received sizable, but smaller, donations from Exxon Mobil, State Farm, and General Electric.

In 2003, as CSE was on the way to becoming Americans for Prosperity, it was the same pattern. David Koch provided $850,000 for the new entity—nearly ten times larger than the average of its other donations in that first year. Americans for Prosperity and CSE may be "true" grassroots organizations—but they're ones substantially underwritten by the Kochs.

Why did CSE split into two new organizations—Americans for Prosperity and FreedomWorks—beyond the now obvious need to distance CSE from the tobacco documents made available that same year in the Legacy archive, which would start connecting the dots on the Kochs' power plays?

It's already been mentioned that CSE and the CSE Foundation "developed different visions." However, the reason for the split may also have been due to a serious disagreement with former House majority leader Dick Armey, who'd taken over CSE after leaving Congress. Unlike Ron Paul, Armey was a real Washington insider—the sort of traditional, institutional

Republican politician that Rich Fink and the Kochs almost certainly don't like or trust.

It is likely that Armey wished to take CSE in a direction that the Kochs weren't interested in, so they split rather than force the issue with a very public leader. Nothing has been written (at least that is publicly available) about the scope or nature of the differences, so the specifics are impossible to discern. Jane Mayer, in *The New Yorker,* merely calls them "internal rivalries."[1] What's important, though, is to note that the pieces were already solidly in place behind the scenes to maintain a CSE mind-set at FreedomWorks, which allowed the media to focus so much of its attention there, and not on AFP. For example, Chicago businessman Dick Stephenson was on CSE's board the year of the split and has been part of the Kochs' donor network. A half dozen political, research, and political grassroots network leaders from the Koch/CSE days—including Matt Kibbe, Wayne Brough, David Kirby, Russ Walker, and state directors from big states—went with FreedomWorks.

As part of the split, Stephenson became committed to FreedomWorks. But, as *The Washington Post* and others reported, Stephenson was instrumental in easing Armey out of FreedomWorks in 2012 (with a twenty-year, $8 million buyout) and returning it into the hands of the Tea Party movement leaders who'd cut their teeth inside CSE under Rich Fink's tutelage and Charles Koch's influence. So did Charles Koch and Rich Fink bide their time and wait Armey out, then watch as Stephenson forced him out and returned it to the old CSE hands? It sure looks that way from the outside.

FreedomWorks was likely a sideshow for the Kochs, or a useful diversion. Their interests have clearly been with Americans for Prosperity since the split and in building the cornerstones of a real state-based political, grassroots, academic, policy, and propaganda network. It was critical to have their game plan fully in place, assembled through their donors and trusted leadership, in 2008 and early 2009—just in time to capitalize and fully launch the Tea Party movement as it seemingly "spontaneously" appeared.

The spokes of that Tea Party movement-in-waiting were created in partnership with AFP at the hub and, until recently, appeared disconnected. But a careful review of the ways in which their financial backing ramped up in the months before the spontaneous outburst of Tea Party activity in the spring of 2009 indicates that they were all built as part of what Rich Fink and Charles Koch have always wished to assemble—a real, connected network with the intellectual, political, academic, and "boots on the ground" grassroots muscle capable of redirecting the Republican Party from the outside at first, and then the inside.

In leading up to that effort at the end of 2008 and in early 2009, Rich Fink returned in force to take firm control of Americans for Prosperity and its work. He began to show up again on boards of Koch-funded entities that are central to the network. He brought back Nancy Pfotenhauer—who had run Koch Industries' DC office as well as the Koch-funded Independent Women's Forum—as AFP's first president. She spent several years with him building up AFP, before handing it over to Fink's next protégé, Tim Phillips, and leaving to work for John McCain's presidential campaign.

By 2008, a new Koch Tea Party–styled network was fully formed and ready to challenge the institutional Republican Party in DC. All it required was a suitable opponent, which they received in the form of presidential candidate Barack Obama, and a spark to ignite the Tea Party fervor and movement that had been more than a decade in the making.

20

☆ ☆ ☆

Five Pillars

Over the years, Rich Fink and his various Koch protégés have occasionally talked publicly about what would be needed to take over one of the two national political parties from the outside and place Libertarian, free-market principles at its center.

It would take:

1. an extensive academic network to support it intellectually;
2. policy networks in every state to draw on that intellectual underpinning from hundreds of American universities;
3. a true political grassroots alliance that extended to all of those state capitals and worked closely with the academic and policy network;
4. a propaganda arm that could bring tightly controlled messaging and narratives to the fore in the state networks in a way that looked like independent journalism;
5. and a national coordinating group that could enforce discipline in what would otherwise be a chaotic, unruly, wildly disconnected political network that ran the gamut from the patriot movement to American exceptionalism.

As luck—or careful, strategic planning—would have it, just such a highly leveraged network with these very pillars was in place as the Tea Party movement appeared to emerge from nowhere at the start of President Obama's first term in office. That Tea Party movement looked an awful lot like the efforts the Kochs' CSE had led in the Clinton and Bush years—just with more money, broad state-based causes, better-trained leaders, and a willingness to integrate and coordinate more efficiently with each other.

According to publicly available IRS records, the five essential pillars of just such a Tea Party movement network were all funded and in place by that spring of 2009—the Sam Adams Alliance to direct grassroots efforts; the Franklin Center for Government and Public Integrity to direct propaganda efforts in state capitals across the United States; the State Policy Network to coordinate funding and free-market policies at state-based think tanks; hundreds of grants from the Koch foundations to American universities that were linked in through SPN; and, of course, CSE's successor, Americans for Prosperity, built to coordinate the effort nationally.

All of them saw their budgets expand significantly as Obama ran for the White House and then took office—months or even a full year before the Tea Party movement erupted into public view. This explains why the Tea Party movement was able to mobilize, spread, and network so rapidly, as if by magic.

The Sam Adams Alliance was started by Eric O'Keefe, a well-known leader from the Koch donor network who once worked for CSE's Citizens for Congressional Reform. The alliance's budget more than doubled overnight—from $1.8 million in 2007 to $4.2 million in 2008, according to its 2008 IRS Form 990.

Of all the main groups in the network, the Sam Adams Alliance (SAA) signaled its clear intent nearly a year before the advent of the Tea Party movement. During the summer of 2008, SAA began to clear the path for the Tea Party movement at a series of training sessions in Texas, Illinois, and Colorado. Its name, of course, signaled its intent as well. Sam Adams was the brewer in 1773 who concocted the Boston Tea Party scheme in the first place.

In fact, SAA had been quietly working toward a Tea Party moment for nearly two years. In a November 2006 fund-raising letter, O'Keefe said, "We aim, in short, to be the premier networking station for citizen volunteers, donors and local leaders who want to . . . put citizens back in charge of government" by building "freestanding, effective, and lasting networks in states across the nation."

SAA held meetups with state chapters of Americans for Prosperity for months leading up to Santelli's rant to organize angry citizens willing to do something about taxes, regulations, and spending in DC—the well-refined CSE and tobacco-industry playbook. It also promoted the efforts by Ron Paul in 2007 to re-create similar Boston Tea Party stunts.

In July 2008, Americans for Prosperity launched RightOnline, a conference "about advancing liberty and prosperity for all Americans by leading the way to more effective and informed online activism," according to their Web site. At the first RightOnline.com gathering—in Austin, Texas, that same month—trainers from the Sam Adams Alliance explained how to build the Tea Party community, complete with, again, the same CSE and tobacco-industry playbook.

According to *The New York Times*,[1] Emily Zanotti, one of the Alliance's trainers, quoted Sam Adams and referenced the Boston Tea Party often and rallied those at the conference to "join together as communities to act as watchdogs" at the state and local level." Literally the moment Santelli's diatribe occurred at the Chicago Mercantile Exchange, the Sam Adams Alliance moved into action. Eric Odom, its new media director, had Tea Party Web sites, Facebook pages, and Twitter streams up and running within hours. Then, as the Tea Party movement spread, the SAA training and new social media network was there to spur it on, including the creation of new efforts such as the Patriot Action Network.

Both Odom and the SAA trainers had developed a waiting pool of online activists who mobilized instantly. The day after Santelli's rant, for instance, Phil Kerpen from Americans for Prosperity[2] created a Facebook group "Rick Santelli is right, we need a Taxpayer Tea Party"—which was managed by Odom. Until a few days before the Mercantile Exchange event, the Sam Adams Alliance had offered to take in interns for their state-based network through the Charles G. Koch Summer Fellow Program, administered by the Institute for Humane Studies[3] and the State Policy Network, according to a Wayback Machine Web snapshot of the fellowship program. The reference to the Koch fellows program no longer exists on that page.

But the Tea Party movement also needed messaging and propaganda to spread virally from state to state. In late 2008 and early 2009, just such an entity emerged in the Franklin Center—creating dozens of seemingly independent media outlets virtually overnight in state capitals that served as a networked echo chamber for the Tea Party movement.

Also run by leaders from the Koch donor network and funded by Donors Trust, the Franklin Center spun out from the Sam Adams Alliance and saw its budget go from zero dollars in 2008 to $2.3 million in early 2009, according to IRS records. Today, the Franklin Center coordinates fifty-five interlocked news sites covering politics in thirty-nine states that all follow the same antitax, antiregulation, antispending Tea Party script.

Jason Stverak, the Franklin Center's president, was the regional field director for the Sam Adams Alliance. The Franklin Center's director of donor relations, Matt Hauck, worked for the Charles G. Koch Foundation. Erik Telford left AFP to head up its strategic initiatives outreach. In early 2009 a member of the Franklin Center's original board of directors was Rudie Martinson, who worked for Americans for Prosperity in North Dakota. For years, one of the two physical addresses for the Franklin Center was a post office box at the UPS store in Bismarck, North Dakota.

The State Policy Network, also run by leaders from the Koch donor network, saw its budget boom in 2008 and 2009—just in time to take full advantage of the Tea Party movement. According to IRS records, its budget jumped to nearly $4 million in 2008. SPN's network of state-based think tanks brought the policy underpinning to the Tea Party movement. But, according to IRS records, it also coordinated Koch foundation grant-making activities at hundreds of American universities. In 2006, for instance, it spent $872,505 on efforts to "recruit adjunct scholars willing to serve on the boards of advisors of state-based think tanks" and to "produce a media guide for use by members."

SPN's executive vice president and operations director, Tony Woodlief, was the president of the Mercatus Center, which Rich Fink and Charles Koch had established at George Mason University to serve as the hub for its academic network. Daniel Erspamer, SPN's vice president for strategic partnerships, was the director of development at Americans for Prosperity from 2004 to 2009 and was with the Charles G. Koch Foundation before that.

The president of SPN, Tracie Sharp, caught a bit of flak for describing SPN at its annual meeting as the think tank equivalent of the giant global chain Ikea—where SPN provides a think tank "catalogue" for its network showing "what success would look like," according to Jane Mayer in *The New Yorker*.[4] In the audience were representatives from the constellation of Koch groups, including Koch Industries, the Charles Koch Institute, the Charles G. Koch Foundation, Americans for Prosperity, and Freedom Partners, according to a recent report by the Center for Media and Democracy.[5]

Instead of Ikea-like catalog pictures, SPN provides visions of state policy projects that align with its agenda, which covers the usual antitax, antiregulatory, antispending rhetoric. "The success we show is you guys. Here's how we win in your state," Sharp said, according to *The New Yorker*.[6] She also described to the assembly how SPN's agenda is shaped by its donor network. "The [SPN] grants are driven by donor intent. The donors have a very specific idea of what they want to happen.

"These aren't just little think tanks that are doing nonpartisan research based on what's happening in the state and really reflective of the culture of those states," Lisa Graves, the Center for Media and Democracy's executive director, told *Politico*.[7] "These are a lot of groups that put together pretty cooked books on the issues they are peddling."

Sharp takes issue with CMD's characterizations. "Every [SPN] think tank . . . rallies around a common belief: the power of free markets and free people to create a healthy, prosperous society," she told *Politico*. "They eschew a top-down, DC-centric approach to running people's lives. . . . There is no governing organization dictating what free-market think tanks research or how they educate the public."

Various philanthropic foundations associated with the Koch family now provide grants to more than 250 American universities, with training to recruit adjunct scholars, messaging, and media guides coordinated by SPN. That extensive academic network project began years earlier—but skyrocketed the year before the Tea Party movement began. Koch foundation grants to American universities were $2.6 million in 2007—but jumped to $6.1 million in 2008 and then to $13.5 million in 2009. Two years ago, Greenpeace compiled a list[8] of Koch Foundation grants to universities, which are in every state and range from big grants such as $1.3 million to Florida State University and $1 million to Clemson in South Carolina, to smaller grants such as $27,500 to Penn State and $47,000 to Utah State. The total, from 2005 to 2014, was more than $50 million—but the huge jump occurred the year before the Tea Party movement began.

At the center of the hub of activity is CSE's successor, Americans for Prosperity. It, too, was fully prepared and ready to act when the Tea Party movement kicked into high gear in February of 2009. Since its transition from CSE in 2003–4, Americans for Prosperity saw its budget leap to more than $10 million in early 2009, according to IRS records.

As the Tea Party movement took form, AFP was seemingly connected everywhere. Its state directors, especially in the bigger states, were coordinating Tea Party rallies. And, of course, the long-running alliance with the tobacco industry that began with CSE carried forward to its successor. AFP takes pro-tobacco positions, defending the tobacco industry against excise tax hikes as CSE did and using academic studies and policy reports to fight efforts to regulate secondhand smoke in the workplace.

The 2005 effort by AFP's Texas state director, Peggy Venable, to kill off a proposed smoking ban in that state is an obvious example. There are many others, in every year since AFP succeeded CSE as the Kochs' third-party coordinating group. Venable's description of AFP's opposition to the Texas smoking ban as an intrusion on private property rights, a tactic refined by Philip Morris and CSE in the 1990s in other states, is too perfect a match to be a coincidence. So is the 2008 AFP opposition to a cigarette excise tax in Illinois centered on arguments that it would cost jobs; AFP's 2009 opposition to another indoor-air-pollution law on behalf of the tobacco industry in Missouri, this time based on the public policy argument for personal liberty and jobs; or its 2009 campaign on behalf of Philip Morris's parent company, Altria, to respond to Virginia's smoking ban efforts.

By early 2009, then, the five pillars of all that was necessary to mobilize, train, network, message, and coordinate the Tea Party movement—refined by CSE and tobacco industry playbooks over the years—were in place. All of these groups were fully ready to take advantage of the Tea Party movement.

Even efforts such as the national tour by Tea Party Patriots' founders Jenny Beth Martin and Mark Meckler—who previously had no connections to the Koch network—were stage-managed and surrounded by the Koch donor network efforts. A year after their tour—and after names from the Koch donor network surfaced publicly—*Mother Jones* wrote that the *Patriot One* private jet they'd flown on for that Tea Party tour to rally the movement was owned by Ray Thompson, a member of the Koch donor network, who provided the jet from his manufacturing company in Kalispell, Montana.[9]

In a rare interview with a friendly journalist at *The Weekly Standard* designed to burnish his public image in 2011 following repeated public attacks by Obama White House officials, Charles Koch may have said more than he cared to about what they'd finally managed to achieve on the cusp of the Tea Party movement. Asked about the rise of the Tea Party to oppose Obama and his vision for the country, he said he was in awe of its power and strength: "The way it's grown, the passion and the intensity, was beyond what I had anticipated."[10]

21

☆ ☆ ☆

The Sam Adams Alliance

In 2006—two years after the Kochs and Rich Fink had dissolved Citizens for a Sound Economy and replaced it with Americans for Prosperity, and three years before the virgin birth of the Tea Party movement in Chicago—Americans for Limited Government held a conference for libertarian and free-market activists, says journalist Lee Fang, author of *The Machine*. ALG was another of the longtime Koch network allies and had worked closely with CSE over the years. Later ALG would receive substantial funding in 2010 and 2012 as the Koch donor network ramped up its political efforts, according to media coverage and tax forms, said Fang.[1]

The 2006 conference, in Chicago, was organized around opposition to taxes and big government, reported Laura Oppenheimer, a staff writer for *The Oregonian* of Portland, Oregon.[2] The attendees coalesced around what they believed was a brand-new political theme that could galvanize populist anger over taxes, regulations, and government intervention: the Boston Tea Party.

Mary Adams, an activist from rural Maine, accepted their activist-of-the-year award in 2006 and dedicated it to Sam Adams, the colonial-era leader who shared her name and led the Tea Party attack in Boston. The group decided that the Tea Party political rhetoric had real power and could serve as a blueprint for a much broader antigovernment effort.

The Sam Adams Alliance emerged from that conference. It was started by Eric O'Keefe, today a well-known leader from the Koch donor network who once worked for CSE's Citizens for Congressional Reform, and former GOP and term-limits campaign consultants.[3] One of the first videos from the group retold the story of the Boston Tea Party and merged that story with the images of the new Sam Adams Alliance staff working phone banks and of antitax protesters marching with Sam Adams Alliance signs.

The Sam Adams Alliance was small at first, but its modest annual budget of $1.8 million in 2007 more than doubled overnight to $4.2 million in 2008 according to IRS Form 990 tax records.

Directed by former CSE operative O'Keefe, the Sam Adams Alliance began handing out cash grants to activists in key swing states in 2007 related to Tea Party themes. Grants went to Tea Party activists in Tennessee, Virginia, and Oregon, where CSE had spearheaded enormous antitax campaigns for the tobacco companies shortly before becoming Americans for Prosperity. In one instance, the Sam Adams Alliance provided a grant to a Chicago-area group that staged a Tea Party antitax revolt alongside Ron Paul volunteers. At the same time, in 2007 and 2008, Americans for Prosperity was convening Tea Party events in other states. Thanks to the seamless transition from CSE to Americans for Prosperity in 2003–4, they already had their network in place. AFP had nearly 2 million people in its network from the start. "I see AFP as having a huge number of boots on the ground," David Koch told *The Weekly Standard* in describing the start of Americans for Prosperity.[4] CSE had forged the path—how to network with like-minded ideological groups and use corporate muscle to build those "boots on the ground."

AFP's Michigan chapter, for instance, formed a coalition with the Michigan Realtors Association and other business groups in 2007—two years before the Chicago Mercantile Exchange event—to host Tea Party events to support corporate tax cuts. "Our April 18th [2007] tax rally will have the tea bag as our theme to draw a parallel to the Boston Tea Party that sparked the American Revolution," Michigan's AFP chapter said in conjunction with the corporate-tax-cut events.[5]

With support from the Kochs' Americans for Prosperity, the Sam Adams Alliance worked hard in all of the most important former CSE network states to elevate the Tea Party themes they'd tested for more than a decade.

Americans for Prosperity sponsored the RightOnline.com conference in Austin, Texas, that summer—the same state where AFP had recently defeated a secondhand-smoke measure in the Texas legislature on the tobacco industry's behalf.

At the conference, the Sam Adams Alliance launched an ambitious national project designed to bring the AFP network into the digital age. "The Sam Adams Alliance . . . has started an ambitious project this year to encourage right-leaning activists and bloggers to get online and focus on local and state issues," *The New York Times* reported in a July 19, 2008, story called "The Sam Adams Project."[6]

"At the RightOnline.com gathering, sponsored by Americans for Prosperity Foundation and others here for conservative bloggers, several trainers talked about the tools provided by the alliance, under umbrellas for each locale," the article said. "Previous sessions were held in Chicago and Denver."

The new digital blogging model was built on activist models on the left such as MoveOn.org and blogging sites such as DailyKos.com, *The Times* reported, in order to mobilize voters online. *The Times* tried to determine the funding sources for the Sam Adams Alliance but said that it got nowhere. "No donors are listed on its 990 tax form, according to public tax filings, and on its Web site, it proudly declares that it respects its donors' right to privacy and to voluntary disclosure, and doesn't accept any government funds. They say they are grateful for 'our judiciary's firm respect for donor privacy.' A check of the filings with the Illinois attorney general's office finds no record that the organization has registered its finances."

The common theme at the Sam Adams Alliance training sessions inside the AFP conference was the American antitax revolution fomented by the Boston Tea Party. "Emily Zanotti, one of the alliance trainers, peppered her talk with conservative bloggers on Friday with quotes from Samuel Adams (think tea party and taxes) and stories of the Founding Fathers as she tried to persuade them to build communities," the *Times* article noted.

It quoted Zanotti telling the AFP conferees at RightOnline.com that the Sam Adams Alliance was bringing the Tea Party revolution into the digital age through its networks. "Without community there would have been no 1776. So we're moving you, one at a time, one blogger at a time," Zanotti said.

While O'Keefe, who founded the Sam Adams Alliance, was not at the AFP conference in Texas, *The Times* referenced a recent column about his strategy in confronting Democrats in key swing states. The approach perfectly aligned with the central strategies that Rich Fink and Charles Koch had built through CSE before morphing it into Americans for Prosperity.

"O'Keefe lists seven capacities that are required to drive a successful political strategy and keep it on offense: the capacity to generate intellectual ammunition, to pursue investigations, to mobilize for elections, to fight media bias, to pursue strategic litigation, to train new leaders, and to sustain a presence in the new media," *The Times* reported. It was capacity building that looked like a national political party.

The Sam Adams Alliance had been building a sustainable Internet presence around Tea Party themes for months. It had targets in South Dakota and Montana, where the blogosphere was especially strong. "Zanotti indicated during her talk that the alliance was working on projects that it wasn't ready to talk about yet," *The Times* said.

But the alliance clearly had big digital network goals in mind, built around the capacities and strategies outlined by O'Keefe. "Zanotti [coaxed] her audience to establish networks, to crosslink, to join together as communities to act as watchdogs. 'We bring bloggers together to police their communities,' she said and later added, 'Tell us what your local government is not doing. . . . How are they spending your money, where is it going?'"

Time and again, the Sam Adams Alliance trainers returned to one of the strongest Tea Party themes: that a relentless network can change history. "Be the tireless minority online, [Zanotti] said, borrowing several times from that Sam Adams quote: 'It does not require a majority to prevail, but rather an irate, tireless minority keen to set brush fires in people's minds.'"

All of this might well have faded away without further scrutiny—except that the Sam Adams Alliance efforts in 2007 and 2008 inside the Americans for Prosperity campaign network came to sudden prominence in the spring of 2009 after Obama had been elected. But in describing the role that the Sam Adams Alliance had played in the 2009 "spontaneous" Tea Party uprising, any sort of historical context was largely lost in the media coverage.

One of the best journalistic efforts to deconstruct the Sam Adams Alliance contribution to the Tea Party efforts came from a special report called "Anatomy of the Tea Party Movement: Sam Adams Alliance" from the *Huff-Post*'s Eyes & Ears Citizen Journalism Unit.[7] After describing O'Keefe's connection to the Kochs through Citizens for a Sound Economy, the report then focused on the role that the Sam Adams Alliance had played in the 2009 events. It started, as in other accounts, with the notion that the Tea Party movement had been born in the spring of 2009.

"Shortly before online activist Eric Odom helped kick-start the Tea Party movement, he was new media director for [the] Sam Adams Alliance," the article reported. "This put him in charge of (among other things) setting up websites, coordinating Facebook groups, managing Twitter accounts and other social networking tasks. Odom's first known acts as a Tea Partier were to set up the OfficialChicagoTeaParty.com site and Facebook pages within hours of Rick Santelli's February rant, then spreading the word through Twitter, initially utilizing #TCOT, a Twitter hashtag for Top Conservatives on Twitter."

The report then described at length the preparations that Odom, O'Keefe, a third Sam Adams Alliance staff member, Ken Marrero, and John Tillman, who had once directed the start-up of Americans for Limited

Government, had made to kick off the Tea Party revolution. By doing so, the *HuffPost*'s Eyes & Ears Citizen Journalism Unit attempted to explain the extraordinarily complicated network of groups and individuals who had worked together for years and came together around the Chicago event to explode the Tea Party themes.

"Within hours of Rick Santelli's rant, Kristina Rasmussen, who had just been hired as the executive vice president by the Illinois Policy Institute (which Tillman ran) that morning, helped kick start the Chicago Tea Party by participating in a February 19 conference call to plan the event," the article said. "Rasmussen, who was then the director of government affairs at [the] National Taxpayers Union, was the second speaker on the call. Tillman also serves on the Sam Adams Alliance's board of directors and was president and COO of [the] Sam Adams Alliance during its start up phase."

A network of groups and organizations were involved in the Tea Party movement's planning beforehand, but the origin was nearly undecipherable due to the interlocking nature of all parties involved. Such a networked strategy had been typical of the CSE network as well for its entire existence before it became AFP. No wonder that any media covering the Tea Party's beginnings had a nearly impossible time unraveling its history or context.

The *HuffPost* article then got even more convoluted. "American Liberty Alliance is not the only Sam Adams Alliance affiliate in this fight, however. American Majority, a self-described 'political training institute' is a 'concept' of [the] Sam Adams Alliance, which in turn describes itself as AM's 'sponsor.' American Majority staff includes George W. Bush speechwriter Ned Ryun; regional field director for Bush/Cheney '04, Lonny Leitner; former Republican state legislator Shari Weber; and former director of operations at the Oklahoma Republican Party, Matt Pinnell."

Why does this matter? Why does a network of three seemingly disconnected groups with bland names—two of which have *American* in them—matter at all in the Tea Party uprising? How does one follow along in the playbook?

Sorting through the network of names and organizations—and matching them to their respective roles—is mind-numbing in its complexity.

But, the article said, it was apparent in hindsight that the Tea Party movement had been long in the planning stage, with deep connections to the Koch donor network—all of which was systematically painted over after the fact.

"Long before [the] Sam Adams Alliance's recent website redesign, they altered an internship recruitment page that connected [the] Sam Adams Alliance to Koch Industries. 'Interested parties can apply for a Sam Adams Alliance internship through the Charles G. Koch Summer Fellow Program administered by the Institute for Humane Studies and the State Policy Network.'

"The internship is still listed on the IHS website. Charles Koch founded IHS," the report stated. "The internship page existed up until the site's ongoing redesign, but recently the Koch reference was absent from the Sam Adams Alliance website. An article in *Playboy* magazine . . . claimed the Koch reference was scrubbed on Feb. 16. Three days later, Santelli's supposedly-spontaneous rant kick-started the Tea Party movement."

So while this investigative report went into the bramble bushes as far as it possibly could to untangle the Chicago event and found enough to question the spontaneous nature of the event and the network behind it, its ability to go more deeply behind the Koch donor network connections was limited. Finding the power source behind the Chicago Tea Party event— and the Sam Adams Alliance's role in paving the way for its launch—was elusive.

But a look at the citizen network the Sam Adams Alliance and its affiliates linked to reveals a clear road map . . . directly to the exact, same network claimed by CSE and then Americans for Prosperity. When the Patriot Action Network created by Eric Odom in 2008 claimed an immediate network of nearly 2 million members and staked its claim that "We Are the Tea Party" almost overnight, it could have acquired that network so quickly in only one logical place.

"Patriot Action Network is one of the nation's largest conservative social action networks, serving hundreds of thousands of citizens every
month," its Web site said. "We are united by our passion for re-establishing
Constitution-based liberty and limited government through dialogue, debate, legislation and elections. Not only is the Patriot Action Network the
largest active social hub of the Patriot Movement . . . we're also the official
social action network of Grassfire Nation and the 1.8 million Patriot members of Grassfire.com."

The Grassfire.org Alliance, a nonprofit 501(c)(4), launched in 2000,
described itself as "an online conservative issues advocacy organization"
and claimed that it was a grassroots organization. It largely disappeared in
2007 and then launched a "Join The Resistance" campaign in 2008 to "hold
off as much of the Obama agenda as possible."[8]

Building actual, real citizen grassroots members is generally the hard
work of national political parties. But the tobacco companies had long ago
learned how to mirror that effort through their successive campaigns (with
the Kochs' CSE as their key third-party ally directing traffic) ranging from
COFIRE in the Reagan years to the Mobilization Universe in the second
Bush administration. The Sam Adams Alliance, by accident or design, benefited from those earlier efforts.

When the Sam Adams Alliance announced, in November 8, 2006, that
it aimed "to be the premier networking station for citizen volunteers, donors, and local leaders who want to make real change and put citizens back
in charge of government," it had a rich playbook to work from and a road
map that had been tested from Enough is Enough to Get Government Off
Our Back.

Like so many of the other seemingly disconnected groups inside the
network—the CART and COFIRE coalitions during the Reagan and
Bush years, for instance—the Sam Adams Alliance eventually outlived its
usefulness and faded away, further obscuring the origins of the long rise of
the Tea Party movement. In 2010, writes journalist George Montbiot, the
alliance provided three quarters of the funding for another conservative

group called American Majority, which has a similar mission to train grass-roots political leaders in the Tea Party movement.

By 2013, many of its activities had morphed into American Majority, where one of its founder, Eric O'Keefe, has helped guide and lead the organization, according to SourceWatch. American Majority now trains thousands of Tea Party candidates for local offices across the Untied States. In 2008, the year in which American Majority was formed, 88 percent of American Majority's funding came from a single donation of $3.7 million, Montbiot wrote.

Today, American Majority has essentially replaced the mission of the Sam Adams Alliance. "American Majority has conducted over 800 train-ings in 45 different states, training over 30,000 new leaders and activists." It bills itself as the "organizing arm for conservatives" to "put in place the nation's new, conservative grassroots infrastructure." Like its predecessor, American Majority is "dedicated to developing a new generation of Amer-ican leadership that will reject the self-destructive policies associated with government expansion," its Web site says. So while the Sam Adams Alliance served its purpose, and then faded from the scene, its mission and spirit are very much alive and well.

22

☆ ☆ ☆

Propaganda "Dressed Up as Journalism"

Medora is a small, seasonal tourist town in the Badlands of western North Dakota, about 25 miles from the Montana border. It has a population of less than one hundred. It went for John McCain for president by a three-to-one margin in 2008. A handful of small stores are in the center of the town—some gift shops, a bookstore, an ice cream shop, two restaurants, a museum, and a hotel that's full during tourist season.

Around the corner from downtown is the Rushmore Mountain Taffy and Gift Shop (not to be confused with the Rushmore Mountain Taffy Shop at the base of Mount Rushmore in South Dakota). You wouldn't know it by looking at it, but the Medora taffy shop was the first legal home of a media organization that now provides a significant amount of political news coverage in thirty-nine state capitals through fifty-five interconnected news sites, according to a local reporter who was curious about the entity and asked around.[1]

At the start of 2008, the Franklin Center for Government and Public Integrity had a budget of zero dollars. Its legal home was the taffy shop in Medora. By 2009 the Franklin Center's budget had jumped to $2.4 million, according to IRS tax records. That's a spectacular leap for a nonprofit, especially in Medora.

It was almost as if someone wished to utilize the charter concept of the Franklin Center—developing individual but interlinked news centers across the United States that would all promote the same messages—for other purposes and therefore infused it with a mountain of funding and network support. Intriguingly, this was a year before the Tea Party movement seemingly sprang from nowhere and spread like a prairie fire to the thirty-nine state capitals where the Franklin Center now operates its news sites.

The Franklin Center has a second address—a post office box in Bismarck, North Dakota, where mail is forwarded east to Old Town Alexandria, near Washington, DC. North Dakota law requires that nonprofits have a "physical address," not just a forwarding address or a post office box. So, for years, the Franklin Center's registered agent was at the taffy shop, while the mail was forwarded from the UPS store in Bismarck.

The Franklin Center's president is Jason Stverak. He used to be the executive director of the North Dakota Republican Party. He also ran Rudy Giuliani's presidential campaign efforts in the state. But just prior to starting the Franklin Center, he was the regional field director for the Sam Adams Alliance, where, according to his Franklin Center bio, he "worked with state groups and associations committed to promoting the free-market policies" that are now embedded in every political story that the network's reporters write about in state capitals across the country.

"An expert in non-profit journalism, Jason works to promote social welfare and civil betterment by leading initiatives that advance investigative journalism," his Franklin Center bio reads. "His support of non-profit journalism has played a vital role in exposing corruption in our elected officials and encouraging transparency in government."

The Franklin Center grew from nothing in 2007–8 to the largest network of local political reporting in the country almost overnight. Its fifty-five news sites generally cover political events or issues from an antitax, antiregulation, or antispending frame. While each of the sites has its own team of local reporters, they generally tend to share common themes across the entire network of coverage, recent studies have shown. Government is either working badly and needs to be exposed; or local initiatives are spending far too much money; or politicians are unjustly pushing for excise taxes on oil or gas or cigarettes; or the local governments are burying citizens in regulations and bureaucracy.

The Franklin Center describes most of its reporters in the state capitals as "watchdogs," constantly looking for excise taxes that need to be rolled back or government initiatives and regulations that need to be curtailed. The organization was built to "address falling standards in the media as well as a steep falloff in reporting on state government," its mission statement says. It "provides professional training; research, editorial, multimedia and technical support; and assistance with marketing and promoting the work of a nationwide network of non-profit reporters." It supplements that watchdog reporting in state capitals with its "newly launched Citizen Watchdog program that trains ordinary citizens to report from local communities."

In many of the state capitals across the United States, especially in the less populated red states, the Franklin Center news sites are a significant source of local and statewide political news. "Specializing in state and local government, [the] Franklin Center has focused its efforts on reaching maximum penetration within small and mid-sized media markets—on driving a conversation about transparency, accountability, and fiscal responsibility at the grassroots level and putting a human face on public policy," it says. "We specialize in reaching a layman's audience through local media, coordinating our nationwide network to ensure that we are hitting this audience in every state.

"[The] Franklin Center was founded in 2009 to help fill the void created as the nation's newspapers cut back on their statehouse news coverage and investigative reporting in the wake of falling circulation and revenues. Our goal is to provide fresh, original, hard-hitting news content that is published on our own Web sites and in traditional media sources."

While each of the local sites and reporters cover their own beats and stories, they all share a common goal and platform. "All publications have a mission and a voice. We are unabashed in ours: to spotlight waste, fraud and misuse of taxpayer dollars by state and local governments. We always ask these questions when reporting on events: What does this mean for taxpayers? Will it advance or restrict individual freedom? We look at the bigger picture, provide analysis that's often missing from modern news stories, and do more than provide 'he-said, she-said' reports from the state Capitol. Our journalists look for the back story and offer much-needed perspective on the day's news."

That context—multiple news outlets with the same underlying themes—is what makes the Franklin Center unique. State legislators have come to accept a certain style of coverage from its local news sites, which have names such as KansasReporter.com, PlainsDaily.com, or CapitolBeatOK.com, and they are rarely disappointed. The state legislators and local readers also aren't generally aware that a national center is directing traffic.

Beyond its news sites and paid reporters, the Franklin Center also trains an army of citizen journalists who will blog and comment on taxes and government in state capitals. "We're leaders in the new wave of non-profit journalism. We have reporters, news sites, investigative journalists and affiliates across the country—and we're growing. In addition to our nationwide team of professional journalists, we are expanding our reach into citizen journalism," it says. "We provide training to these citizen watchdogs so that they can better employ journalistic standards as they keep their local governments accountable through their blogs and Web sites. While distinct from our journalism efforts, this new wave of information activism will help fulfill Franklin's vision of creating a more vibrant democratic society based on accountability and open government."

Like the Sam Adams Alliance training sessions that were conducted under the umbrella of Americans for Prosperity in the year or so prior to the Chicago Tea Party event, most of the Franklin Center's training sessions for citizen journalists are likewise conducted in partnership with Americans for Prosperity.

A training session in Omaha, Nebraska, in the fall of 2013 is a good example of this partnership. The session was free, sponsored by the Nebraska AFP chapter. The Franklin Center ran it for two nights (and included conservative activist James O'Keefe, who filmed ACORN events under cover, creating a firestorm of controversy).

"Nebraska and our nation are in a fiscal crisis," the AFP's Facebook event page said, describing the training session. "You've heard the egregious examples of waste, fraud and abuse on a daily basis. We can no longer afford to sit by and wait for the government or mainstream media to fully inform the public about what's going on behind closed doors. The time has come to stand up and take action. Together, we can begin the hard, but important job of taking back America."

In an era where old media is being replaced rapidly by digital media and citizen journalism, nonprofit media organizations are paying close attention to the ways in which philanthropy is intersecting with journalism. They are amazed at the rapid growth of the Franklin Center because it has been extraordinarily successful at a time when local investigative journalism efforts—even those supported by philanthropy—have struggled to take hold. Even the largest news organizations in the world are struggling to survive.

The New York Times has gone through several rounds of buyouts and forced layoffs in the last three years, for instance. Every major newspaper in the country is struggling with the transformation to the digital age of media. An *American Journalism Review* in 2009 found that the number of reporters covering state capitals had fallen 30 percent since 2003.

Yet the Franklin Center flourishes. Why? Because it has deep financial pockets and no worries about its funding. *National Journal* reported that the Sam Adams Alliance provided the seed money to launch the Franklin Center in the months prior to the Chicago Tea Party event, taking the funding from zero to $2.4 million in 2009, then to $3.7 million the following year.[2]

Besides operating a group of paid national reporters who focus on state capitals as well as a group of citizen journalists blogging in these state capitals, the Franklin Center also supplies grants to each of the fifty-five sites in the thirty-nine state capitals.

Its success—basically, the reason that it has no need to fight for its survival when every other local digital journalism effort does—is almost certainly due to its connection to the Koch donor network. Like other related groups with operations in the DC area, the Franklin Center benefits greatly from the Koch donor network's Freedom Partners.

The Franklin Center's director of donor development, Matt Hauck, worked for the Charles G. Koch Foundation. Its senior vice president in charge of strategic initiatives, Erik Telford, worked for the Kochs' Americans for Prosperity before joining the Franklin Center. The founding board member who set it up was Rudie Martinson, who helped run Americans for Prosperity in North Dakota. Martinson is still on the Franklin Center's board. One of the founders of the Franklin Center, John Tsarpalas, is a past president of the Sam Adams Alliance and director of the Illinois Republican Party.

The Franklin Center operation works quickly and efficiently. Here's a good example, from a report by the Center for Media and Democracy.[3] In 2012, the Idaho legislature took up a bill that was designed to keep minors from going to commercial tanning salons. It was uncontroversial—other states have instituted similar restrictions for minors due to concerns about the dangers of skin cancer—until the *Idaho Reporter* (one of the Franklin Center's news sites) took up the issue in force. It posted six stories on the tanning-bed bill between February 16 and March 22 of that year, claiming that passing such a bill represents a "huge overreach by the state . . . an infringement upon a family's right to make these kinds of choices."[4] A state Senate committee then voted the bill down.

Former Reuters chief White House correspondent Gene Gibbons conducted a review of statehouse coverage by traditional media outlets shortly after the spontaneous combustion of the Tea Party movement in 2009—and ran smack into the Franklin Center network. He was surprised at what he found, he wrote in his study for the *NiemanReports* publication of the Nieman Foundation for Journalism at Harvard in 2010.[5]

"For the most part, the people in charge of these would-be watchdog operations are political hacks out to subvert journalism in their quest to grab and keep power using whatever means they have to do so," Gibbons wrote. "At the forefront of an effort to blur the distinction between statehouse reporting and political advocacy is the Franklin Center." He added that such efforts were "political propaganda dressed up as journalism."

Gibbons interviewed Jason Stverak in the spring of 2010 for the Nieman Foundation report. Stverak told him that the Franklin Center journalists were held to the same journalism ethics as those from traditional newspapers. They should be judged "based upon the content that they produce," Stverak said.

But when Gibbons looked into how the Franklin Center went about its business, he indeed found "political propaganda dressed up as journalism." Four months after he interviewed Stverak, Gibbons wrote, "The Franklin Center cosponsored and played an active role in a two-day conference organized by Americans for Prosperity Foundation. The Right Online Agenda conference included such breakout sessions as 'Intro to Online Activism' and 'Killing the Death Tax' and featured speakers such as conservative U.S. Representative Michele Bachman of Minnesota and Tea Party activist Sharron Angle, a Republican who was then running against Harry Reid in the election for U.S. Senate in Nevada. No Democratic legislators were included in the program. The finale of the Las Vegas conference was a 'November is Coming Rally.' "

But Gibbons also said that this was likely the future of some form of journalism and cited conservative columnist K. Daniel Glover in a subsequent report in June of 2010 on the trends for the Kennedy School of Government's Joan Shorenstein Center on the Press, Politics and Public Policy.

"Once conservatives realize they can conduct great investigations that expose the flaws of intrusive government and the special interests that corrupt it, you will see more of them embracing that kind of journalism," Glover told him. "Mainstream publications like the [*Washington*] *Examiner* and organizations like the Franklin Center . . . which helps support and fund budding watchdogs, are showing them the way."

The Franklin Center sites also clearly drive follow-on news coverage, often uncritically. Its *Wisconsin Reporter,* for instance, once sponsored a poll that found more than 70 percent of people in the state supported an effort by Governor Scott Walker to cut the collective bargaining rights of the state's public sector workers—a fight that angered the unions of teachers and other public sector workers. National news organizations, including MSNBC, picked up the coverage and reported on the poll.

In his study, Gibbons found a highly leveraged network of sites: "The State Policy Network–Sam Adams Alliance–Franklin Center troika is at least loosely associated with more than a dozen other conservative groups funding news sites in various states."

By 2011, according to CMD and others, the Franklin Center had more than tripled in size from its 2009 start. Donors Trust, a 501(c)(3) charity whose Web site says they encourage giving to "fund organizations that undergird America's founding principles," alone provided $6.3 million to the Franklin Center in 2011, according to those reports. *Mother Jones* called Donors Trust "the dark-money ATM of the conservative movement" in a 2013 article.[6] The Franklin Center was the second-largest recipient of Donors Trust funding in 2011. A central contributor to Donors Trust is the Knowledge and Progress Fund founded and run by Charles Koch.

Today, Franklin Center reports make the national news circuit through the Fox News Channel, the *Washington Examiner,* and *The Daily Caller* and hit the front page of the *Drudge Report* consistently. For instance, at the end of October 2014—just a few days before the midterm elections, its *Wisconsin Reporter* story about Governor Scott Walker's opponent in his reelection fight (Democratic gubernatorial candidate Mary Burke) was highlighted by Rush Limbaugh.[7]

"Now this story hit," Limbaugh said on his popular, syndicated radio program. "It's a story about Mary Burke, the Democrat candidate there, and how she was fired from the family business for incompetence. Whatever the family business is, she was fired from it. She's seeking the governorship in Wisconsin, and the point is, if her own family had to discharge her from the family business because of how much she gunked it up, then what business does she have being elected governor?"

Needless to say, Burke contested the news story. But the damage was done, with little time to deal with it publicly before the election.

One thing is also obvious from this episode. What began as a novel concept—shaping media coverage from a libertarian perspective by *becoming* the media and presenting only one side of an issue—in the years and months prior to the spontaneous rise of the Tea Party in Chicago in 2009 may now, according to Gibbons and others studying the intersection of philanthropy and journalism, become the norm for the way in which news is conveyed in American democracy.

23

☆ ☆ ☆

Capturing the States

Thomas Roe was a member of President Reagan's kitchen cabinet.[1] Reagan once suggested to Roe that he start a network of policy councils modeled after DC think tanks. They could have the same sort of influence, but at the state and grassroots level. Roe did just that and founded the State Policy Network soon thereafter.

Roe was proud of the SPN and its ambition. "You capture the Soviet Union—I'm going to capture the states," Roe told a Heritage Foundation trustee during the Reagan era, according to an interview with Lee Edwards for his book on the twenty-five-year history of the Heritage Foundation.[2]

Its founding executive director, Byron Lamm, was from my hometown of Fort Wayne, Indiana. While SPN has since relocated its national headquarters to a suite of offices in Arlington, Virginia, to more easily take advantage of the funding pool available to the Donors Trust and Freedom Partners colocated there, its roots still run deep in the Hoosier state.

It was one of the reasons that Indiana's GOP governor Mike Pence was one of just two or three potential GOP presidential contenders for 2016 virtually guaranteed inner-circle status with the Koch donor network that raised and spent hundreds of millions of dollars in the 2014 midterm federal elections. The network of state policy councils that serve as the backbone of the free-market movement was born in Indiana. It didn't hurt that Pence's former chief of staff, Marc Short, runs Freedom Partners, which coordinates much of the Koch donor network's political spending. However, when Pence signed the Religious Freedom Restoration Act into law in Indiana in March 2015, and he was caught in a culture war, his dreams of being a GOP presidential candidate ended.[3]

The State Policy Network has been around for a considerable time. But the true nature of its origins—beyond anecdotal stories about President Reagan's offhand comment, or Roe's subsequent comment to an interviewer about his ambition to "capture the states"—wasn't known until the internal tobacco-industry documents became available in UCSF's Legacy archive.

A July 10, 1991, letter from the executive director of the American Legislative Exchange Council, Sam Brunelli, to a senior vice president of the Tobacco Institute, Kurt Malmgren, makes those origins quite clear. The State Policy Network was a creation of ALEC—an organization that creates "model" bills for state legislators based on corporate funding, which has come under fire for defending "stand your ground" gun laws in the states, prompting an exodus of some of its prominent corporate funders.

In the letter, Brunelli makes the case to the Tobacco Institute for tobacco funding and support for the State Policy Network. As part of his letter he included a report that shows the Kochs' Citizens for a Sound Economy as one of the four key national organizations leading the coordination of the state policy councils (along with the National Rifle Association and two others).

"Our energy and effort goes into winning the public policy debate, and championing a free market economy . . . a pro-business, pro-growth, pro-freedom, limited government agenda," Brunelli wrote to the Tobacco Institute. As proof of their effectiveness and their ability to deliver on the tobacco industry's political strategies, he described the network of policy councils under its direction, coordinated by the Kochs' CSE. "ALEC is now at center stage, at the cutting edge of the public policy debate being waged in state capitols across the country."

Like CSE, the State Policy Network refined its approach over the years and grew in stature and funding. But in 2008, the year prior to the Chicago Tea Party event—working with the Kochs' university network of funded scholars, ALEC, and the Koch donor network—SPN saw its budget jump by 50 percent, to $4 million.

Its principal task in 2008, according to IRS tax records, was to coordinate policy language among hundreds of adjunct scholars at dozens of universities that had received funding from the various Koch foundations. A single line item for nearly $1 million in its budget that year was to "recruit adjunct scholars willing to serve on the boards of advisors of state-based think tanks; produce a media guide for use by members; create an economic and regulatory index which compares different levels of regulation and taxation in various states." It's not surprising, then, that these same State Policy Network councils create the tax analytics used as the basis of efforts by the Kochs' Americans for Prosperity and ALEC to oppose excise taxes on cigarettes or as the rationale to roll back regulations on corporations.

Since the Chicago Tea Party days, the State Policy Network has continued to grow in leaps and bounds, reflecting the appetite for its policy directives to help fuel political grassroots efforts. By 2011, the combined revenue of SPN's affiliated network had grown to $83 million, while its national budget had increased to $8 million, mostly due to funding from Donors Trust and the Donors Capital Fund, which coordinate the funding of the Koch donor network, according to *Politico*, which based its reporting on a study by the Center for Media and Democracy.

SPN's executive director, Tracie Sharp, dismissed the CMD study, telling *Politico* that the councils were "fiercely independent" and not coordinated. But she insisted that all think tanks rallied around a "common belief: the power of free markets and free people to create a healthy, prosperous society." [4] Whether that's true or not may not matter. The reality is that some policies appear everywhere all at once, as if by magic. Before Ted Cruz became a GOP senator from Texas, he wrote a report for one of SPN's leading lights, the Texas Public Policy Foundation, arguing that President Obama's health care reform bill violated states' rights in the Tenth Amendment.

"That report is one of the many sorts of reports that are penned by various individuals . . . that then spread like wildfire through the rest of the affiliates," Rebekah Wilce, the author of the CMD study, told *Politico*. "And in the individual states where they are published basically verbatim, you can't see where they came from, or the author's name is not published on them."

In late 2013, however, the *New Yorker* reported that Sharp's characterization of the "independence" of the SPN network wasn't quite true. Notes provided to *The New Yorker* on what was said during the SPN's recent twenty-first annual meeting show that the network generally does what its donors want, as well as providing a blueprint for how to plug and play various policy ideas on the corporate donors' wish list.[5] A 2013 State Policy Network budget proposal also makes it clear that SPN's national leadership directs much of the funding from the donor network to its affiliates in the states. The budget document itemizes the amounts that each SPN affiliate is likely to receive from the national coordinating office, according to *The Guardian*.[6] What's more, in 2012, a list of the 2010 funders of Senator Cruz's former SPN affiliate, the Texas Public Policy Foundation, which was inadvertently disclosed to the IRS, makes it clear the way in which the national donors direct funds to the state affiliates. Koch Industries gave $159,000 directly to the Texas affiliate Senator Cruz worked at, along with $69,000 from a Koch family foundation.

SPN and its affiliate network saw its budget increase exponentially starting two years prior to the Chicago Tea Party event, then accelerate in recent years largely because it sits at the center of the Koch donor network historically. As mentioned earlier, SPN's executive vice president, Tony Woodlief, was the president of the Mercatus Center at George Mason University, which Rich Fink and Charles Koch established to coordinate research and funding to hundreds of academics at American universities. And Daniel Erspamer, who directs strategic partnerships and manages donor development for SPN, was the director of development for Americans for Prosperity and worked in development for the Charles G. Koch Foundation prior to that.

SPN also has kept its ties to the tobacco industry intact since the early 1990s—continuing to do its bidding as recently as 2014, according to several reports and stories. Lee Fang has reported that SPN has consistently "package[d] its resistance to tobacco taxes and health regulations as part of a 'freedom agenda' for conservatives." Altria/Philip Morris included SPN on its list of organizations it donated to as recently as 2012. SPN's affiliates have led efforts to oppose public-smoking bans and cigarette excise taxes in Ohio and elsewhere for nearly two decades.

"The funding behind SPN closely resembles a client-based relationship," the CMD study said. "When the Bradley Foundation wants to launch an effort to privatize public schools, its funding to SPN entities goes a long way in producing agenda-driven research and lobbying state legislatures to implement a voucher system," the CMD study said.[7]

"When the Koch brothers want to see lower corporate taxes and fewer pollution regulations so Koch Industries can see higher profits, contributing to right-wing think tanks that aggressively call for lowering or eliminating corporate taxes and removing environmental regulations serves as an investment that aids their corporation as well as their personal agenda," it said. "When tobacco companies like Reynolds, American, or Altria/Philip Morris want to avoid tobacco taxes and health regulations, reports by SPN groups in many states can help inspire local resistance."

What all of this illustrates is that SPN has built a successful and well-funded network in state capitals over the past two decades and coordinates its activities closely with its allies such as Americans for Prosperity, the Franklin Center, and the academic network created from the Mercatus Center. The model has been refined from the early 1990s onward and accelerated in the years just prior to the Chicago Tea Party event at the start of the Obama administration.

24

☆ ☆ ☆

Structure of Social Change

When Charles Koch and Rich Fink established the Mercatus Center at George Mason University in the 1980s, their plans were modest. They wanted the center to serve as the intellectual, academic fountainhead for the policy and political work of aligned groups in Washington. It later also served as a sort of administration-in-waiting during the Clinton administration. Regulatory experts such as Wendy Gramm and Susan Dudley associated with Mercatus worked in key posts during the Bush administration.

That strategy changed completely in 2008, a year before the Chicago Tea Party event, when it became apparent that a Democratic presidential candidate could potentially seize the White House.

Until 2008, the Charles Koch Foundation had given the bulk of its annual support to the Mercatus Center, with much smaller amounts going to a handful of other like-minded organizations. The year CSE began to dissolve (2003) is typical. That year, the Charles Koch Foundation gave nearly $2 million to the Mercatus Center, and just fourteen other groups received grants ranging from $25,000 to the Acton Institute to $71,000 to the Federalist Society.

But that all changed in 2007–8, two years before the Chicago Tea Party event. In 2007, the Charles Koch Foundation began to provide grants directly to many more than just the half dozen schools they'd supported prior to then in order to supplement the salaries of professors and directly connect adjunct scholars' research projects to the State Policy Network's political work in state capitals.

The first wave of new grants went to about two dozen universities, ranging from grants to big public ones such as Florida State ($50,000) to grants to schools in less populated states such as Montana State ($11,000). The programs and policy work were coordinated by both the Mercatus Center, which Rich Fink had started for the Kochs, and the State Policy Network, which received a grant of $1 million to coordinate the academic network that was slated to expand rapidly.

In 2008, the number of universities across the country receiving funding and direction from SPN and Mercatus tripled. In 2009, those receiving Koch funding doubled on top of this again, and it has grown every year since. Other foundations connected to the Koch family began making grants to universities as well, beginning in 2008, increasing the budget again. The Mercatus annual budget now is more than $13 million.

All told, the various Koch family foundations have provided more than $50 million to 250-plus American universities since the trajectory began in 2008—all of it coordinated by Mercatus and directed by the State Policy Network to shape the work of the adjunct scholars in the academic network.

"Charles Koch has rapidly expanded giving to universities, sending $50 million to . . . institutions of higher education from 2005–2012. Koch's investments in universities has skyrocketed in recent years, from just seven schools in 2005 to about 250 today," Greenpeace said in a report about the Koch academic network.[1]

"This massive shift in investment comes at the supervision of Koch Industries executive Richard Fink. Fink's political strategy, the 'Structure of Social Change,' is built around universities, which provide ideas for Koch political groups to manufacture into policies they later advocate for," the group said.

Daniel Schulman, a journalist and author of *Sons of Wichita: How the Koch Brothers Became America's Most Powerful and Private Dynasty*,[2] detailed Fink's political strategy, and his associated concept, the Structure of Social Change, in a profile of him for *The Politico 50*.[3] Fink resisted the profile, he told Schulman, because he preferred to remain in the background. Schulman went ahead anyway and included Fink in his list. The profile was called "Charles Koch's Brain."

"Fink doesn't want to be profiled. He hates the idea, actually. And he'd really rather not be featured on *The POLITICO 50*, for which he protests he's not even a 'viable' candidate," Schulman wrote. "It doesn't matter to Fink that you know who he is, or that he has served for decades as chief political adviser to one of the world's wealthiest and most powerful businessmen. He prefers to operate in the background, thinking one move ahead in the ideological chess game that has been his life's work, as a trusted confidant to billionaire industrialist Charles Koch and an architect of a remarkable political ascent that has earned Charles and his brother David the grudging acceptance of the GOP establishment—and the venom of the left.

"The 63-year-old, silver-haired strategist, a man largely unknown outside a small circle of like-minded conservative operatives, has spent more than 30 years overseeing Charles's multifarious philanthropic, political and public policy endeavors—the 'Kochtopus,' to its detractors. He is officially an executive vice president of Koch Industries, where he has spent much of his career overseeing the company's legal, lobbying and public affairs divisions, and integrating them into a single unit that was eventually dubbed Koch Companies Public Sector. In that role, Fink has become one of the most powerful political players in America—and he's done it without attracting almost any attention to himself."

Fink was clear about the steps to bring about a political revolution, and a university network was critical to that effort, he told Schulman. "What we needed to do was build the foundations for a spontaneous order for free-dom and that included a multifaceted, integrated structure of social change," Fink said. The epicenter of that "multifaceted, integrated structure of social change" began with the university network. "To facilitate the production of [the necessary] raw materials, Koch pumped millions of dollars into hun-dreds of universities," Schulman wrote. "These contributions—which to-taled nearly $31 million from 2007 to 2011 alone—have gone to endow professorships, underwrite free-market economics programs and sponsor conferences for libertarian thinkers."

The Koch donations to the universities come with strings attached. "Evidence at schools like George Mason University, Florida State University, Clemson University and Suffolk University fits a familiar pattern: Charles Koch expects a specific return on his large investments," Greenpeace noted in their "Koch on Campus" report. "Koch-funded university programs tend to promote a specific agenda, at the expense of independence and academic freedom. Few grant agreements are publicly available, leaving students at most universities in the dark about the influence of Koch and other cor-porate donors."[4]

An investigative report from the Center for Public Integrity during the fall of 2014,[5] for instance, looked more closely at a Koch foundation grant to Florida State. Their investigation was based on sixteen pages of previ-ously unpublished e-mails about the grant requirements.

"In 2007, when the Charles Koch Foundation considered giving mil-lions of dollars to Florida State University's economics department, the offer came with strings attached," the CPI report said. "First, the curriculum it funded must align with the libertarian, deregulatory economic philosophy of Charles Koch, the billionaire industrialist and Republican political bank-roller.

"Second, the Charles Koch Foundation would at least partially control which faculty members Florida State University hired. And third, Bruce Benson, a prominent libertarian economic theorist and Florida State University economics department chairman, must stay on another three years as department chairman—even though he told his wife he'd step down in 2009 after one three-year term."

Benson noted in a November 2007 memorandum that the Charles Koch Foundation would not just "give us money to hire anyone we want and fund any graduate student that we choose. There are constraints," CPI said. "Benson later added in the memo: 'Koch cannot tell a university who to hire, but they are going to try to make sure, through contractual terms and monitoring, that people hired are [to] be consistent with 'donor intent.'"

There's no great mystery about why Fink and the Kochs would turn to academia to intellectually fuel social change that would protect, promote, or defend business interests. The tobacco industry forged that path for decades, starting in the 1950s, through its Council for Tobacco Research.

Philip Morris created the Council for Tobacco Research in the 1950s to manufacture studies and reports that questioned the science that showed smoking caused lung cancer and other health problems. Most of the council's money was spent on advertising and marketing the flimsy research behind the studies. The tobacco industry's academic network was described by *The Wall Street Journal* in 1993 as "the longest-running misinformation campaign in US business history." The council was closed down in 1999.

It took decades for the national media and federal courts to unravel the complex web of academic reports written primarily to protect the tobacco industry. In later years, as the political fights surrounding the tobacco companies intensified, their academic network became their refuge of last resort in many instances. For decades the Council for Tobacco Research shielded the tobacco industry from questions about the dangers of smoking, until established science became too overwhelming.

But anyone studying the ways in which academic reports gain credibility and serve as the intellectual basis of policy fights has a clear road map from the tobacco industry's academic network. It worked quite well for nearly two decades.

The Kochs' CSE and then Americans for Prosperity have seen, firsthand, how academic reports have fueled social change, politically benefiting their tobacco industry partners. The concept is as utilitarian as any that has ever existed in the bare-knuckled intersection of policy and politics.

25

☆ ☆ ☆

A Blueprint Years in the Making

If the 14 million internal tobacco industry memos and documents show one thing clearly, it is this: political campaign networks built to defend and promote large corporate interests with integrated goals, messaging, targets, and allies simply don't materialize overnight. The funding and strategies behind them take years to develop before reaching maturity. And they build on each other over time.

The Donors Capital Fund, a supporting organization associated with its parent organization, Donors Trust, is precisely such an idea that took time to nurture before reaching maturity. It was built to network and leverage political and ideological campaign funding. It was formed around the time that the Kochs' Citizens for a Sound Economy—as the central, coordinating third-party ally of the tobacco industry and other corporate interests—dissolved and Americans for Prosperity emerged in its place.

Charles and David Koch are widely credited with the creation of the Donors Trust concept as a way to pool contributions from a variety of funders interested in supporting the antitax and antiregulation principles of limited government. It is the backbone of the Koch donor network.

Donors Trust is the parent company. According to the Donors Capital

Fund Web site, if a client plans to maintain a balance of over $1 million, then Donors Trust refers clients to Donors Capital Fund. "Donors Capital Fund is an IRS-approved, 501(c)(3), 509(a)(3) supporting organization that is associated with Donors Trust, a public charity and donor-advised fund formed to safeguard the charitable intent of donors who are dedicated to the ideals of limited government, personal responsibility, and free enterprise," its mission statement says.

The Kochs began to pool their own philanthropy through Donors Capital after 2003 and advised others to do so as well.

What exactly are Donors Capital Fund and Donors Trust? As the Center for Media and Democracy reports, "Both funding organizations are called 'donor-advised funds,' which means that the funds create separate accounts for individual donors, and the donors then recommend disbursements from the accounts to different non-profits. They cloak the identity of the original mystery donors because the funds are then distributed in the name of DT or DCT, contributing another step to what has been called a 'murky money maze.' . . . The twin Donors organizations are advertised as a way for very wealthy people and corporations to remain hidden when 'funding sensitive or controversial issues.' "[1] By 2009, as the Tea Party was supposedly springing forth naturally and not by design, Donors Capital and Donors Trust had already grown to immense proportions. More than $300 million was re-granted through the Donors Capital Fund and Donors Trust between 2002 and 2010, according to IRS tax forms and several studies. The Knowledge and Progress Fund, controlled by Charles Koch and managed by Rich Fink, has given only to Donors Capital and Donors Trust since 2005.

"What you see is that as the contribution of donors has increased over the 2003-to-2010 timeframe, the contribution of other [Koch] foundations has declined. Koch went from a high of 9 percent of the funding flow in 2008 to 1 percent in 2010," Drexel University sociologist Robert Brulle told *Frontline* in October 2012.[2]

"We do know that the Koch brothers have made significant contributions to Donors Trust through their foundation called the Knowledge and Progress Fund. They gave $1.25 million in 2007, $1.25 million in 2008, and then $2 million in 2010 to Donors. We don't know where it went after it goes to Donors, because it's not necessarily a one-for-one giving."

The mission of Donors Capital as described on its Web site is direct: "Over the years, it has become all too common to see philanthropic capital stray from the original donor's wishes and be used for purposes other than what they intended. Donors Capital Fund was established as an antidote for those donors who wish to see their charitable capital used for liberty during their lifetime and beyond."

What it funds, and why, is also clear. "Donors Capital Fund only supports a class of public charities firmly committed to liberty. These charities all help strengthen American civil society by promoting private initiatives rather than government programs as the solution to the most pressing issues of the day in the areas of social welfare, health, the environment, economics, governance, foreign relations, and arts and culture."

The Donors Capital concept had become fully realized by 2009—the year of the supposed spontaneous grassroots birth of the Tea Party movement. It disbursed nearly $60 million that year to more than two hundred organizations that had all signed on to the antitax and antiregulation concepts of liberty and free enterprise, IRS records show.

The list of recipients in 2009 includes essentially the entire universe of groups in the network built to campaign around these ideals. Dozens of groups received Donors Trust funding in small amounts. But the cornerstones of the Tea Party–styled movement that had been perfected for more than a decade received substantial sums. They received "most favored status" in the Koch donor network. Just fourteen groups received more than $1 million from Donors Capital that year. Americans for Prosperity was at the front and received more than all others. The Franklin Center received $2.3 million. The Sam Adams Alliance received $3.2 million. The State Policy Network received $2.5 million. Americans for Limited Government Research received $2.2 million. The Mercatus Center received $1.2 million.

Tea Party leaders and spokespeople have long disputed any suggestions that they're coordinated, directed, coached, trained, or funded through this network. But even a cursory look at connections to the leaders of some of the groups quoted in the myriad media stories about the Tea Party movement from 2009 onward all have one thing in common—a connection in some fashion to the Kochs' Americans for Prosperity and its affiliate network.

For instance, Americans for Prosperity funded and coordinated Carol Waddell's "Waco Tea Party's grassroots campaign, leadership and activist survival school." AFP trained Tim Savaglio and his Tea Party group. Margie Dresher works for AFP. Toby Marie Walker earned AFP's "Tea Party of the Year" in 2010. AFP funded Tom Zawistowski's Tea Party conference. Jennifer Stefano is AFP's state director in Pennsylvania. Jaime Radtke has an affiliate alliance with AFP. Larry Norvig's Tea Party group runs AFP campaigns in Virginia. Tim Curtis speaks at AFP campaign events. AFP ran tactics and messaging strategy training for Susan McLaughlin's Tea Party group in Ohio. This is just a partial list of Tea Party spokespeople quoted or featured by ABC News, the Associated Press, Reuters, CNN, *The Wall Street Journal, Business Insider, Newsday,* and others in 2009 and beyond.

None of these local or statewide Tea Party leaders are necessarily or even knowingly doing the bidding of either the Koch donor network or Americans for Prosperity. That isn't the point. What is relevant, and what almost never makes it into media coverage of the Tea Party movement, is that they are part of a highly organized and leveraged political network that has a great deal of funding behind it.

Big, complicated political grassroots campaign efforts are exceedingly difficult to parse in real time. The tobacco industry's campaign to derail Hillarycare, or to develop the Allied Forces concept to defend against concerted attacks on the tobacco companies through broader antitax and antiregulatory fights, weren't identified until after the internal tobacco documents were released and public health researchers were able to discern the full scope of the campaign. Details about coalitions such as Enough is Enough or Get Government Off Our Back likewise only emerged years later.

When a political campaign network assembled itself against President Obama's health care reform initiative—with themes, messages, and tactics pulled from essentially the same tobacco industry playbook that had derailed Hillary Clinton's health care reform efforts more than a decade earlier—it wasn't until the fall of 2013 that the nature of that effort started to emerge.

The New York Times published an investigative story on October 5, 2013, about how a coalition of conservative activists, led by former attorney general Ed Meese, met at the start of Obama's second term to find a new way to attack Obamacare.[3]

"Their push to repeal Obama's health law was going nowhere, and they desperately needed a new plan. Out of that session came a 'blueprint to defunding Obamacare'—signed by Meese and leaders from more than three dozen conservative groups," *The Times* reported. "It articulated a take-no-prisoners legislative strategy that had long percolated in conservative circles: that Republican leaders could derail the health overhaul if conservative lawmakers were willing to push fellow Republicans—including their cautious leaders—into cutting off funding for the entire federal government."

This coalition shut down the federal government in the fall of 2013. While the campaign effort seemed to emerge abruptly, it was months and years in the making—and extraordinarily well supported, the *Times'* investigation found.

"To many Americans, the shutdown came out of nowhere," the *Times* story said. "But . . . the confrontation that precipitated the crisis was the outgrowth of a long-running effort to undo the law, the Affordable Care Act, since its passage in 2010. That effort was waged by a galaxy of conservative groups with more money, organized tactics and interconnections than is commonly known."

Despite polls showing that the American public was divided on the law and its impact, the Tea Party caucus in Congress was "excited about drawing a red line against a law they despise" and was willing to force the federal government to shut down to defund it. But the effort to shut down the government over Obamacare was just the latest chapter in a long-running story, *The Times* found.

"The current budget brinkmanship is just the latest development in a well-financed, broad-based assault on the health law, Obama's signature legislative initiative," *The Times* reported. "Groups such as Tea Party Patriots [and] Americans for Prosperity . . . are all immersed in the fight."

Financing for the coalition came from the Koch donor network. "The billionaire Koch brothers, Charles and David, have been deeply involved with financing the overall effort. A group linked to the Kochs, Freedom Partners Chamber of Commerce, disbursed more than $200 million last year to non-profit organizations involved in the fight."

But as detailed as the *Times'* investigative piece was, it struggled to explain the Koch donor network's true aim in the effort. Was it to shut down the federal government or to provoke public anger and concern among Americans about the health care law?

"Not all of the groups have been on board with the defunding campaign. Some, like the Koch-financed Americans for Prosperity, which spent $5.5 million on health care television advertisements over the past three months, are more focused on sowing doubts about the law. But all have a common goal, which is to cripple a measure that Texas Sen. Ted Cruz, leader of the defunding effort, has likened to a horror movie," *The Times* said.

"We view this as a long-term effort," said Tim Phillips, president of Americans for Prosperity. AFP would spend "tens of millions" of dollars on a "multi-front effort" that included working to prevent states from expanding Medicaid under the law. AFP's goal was not to defund the law, but to abolish it altogether. "We want to see this law repealed," Phillips said.

While it appeared that the Tea Party movement was somewhat split on the true aims of the effort, their shared common goal was evident. "In the three years since Obama signed the health measure, Tea Party–inspired groups have mobilized, aided by a financing network that continues to grow, both in its complexity and the sheer amount of money that flows through it," *The Times* found.

"A review of tax records, campaign finance reports and corporate filings shows that hundreds of millions of dollars have been raised and spent since 2012 by organizations, many of them loosely connected, leading opposition to the measure." At the center of the effort are Charles and David Koch and their donor network.

"One of the biggest sources . . . is Freedom Partners, a tax-exempt 'business league' that claims more than 200 members, each of whom pays at least $100,000 in dues," *The Times* said. "The group's board is headed by a longtime executive of Koch Industries, the conglomerate run by the Koch brothers, who were among the original financiers of the Tea Party movement. The Kochs declined to comment."

The effort to defund Obamacare by shutting down the federal government didn't succeed—and nearly derailed the Republican Party's political chances of recapturing the Senate in the midterm elections. But American voters are either forgiving or forgetful because the Senate turned over to the GOP a year later. So the Tea Party movement and its donor network, in the end, may have gotten precisely what it had hoped for—a public, highly orchestrated attack on President Obama's signature health law that diminished its effectiveness but, in the end, did no significant, lasting damage to the GOP brand or its chances in national elections.

26

☆ ☆ ☆

Winning

While Rich Fink has run the network, and David Koch has chaired many of the key hubs, Charles Koch has remained largely behind the curtain over the years, pulling the strings. If there is a theory of political change behind the movement, it is Charles Koch's theory of change.

Steady, relentless growth seems to be built into Charles Koch's DNA, and it is reflected both in his business and politics. Since inheriting a relatively small enterprise in Kansas from his father, Fred, Charles Koch has built the company into a globe-straddling enterprise. Koch Industries is two thousand times the size of the company that Fred Koch built—the second-largest private company in the United States, employing more than seventy thousand people in sixty countries, with businesses that range from cattle and paper to oil, chemicals, and commodities trading.

His free-market economic philosophies largely come from Ludwig von Mises, an Austrian economist revered by Libertarian leaders. "The issue is always the same: the government or the market," Mises once famously said. "There is no third solution." Charles Koch's 2007 management book, *The Science of Success*, goes into some detail about "destructive compensation schemes" such as built-in cost-of-living raises for employees. And, of the two brothers behind the network, Charles most passionately believes that government regulations are harmful and that government should be as small as possible.

So it should come as no surprise that Charles Koch has built his political network every bit as aggressively as he has his business.

How much have the Kochs spent on politics? Public tax records between 1998 and 2008 reveal the following: the Charles G. Koch Charitable Foundation, more than $48 million; the Claude R. Lambe Charitable Foundation (which dissolved in 2013), more than $28 million; the David H. Koch Charitable Foundation, more than $120 million; Koch Industries, more than $50 million just on lobbying. And KochPAC, Koch Industries' political-action committee, "has donated some eight million dollars to political campaigns, more than eighty per cent of it to Republicans," reported *The New Yorker* in August 2010). And those are only the monies that can be traced. Considerably more than this has certainly been spent anonymously.

From its roots at CSE, then through Americans for Prosperity, a 2013 study by the Center for Responsive Politics (CRP) identified seventeen non-profit groups backed by Charles Koch's donor network that had received more than $400 million in the 2011–12 election cycle. And far from becoming discouraged by the election results in 2012, they doubled down in 2014—and found success in the federal midterm elections. But all of that may be just a prelude to 2016, when Charles Koch finally hopes to seize the grand prize that has, so far, eluded him.

"The Kochs haven't just multiplied the wealth of their dad; they've repackaged and amplified his worldview and subsidized the Tea Party movement," Lisa Graves, the Center for Media and Democracy's executive director, told me. CMD has published several reports on various parts of the rapidly growing Koch political network.

Each part of the Koch-sponsored political network has its assigned task, from voter data sets to youth outreach—much as a corporation assigns key roles and responsibilities. According to the tax returns reviewed by CRP, the network spanned a dozen limited liability companies with indecipherable names such as ORRA LLC.

Lloyd Hitoshi Mayer, a University of Notre Dame Law School professor who studies the tax issues of politically active nonprofits, told *The Washington Post*[1] (which conducted the tax review jointly with the Center for Responsive Politics) that he had never seen a network with a similar design in the tax-exempt world.

"It is a very sophisticated and complicated structure," said Lloyd Hitoshi Mayer. "It's designed to make it opaque as to where the money is coming from and where the money is going. No layperson thought this up. It would only be worth it if you were spending the kind of dollars the Koch brothers are, because this was not cheap."

Colleagues on Wall Street, in high finance, and in corporate boardrooms admire this systematic approach toward building business and political networks around strategic roles and responsibilities. "He has no peer in the business and political world today," someone who worked for Charles Koch for years (and greatly admires both his business and political philosophies) told me.

Charles Koch has rarely spoken in public about his motivations in building a political movement, or why both his funding and his donor network should remain secretive. In one of just a few interviews by him, he told *Forbes* magazine in late 2012 that secrecy was a necessity.[2]

"We get death threats, threats to blow up our facilities, kill our people. We get Anonymous and other groups trying to crash our IT systems," he said. "So long as we're in a society like that, where the president attacks us and we get threats from people in Congress, and this is pushed out and becomes part of the culture—that we are evil, so we need to be destroyed, or killed—then why force people to disclose?"

For all of his efforts to build a game-changing political movement, however, 2016 will be the great test. For all of his success, the White House has eluded him. He has spent the better part of several decades preparing for this moment. Charles Koch may not have many more presidential political cycles left to see his carefully constructed, highly ambitious, and well-rehearsed political dream reach the finish line. Since he is nearing eighty, the 2016 presidential election could be his last personal effort to bring to fruition what he and Rich Fink mapped out more than twenty years ago when they left the dysfunctional Libertarian Party behind and took dead aim at the center of the Republican Party.

His creation is now fully formed and operational. Americans for Prosperity spent more than $122 million in 2012 during the presidential campaign season, according to a detailed information summary it was required to file with the Colorado secretary of state. According to an analysis by the Center for Public Integrity (CPI), that's more than the total amount the group had spent during its entire post-CSE days. It was also a fivefold increase over what AFP had spent in 2010 when the Republicans regained control of the House.

More than $30 million was spent on ads to convince voters not to vote for Obama, according to the CPI analysis. Freedom Partners, the new 501(c)(6), spent $250 million raised from the two hundred–plus Koch donor network in 2012, according to newly released tax records. A portion of AFP's budget in 2012 came from Freedom Partners.

The Republican Party's voter database efforts were a dismal failure in 2012, by nearly all accounts—and clearly outmatched by the Obama and Democratic Party efforts. The Kochs' well-guarded Themis voter database project is well along in its development, however, and was instrumental in the 2014 midterm elections. It will be fully developed in 2016. It got an initial trial run nationally with Governor Tim Pawlenty's brief presidential campaign efforts, according to FEC records. Network partners such as the State Policy Network and the Franklin Center are now fully embedded in nearly every state capital.

There is no reason to believe that this sort of effort will slow down. If anything, it will accelerate. What will change, however, is the strategy—and perhaps the path to the ultimate prize. In fact, it may already be shifting.

If this is, in fact, the network's best chance to alter the core of the Republican Party for good and seize the White House while Charles Koch is still actively directing the network, then it will need to make a difficult, but strategic, decision.

Right now, the Tea Party movement that the Koch network has shaped and managed for the better part of two decades is threatening the center of the institutional Republican Party in Washington and is clearly struggling to remain part of the GOP family. Old political tensions, subsumed in the common goal of defeating Obama, are surfacing again in DC.

The Conservative Action Project, cochaired by CSE's former distinguished fellow David McIntosh, lobbed a hard-edged warning at the House Republican leadership expressing its extreme displeasure over the dismissal of Paul Teller—the executive director of the conservative Republican Study Committee, who complained publicly about the 2013 budget deal hammered out by former GOP vice-presidential candidate Paul Ryan and was let go by leadership as a result. In a letter made public by Heritage Action signed by McIntosh and cosigned by leaders from nearly every corner of the Koch network, they put the House GOP leadership on notice.

"We are saddened and outraged that an organization that purports to represent conservatives in Congress would dismiss a staff member for advancing conservatism and working with conservatives outside of Congress. Given this action, and earlier comments by the Speaker, it is clear that the conservative movement has come under attack on Capitol Hill today," wrote McIntosh and leaders from the Tea Party Patriots, the Tea Party Express, FreedomWorks, Heritage Action, 60 Plus Association, Americans for Limited Government, and others.

Missing from the list, however, was Americans for Prosperity, the centerpiece of the Koch network, as well as the State Policy Network and the Franklin Center. What's more, Koch Industries—in a generic letter to senators—went out of its way to distance itself from the efforts by essentially this same group to conspire to shut down the federal government in an effort to defund Obamacare. In short, the foundation of the Koch net-work, including its cornerstones, was conspicuously absent.

So has the Koch network changed directions or shifted strategies? Is it no longer playing hardball in Washington, DC, as it has for twenty years? Is it no longer deploying the Tea Party movement it constructed? Possibly not. What seems more likely is that the brain trust has decided it's time to finally win the one, big prize that has always eluded it since the early days when Charles and David Koch first left the Libertarian Party on the long journey to remake the GOP by changing the definition of what it means to be a conservative in America.

House and Senate victories are certainly worthwhile efforts. But winning the White House—with a candidate of your own—is the ultimate prize in any political movement. And winning the White House requires more than money and networks. It also requires a compelling narrative that can attract a majority of voters rather than divide them.

The new strategy will, most likely, center on a GOP presidential candi-date who is willing to speak to, energize, and mobilize the Koch network, but who can also build bridges to the institutional, established parts of the Republican Party.

Before he nearly self-destructed over the George Washington Bridge in-cident, that candidate might well have been New Jersey governor Chris Christie. David Koch went out of his way to try to convince Christie to run against Mitt Romney in 2012. According to *Mother Jones,* the Kochs invited Christie to sneak out of New Jersey to give a keynote talk at a Koch donor network meeting on June 26, 2011.[3]

Until recently, they may have seen their greatest opportunity to finally win their biggest prize in Governor Christie. Their hearts were also with Wisconsin governor Scott Walker (whom their network rescued from politi-cal oblivion) until he withdrew from the 2016 presidential campaign. But their imperative to finally win the White House could lead them to build whatever bridges they must to make sure that they back a winner in 2016— at almost any cost.

Because his father was once chairman of AFP's predecessor, Senator Rand Paul clearly holds a fond place in the hearts and minds of Charles and David Koch. But some of Paul's views, especially on the military, are far outside the norm of traditional GOP politics, which may make his national candidacy difficult in a general election.

Until he stumbled badly over the Religious Freedom Restoration Act, Indiana governor Mike Pence was well positioned as a favorite son in the Koch network. Pence fought the Kochs' fights in the House of Representatives as the chairman of the House Republican Conference (the same springboard John Boehner used to jump to House Speaker, with the support of the Kochs' third-party allies such as CSE).

Pence is a firebrand conservative on social issues such as abortion and a respected political voice for evangelical Christians, but he is also an antitax conservative figure cut from the same cloth as Charles Koch. Pence's signature effort to date is a rollback in corporate tax rates that AFP's leadership holds up as a model for other governors. AFP president Tim Phillips refers to Pence as "one of our favorite governors."

But, more important, several key former Pence aides on his personal and conference staff from his House days are now running the financial and political efforts at the Kochs' Americans for Prosperity and Freedom Partners. Marc Short, who was Pence's chief of staff on the Republican conference in the House, runs Freedom Partners and is at the head of the table when hundreds of millions of dollars from the Koch donor network are spent in national election cycles. Initially, GOP political operatives had assumed that these moves were meant to prop Pence up. But the religious freedom fiasco ended those efforts—though he may make an interesting vice presidential running mate.

The Kochs pledged to spend nearly $1 billion from their donor network in the 2016 election cycle—an unheard of amount for a third-party group to spend in a national election in America. They pledged to support a number of GOP presidential candidates in the primaries, preserving the ability to coalesce around a potential winner in the general election. A nominee like Donald Trump could test the limits of their support, though Trump has clearly done well within the national grassroots political movement the Koch donor network and tobacco industry has built. This is one reason (among others) that political reporters followed Trump so closely once he'd entered the GOP primaries in the summer of 2015.

The leadership of Charles Koch's donor trust has said publicly that they will not deploy his immensely powerful and well-financed political network—which now rivals that of the institutional Republican Party itself—until a GOP nominee is finally chosen in the 2016 presidential primary system. While that is certainly true in practice, every candidate in the field except Donald Trump has done everything possible to court that donor network relentlessly.

Out of all the choices in what began as a huge, unruly pool of GOP presidential hopefuls, rising star Sen. Marco Rubio (R-FL) could emerge as the network's logical standard-bearer. Rubio may, in fact, be the last man standing—and the candidate that the Koch donor network swings in behind. Rubio wowed the 200-plus wealthy contributors of the Koch donor network at several key meetings throughout 2015, and immediately proceeded to raise tens of millions coming out of these closed-door appearances before the Koch donor network, according to several media accounts.

But one thing is certain. Charles Koch will play to win in 2016. His personal and professional history makes this clear. He learns from his mistakes, refines operations, and advances forward relentlessly in pursuit of singular goals.

The 2016 presidential campaign will, in many ways, be a personal fulfillment of decades of efforts to master the national political system. The long rise of the Tea Party movement—and the political education of Charles and David Koch from their entry into politics in the early, marginal efforts of the Libertarian Party to their roles now as kingmakers dictating central themes inside the GOP establishment orchestrated by their academic, policy, grassroots, media, and political networks and refined through decades of work with campaigns built and financed by the tobacco companies—makes this clear to anyone with eyes to see.

In truth, Charles Koch has no choice in 2016. He's built a unique, unprecedented political movement that was designed to use corporate principles, funding, and interests to control at least one national party. It has achieved success everywhere—except at the White House. So he has to win the presidency. In the end, after all, just one thing really matters in politics—winning. Everything else is just second place.

ACKNOWLEDGMENTS

☆ ☆ ☆

Thanks to:

The Legacy Tobacco Documents Library at the University of California, San Francisco.

Amanda Fallin, Rachel Grana, and Stan Glantz for their groundbreaking study, and individual interviews.

All others I interviewed—both named and confidential—who gave of their time and extensive knowledge in the search for truth and connections.

My relentless, positive-storm family and Ramona Cramer Tucker, who assisted in research.

Tom Dunne and Peter Joseph, who believed in this book and helped refine it in immeasurable and important ways.

Victoria Skurnick, who saw what this book could become before others did.

APPENDIX 1
Acronyms

☆ ☆ ☆

AFP: Americans for Prosperity

ALEC: American Legislative Exchange Council

ALG: Americans for Limited Government

API: American Petroleum Institute

ATR: Americans for Tax Reform

CAP: Center for American Progress

CAP: Conservative Action Project

CART: Citizens Against Regressive Taxation

CAUTI: Californians Against Unfair Tax Increases

CMD: Center for Media and Democracy

COFIRE: Coalition for Fiscal Restraint

CPI: Center for Public Integrity

CSE: Citizens for a Sound Economy

DNC: Democratic National Committee

EIE: Enough is Enough

FDA: Food and Drug Administration

FP: Freedom Partners

FW: FreedomWorks

GGOOB: Get Government Off Our Back

GOP: modern day, Grand Old Party; original meaning in 1875, Gallant Old Party—
    referring to the Republican Party
IG: Inspector General
NIH: National Institutes of Health
NRDC: Natural Resources Defense Council
NSA: National Smokers Alliance
PAC: Political Action Committee
RICO: Racketeer Influenced and Corrupt Organizations
RJR: R.J. Reynolds Tobacco Company
RNC: Republican National Convention
SAA: Sam Adams Alliance
SPN: State Policy Network
SRG: Smokers' Rights Group

APPENDIX 2
Koch Industries Connections

☆ ☆ ☆

Charles Koch, David Koch, or Koch Industries have funded, launched, or partnered with the following organizations or campaigns, to name a few:

Allied Forces

Americans for Prosperity

Citizens Against Regressive Taxation

Citizens for a Sound Economy

Coalition for Fiscal Restraint

Conservative Action Project

Donors Trust

Donors Trust Capital Fund

Enough is Enough

Franklin Center for Government and Public Integrity

Freedom Partners

FreedomWorks

Get Government Off Our Back

Knowledge and Progress Fund

Mobilization Universe

National Smokers Alliance

R.J. Reynolds Tobacco Company

Sam Adams Alliance

State Policy Network

Tobacco Strategy

APPENDIX 3
Key Events

☆ ☆ ☆

1977: Kochs fund launch of Cato Institute.

1984: David Koch and Rich Fink cofound CSE and set up an academic network hub (now Mercatus Center) at George Mason.

1985: Fink urges Congress to eliminate US Tobacco Program.

1987: Roger Ream, VP of CSE, asks Tobacco Institute for funding.

1988: CSE's rep chairs and runs COFIRE, creating the "no new taxes" heart of the Reagan Revolution. RJR tests its own Tea Party. Philip Morris and RJR build smokers' rights coalitions.

1989: *Philip Morris Magazine*'s "A Tea Party—Boston Style."

1990: Tim Hyde of RJR compares Tea Party movement with twenty-year Reagan Revolution. Philip Morris and RJR develop Tea Party antitax revolt themes.

1993: Philip Morris and CSE propose alliance to create antitax front groups. Clinton submits first budget with BTU tax. CSE flips a single senator's position.

1994: RJR's GGOOB Tea Party flips House of Representatives to Republicans. CSE secretly directs GGOOB's fight against federal regulation of the tobacco industry.

1995: RJR's PR firm explains GGOOB's objective: to "mobilize national and state-level resources to oppose regulations and legislation that is in opposition to RJR's interests." CSE mobilizes national grassroots network of antitax Tea Party movement. Enough is Enough created and led by Roger Ailes.

1996: Hyde directed RJR's connection with CSE and implements strategies of Allied Forces concept led by CSE in Dole/Kemp presidential campaign. Philip Morris contributions to CSE grow.

1998: CSE fights to block the Prop 10 cigarette tax effort in California.

1999: Philip Morris and tobacco industry launch Mobilization Universe. Koch network involved in Tea Party–styled protests. CSE and tobacco industry join forces to try to block RICO suit.

2000: CSE requests at least another $2 million from Philip Morris for Mobilization Universe.

2001: CSE spearheads efforts to convince incoming Bush administration to drop RICO suit against the tobacco industry and any efforts to regulate cigarettes or secondhand smoke.

2002: CSE creates actual U.S. Tea Party Web site (www.usteaparty.com).

2003–4: Inadvertent public release of AFP donors' names reveals CSE relied heavily on Koch funding. CSE and CSE Foundation split. CSE merges with Freedom-Works. CSE Foundation is renamed Americans for Prosperity Foundation.

2005: AFP opposes cigarette excise taxes and indoor-smoking ban in Texas and other states. Koch Foundation grants to universities in every state more than $38 million from 2005 to 2010.

2006: Final judgment of the RICO lawsuit issued, but CSE had morphed into AFP. AFP campaigns against cigarette taxes in four states funded by tobacco industry. Documents show themes and construct of the Tea Party movement.

2007: Ron Paul, CSE's first chairman, holds "Tea Party" money bomb rally to raise millions for his presidential campaign.

2008: The Mercatus Center, linked to grassroots organizers through the SPN, the Sam Adams Alliance, and the Franklin Center receives funding boost. Right-Online.com gathering sponsored by AFP includes SAA trainers using Boston Tea Party playbook refined by tobacco industry and CSE/AFP. New Tea Party–styled network in place to challenge the institutional Republican Party in DC.

2009: Franklin Center creates dozens of media outlets virtually overnight in state capitals. AFP's budget leaps to more than $10 million in February. Tea Party Web sites, Facebook pages, and Twitter streams running within hours of Santelli speech at Chicago Mercantile Exchange on February 19. The day after, AFP creates a Facebook group to support a "Taxpayer Tea Party." Tea Party Patriots' founders Jenny Beth Martin and Mark Meckler begin stage-managed national tour. In October, David Koch says AFP (which organizes Tea Parties) was founded "five years ago" and mentions developing nearly a million activists in the states since 2004.

2010: David Koch denies any role in Tea Party movement, past or present, to *New York* magazine.

2011: Charles Koch denies any connection to the Tea Party but reports the Koch Foundation's achievement in *The Weekly Standard*: "The way it's grown, the passion and the intensity, is beyond what I had anticipated."

2012: AFP opposes California's Proposition 29, bankrolled by Philip Morris and R.J. Reynolds. AFP leads efforts to demonize Obamacare and spends more than $122 million during presidential campaign season.

2013: UCSF researchers Stan Glantz, Amanda Fallin, and Rachel Grana produce groundbreaking study on origins of the Tea Party movement.

2014: $400 million (estimated) of Koch donor network money used in effort to flip US Senate to the GOP. Themis voter database project ready for the 2014 midterm elections.

2015: *Politico* reveals Kochs' plan to shape the 2016 election.[1] *USA Today* reports that the Kochs are considering donating to five GOP presidential prospects—Scott Walker, Jeb Bush, Ted Cruz, Rand Paul, Marco Rubio—and have set a $889 million budget.[2]

NOTES

☆ ☆ ☆

1: An Unholy Alliance

1. I was the editor of Ralph Nader's *Public Citizen* magazine at the start of President Reagan's first term, and then a journalist with Knight-Ridder and others in Washington. I was also Dr. David Kessler's public affairs chief at the Food and Drug Administration during the first Bush administration. The science- and evidence-based concept behind the FDA's decision to declare jurisdiction over the tobacco industry was largely mine—and I fought for it relentlessly, first in the Bush administration and later through public health coalitions built to take on the tobacco wars. I was also Dan Quayle's Senate press secretary, and his communications director at the White House. In addition, I was the National Science Foundation's legislative and public affairs director during both the second Bush administration and then the Obama administration. I've written twenty-four novels for leading Christian publishing houses. People generally make assumptions, but I've never answered the question about my politics.

2. The Koch Family Foundations consist of the David H. Koch Foundation (run by David Koch), the Charles G. Koch Foundation (run by Charles Koch), the Claude R. Lambe Charitable Foundation (now dissolved; previously led by Rich Fink; Charles and his family sat on the board), and the Knowledge and Progress Fund (led by Charles; Rich Fink is the president).

3. Jane Mayer, "Covert Operations," *New Yorker,* August 30, 2010, http://www .newyorker.com/magazine/2010/08/30/covert-operations. Reports that Charles and David Koch own nearly all of Koch Industries, which operates oil refineries in three states, controls four thousand miles of pipeline, and owns a wide variety of products from Brawny paper towels, Dixie cups, Georgia-Pacific, Stainmaster carpet, to Lycra.

4. Andrew Goldman, "The Billionaire's Party: David Koch Is New York's Second-Richest Man, a Celebrated Patron of the Arts, and the Tea Party's Wallet," *New York,* July 25, 2010, http://nymag.com/news/features/67285/. Reveals the beginnings of the company and the family struggles.

5. Bruce Liversey, "How Canada Made the Koch Brothers Rich," May 5, 2015, *National Observer,* http://www.nationalobserver.com/2015/05/04/news/how -canada-made-koch-brothers-rich.

6. Brian Doherty, editor of *Reason,* in Mayer, "Covert Operations."

7. In political circles, the two Koch brothers have funded so many opposition campaigns against Obama administration policies that the Koch network is sometimes referred to as the "Kochtopus" by political campaigners and activists.

8. For more details about the BTU issue, read Dawn Erlandson, "The BTU Tax Experience: What Happened and Why It Happened," *Pace Environmental Law Review* 12, no. 1 (Fall 1994), http://digitalcommons.pace.edu/cgi/viewcontent.cgi ?article=1528&context=pelr.

2: The Playbook

1. Tony Carrk, "The Koch Brothers: What You Need to Know About the Financiers of the Radical Right," Center for American Progress Action Fund, April 2011, https://cdn.americanprogress.org/wp-content/uploads/issues/2011/04/pdf /koch_brothers.pdf.

2. Bill Wilson and Roy Wenzl, "The Kochs' Quest to Save America," October 13, 2012, updated August 13, 2014, http://www.kansas.com/news/special -reports/koch/article1100675.html; and http://www.kansas.com/news/special -reports/article1100668.html.

3: A Critical Bridge: Ron Paul and the "Patriot" Movement

1. To listen to Rick Santelli's speech: http://www.huffingtonpost.com/2014/02 /19/tea-party-santelli_n_4815941.html.

2. Steven Perlberg, "Rick Santelli Started the Tea Party with a Rant Exactly Five Years Ago Today—Here's How He Feels About It Now," *Business Insider*, February 19, 2014, http://www.businessinsider.com/rick-santelli-tea-party-rant -2014-2.

3. Julia A. Seymour, "Santelli: Five Years after His Rant Launched Tea Party," *MRCBusiness*, February 19, 2014, http://www.mrc.org/articles/santelli-five-years -after-his-rant-launched-tea-party.

4. Charles Koch did, however, open a John Birch Society bookstore with one of his father's friends in the 1960s. He resigned from the John Birch Society in 1968 (his father died in 1967).

5. "Frequently Asked Questions," John Birch Society, http://www.jbs.org/about -jbs/frequently-asked-questions.

6. "John McManus at the Rally for the Republic (Part 1 of 2)," YouTube, up-loaded September 4, 2008, https://www.youtube.com/watch?v=obgsT03oqS4; and "John McManus at the Rally for the Republic (Part 2 of 2)," YouTube, uploaded September 4, 2008, https://www.youtube.com/watch?v=fiI25K78X7M.

7. Members of the John Birch Society were intrigued by a group of Austrian economists who promoted free-market ideals. The Koch brothers, in particular, were influenced by the classic liberalism Friedrich von Hayek espoused in his book *The Road to Serfdom*, and his belief in unfettered capitalism. Tea Party supporters, such as talk-radio host Glenn Beck, also promote Von Hayek's work.

4: Smedley Butler, a Fascist Coup, and the American Liberty League

1. "Partisan Aim Denied by Liberty League; Founded to Defend Constitution, Organization Declares in a Statement," *New York Times*, April 20, 1936, http://query .nytimes.com/gst/abstract.html?res=9C01EED9173AE33BBC4851DFB266838 D629EDE.

2. Kim Phillips-Fein, *Invisible Hands: The Businessmen's Crusade Against the New Deal* (New York: W. W. Norton), 2010, 20, http://books.google.com/books?id=g0tCw Ohyl7MC&pg=PA20&#v=onepage&q&f=false.

3. "Partisan Aim Denied by Liberty League."

5: What Drives Charles Koch?

1. Charles G. Koch, *The Science of Success* (Hoboken: N.J.: John Wiley & Sons, 2007), http://www.amazon.com/The-Science-Success-Market-Based-Management/dp/0470139889.

2. Liversey, "How Canada Made the Koch Brothers Rich."

3. David Sassoon, "Koch Brothers Positioned to Be Big Winners If Keystone XL Pipeline Is Approved," Reuters, February 10, 2011, http://www.reuters.com/article/2011/02/10/idUS292515702420110210.

4. W. John Moore, "Wichita Pipeline," *National Journal*, May 16, 1992, http://www.precaution.org/lib/wichita_pipeline_national_journal_19920516l.pdf.

5. "#9 Charles Koch: The Forbes 400 Richest Americans 2009," *Forbes*, September 30, 2009, http://www.forbes.com/lists/2009/54/rich-list-09_Charles-Koch_Z9KL.html.

6. Charles G. Koch, "Why Koch Industries Is Speaking Out," Opinion, *Wall Street Journal*, updated March 1, 2011, http://www.wsj.com/articles/SB10001424052748704288304576170974226083178.

7. Charles G. Koch, "Charles Koch: I'm Fighting to Restore a Free Society," Opinion, *Wall Street Journal*, updated April 2, 2014, http://www.wsj.com/news/articles/SB10001424052702303978304579475860515021286.

8. Daniel Schulman, "Charles Koch's Brain," *Politico 50*, September/October 2014, http://www.politico.com/magazine/politico50/2014/charles-kochs-brain.html.

9. Daniel Schulman, quoted in Jim Kelly, "Koch Classic," Style, *Vanity Fair*, June 2014, http://www.vanityfair.com/style/2014/06/daniel-schulman-koch-brothers.

6: The Man Behind the Curtain

1. Wilson and Wenzl, "Kochs' Quest."

7: Why David Koch Never Loses

1. Goldman, "Billionaire's Party."

2. David H. Koch Charitable Foundation and Personal Philanthropy, Koch Family Foundations & Philanthropy, http://www.kochfamilyfoundations.org/FoundationsDHK.asp.

3. "David Koch Gives Smithsonian a Record $35M for New Dinosaur Hall," *CBSDC*, May 3, 2012, http://washington.cbslocal.com/2012/05/03/david-koch -gives-smithsonian-a-record-35m-for-new-dinosaur-hall/.

4. Goldman, "Billionaire's Party."

5. Brian Doherty, editor of *Reason*, in Mayer, "Covert Operations."

6. Goldman, "Billionaire's Party."

7. Taki Oldham, "The Billionaires' Tea Party—Trailer," https://www.youtube .com/watch?v=uB2d-1PRvO4.

8: Tobacco Documents Trail

1. Amanda Fallin, Rachel Grana, and Stanton A. Glantz, "'To Quarterback Behind the Scenes, Third-Party Efforts': The Tobacco Industry and the Tea Party," *Tobacco Control*, TC Online First, February 20, 2013, doi:10.1136/tobaccocon trol-2012-050815, http://tobaccocontrol.bmj.com/content/early/2013/02/20 /tobaccocontrol-2012-050815.full.pdf+html.

9: COFIRE

1. Michael Monroney, "You Call This Fiscal Restraint?," *Christian Science Monitor*, December 17, 1990.

10: Enough Is Enough

1. Walter Williams, an Americans for Prosperity officer, has often guest-hosted for Limbaugh.

2. Tim Dickinson, "How Roger Ailes Built the Fox News Fear Factory," *Rolling Stone*, May 25, 2011, http://www.rollingstone.com/politics/news/how-roger -ailes-built-the-fox-news-fear-factory-20110525.

11: Allied Forces

1. Jim Estes, "How the Big Tobacco Deal Went Bad," *New York Times*, October 6, 2014, http://www.nytimes.com/2014/10/07/opinion/how-the-big-tobacco-deal -went-bad.html?_r=0.

12: CART

1. Laura E. Tesler, PhD, and Ruth E. Malone, PhD, RN, "'Our Reach Is Wide by Any Corporate Standard,'" *American Journal of Public Health*, July 2010, http://www.ncbi.nlm.nih.gov/pmc/articles/PMC2882403/.

2. Smokers' rights group.

3. "Tobacco Farmers Stage 'Tea Party' Protest," *New York Times*, June 10, 1994, http://www.nytimes.com/1994/06/10/us/tobacco-farmers-stage-tea-party-protest.html.

13: Get Government off Our Back

1. Edwin Chen, "In Shift, FDA Says It Could Classify Nicotine as a Drug," *Los Angeles Times*, February 26, 1994, http://articles.latimes.com/1994-02-26/news/mn-27363_1_nicotine-addiction.

2. Dorie E. Apollonio and Lisa A. Bero, "The Creation of Industry Front Groups: The Tobacco Industry and 'Get Government Off Our Back,'" *American Journal of Public Health*, March 2007, http://www.ncbi.nlm.nih.gov/pmc/articles/PMC1805008/.

3. "American Legislative Exchange Council," *SourceWatch*, Center for Media and Democracy, last modified April 6, 2015, http://www.sourcewatch.org/index.php?title=American_Legislative_Exchange_Council. The American Legislative Exchange Council (ALEC) describes itself as the largest "membership association of state legislators." However, the Center for Media and Democracy says that "over 98% of its revenue comes from sources other than legislative dues, primarily from corporations and corporate foundations." ALEC originally promised "no attempt to influence legislation," but the Center for Media and Democracy reports that "corporations hand state legislators their wishlists to benefit their bottom line. . . . ALEC's agenda extends into almost all areas of law. Its bills undermine environmental regulations and deny climate change (though ALEC has told media it does not do so); support school privatization; undercut healthcare reform; defund unions and limit their political influence; restrain legislatures' abilities to raise revenue through taxes; mandate strict election laws that disenfranchise voters; increase incarceration to benefit the private prison industry, among many other issues." In addition, ALEC has received "an untold amount" from "The Charles G. Koch

Foundation and Claude R. Lambe Foundation" (both Koch Family Foundations), as well as from Koch Industries. "The Koch Associate program of the Charles G. Koch Foundation also provides ALEC and other groups with 'Koch Interns' and 'Koch Fellows' . . . some of whom 'go on to become ALEC staffers.'"

16: Mobilization Universe

1. "CSE President Paul Beckner's Response to Remarks Made by Oracle CEO Larry Ellison," FreedomWorks, June 29, 2000, http://www.freedomworks.org /content/cse-president-paul-beckners-response-remarks-made-oracle-ceo-larry -ellison. Although CSE was running Mobilization Universe on Philip Morris's behalf, CSE president Paul Beckner wrote Oracle CEO Larry Ellison on June 29, 2000 (after Oracle had publicly revealed that their rival Microsoft had hired CSE to campaign on their behalf): "Our job is to recruit, educate, train and mobilize hundreds of thousands of volunteer activists to fight for less government, lower taxes and more freedom. When you question the integrity of CSE and CSE Foundation, you are insulting the values and integrity of the 280,000 citizen activists who volunteer their time and money in our efforts. . . . We do not speak for any special interest. We speak for ourselves and we advocate less government intervention in economic marks. That is all."

18: Seamless Transition

1. "About Us," FreedomWorks, http://www.freedomworks.org/about/about -freedomworks.

2. Mayer, "Covert Operations."

19: Sleight of Hand

1. Mayer, "Covert Operations."

20: Five Pillars

1. Kate Phillips, "The Sam Adams Project," *New York Times*, July 19, 2008, http://thecaucus.blogs.nytimes.com/2008/07/19/the-sam-adams-project/?_r=0.

2. Phil Kerpen, the vice president for policy at Americans for Prosperity, is also a contributor to the Fox News Web site.

3. Rich Fink sits on the board of the Institute for Humane Studies.

4. Jane Mayer, "Is Ikea the New Model for the Conservative Movement?," *New Yorker*, November 15, 2013, http://www.newyorker.com/news/news-desk/is-ikea-the-new-model-for-the-conservative-movement.

5. "Exposed: The State Policy Network," Center for Media and Democracy/ALEC Exposed, November 2013, http://www.prwatch.org/files/spn_national_report_final.pdf.

6. Mayer, "Is Ikea the New Model?"

7. Tal Kopan, "Report: Think Tanks Tied to Kochs," *Politico*, November 13, 2013, http://www.politico.com/story/2013/11/koch-brothers-think-tank-report-99791.html.

8. "Koch on Campus: Polluting Higher Education," Greenpeace/Greenpeace USA, http://www.greenpeace.org/usa/en/campaigns/global-warming-and-energy/polluterwatch/koch-industries/KOCH-POLLUTION-ON-CAMPUS-Academic-Freedom-Under-Assault-from-Charles-Kochs-50-million-Campaign-to-Infiltrate-Higher-Education/.

9. Stephanie Mencimer, "A Secret Tea Party Donor Revealed," *Mother Jones*, October 28, 2010, http://www.motherjones.com/politics/2010/10/tea-party-donor-patriot-one-raymon-thompson.

10. Matthew Continetti, "The Paranoid Style in Liberal Politics," *Weekly Standard*, April 4, 2011, http://www.weeklystandard.com/articles/paranoid-style-liberal-politics_555525.html?page=3.

21: The Sam Adams Alliance

1. Lee Fang, *The Machine: A Field Guide to the Resurgent Right* (New York: New Press, 2013), http://www.thenewpress.com.

2. Laura Oppenheimer, "Anti-Spending Crusaders Gain Steam [Americans for Limited Government Convention]," *Free Republic*, September 5, 2006, http://www.freerepublic.com/focus/f-news/1695774/posts.

3. Ibid.

4. Continetti, "Paranoid Style in Liberal Politics."

5. Darrick Scott-Farnsworth, "Taxes Are Focus of April 18th Rally," *LPM Online*, April 17, 2007, http://michiganlp.org/ENewsletters/N20070417.htm#News211.

6. Phillips, "Sam Adams Project."

7. *HuffPost*'s Eyes & Ears Citizen Journalism Unit, "Anatomy of the Tea Party Movement: Sam Adams Alliance," *The Blog, Huffington Post,* March 18, 2010, http://www.huffingtonpost.com/alex-brantzawadzki/anatomy-of-the-tea-party_b_380662.html.

8. Kyle Mantyla, "The Emerging Right-Wing 'Resistance,'" *Right Wing Watch,* November 19, 2008, http://www.rightwingwatch.org/content/emerging-right-wing-resistance.

22: Propaganda "Dressed Up as Journalism"

1. Chet (no last name), "The Koch Brothers' Slow Poisoning of America," *North-Decoder.com,* April 25, 2011, http://www.northdecoder.com/Latest/the-koch-brothers-slow-poisoning-of-america.html.

2. Julie Kosterlitz, "Conservative Watchdogs Awake," *National Journal,* December 12, 2009.

3. PRW Staff, "How a Right-Wing Group Is Infiltrating State News Coverage," Center for Media and Democracy's PRWatch, July 12, 2012, http://www.prwatch.org/news/2012/07/11636/how-right-wing-group-infiltrating-state-news-coverage.

4. Dustin Hurst, "Underage Tanning Could Mean Misdemeanor, $1,000 Fine," *IdahoReporter.com,* February 16, 2012, http://idahoreporter.com/19276/underage-tanning-could-mean-misdemeanor-1000-fine/.

5. Gene Gibbons, "Statehouse Beat Woes Portend Bad News for Good Government," *NiemanReports,* December 15, 2010, http://niemanreports.org/articles/statehouse-beat-woes-portend-bad-news-for-good-government/.

6. Andy Kroll, "Exposed: The Dark-Money ATM of the Conservative Movement," *Mother Jones,* February 5, 2013, http://www.motherjones.com/politics/2013/02/donors-trust-donor-capital-fund-dark-money-koch-bradley-devos.

7. Rush Limbaugh, "Scott Walker's Opponent Fired by Her Own Family," *Rush Limbaugh Show,* October 29, 2014, http://www.rushlimbaugh.com/daily/2014/10/29/quick_hits_page.

23: Capturing the States

1. Reagan's kitchen cabinet was composed of many conservative, prominent businessmen who served as unofficial advisers, yet were greatly influential in his decision-making.

2. Lee Edwards, *Leading the Way: The Story of Ed Feulner and the Heritage Foundation* (New York: Crown Forum/Crown Publishing Group/Random House, 2013).

3. Adam Wren, "The Week Mike Pence's 2016 Dreams Crumbled," *Politico*, April 1, 2015, http://www.politico.com/magazine/story/2015/04/mike-pence -indiana-2016-116569.html#.VUuMnGd0yfA.

4. Kopan, "Report: Think Tanks Tied to Kochs."

5. Mayer, "Is Ikea the New Model?"

6. Ed Pilkington and Suzanne Goldenberg, "State Conservative Groups Plan US-Wide Assault on Education, Health and Tax," *Guardian*, December 5, 2013, http://www.theguardian.com/world/2013/dec/05/state-conservative-groups -assault-education-health-tax.

7. "Exposed: The State Policy Network."

24: Structure of Social Change

1. "Koch on Campus: Polluting Higher Education."

2. Daniel Schulman, *Sons of Wichita: How the Koch Brothers Became America's Most Powerful and Private Dynasty* (New York: Grand Central Publishing, 2014).

3. Daniel Schulman, "Charles Koch's Brain," September/October 2014, *Politico 50*, http://www.politico.com/magazine/politico50/2014/charles-kochs-brain .html#.VUuZbWd0yfA.

4. "Koch on Campus: Polluting Higher Education."

5. Dave Levinthal, "Koch Foundation Proposal to College: Teach Our Curriculum, Get Millions," Center for Public Integrity, September 12, 2014, updated September 16, 2014, http://www.publicintegrity.org/2014/09/12/15495/koch -foundation-proposal-college-teach-our-curriculum-get-millions.

25: A Blueprint Years in the Making

1. "Donors Capital Fund," *SourceWatch*, Center for Media and Democracy, http://www.sourcewatch.org/index.php/Donors_Capital_Fund.

2. "Robert Brulle: Inside the Climate Change 'Countermovement,'" *Frontline*, PBS, October 23, 2012, http://www.pbs.org/wgbh/pages/frontline/environment/climate-of-doubt/robert-brulle-inside-the-climate-change-countermovement/.

3. Cheryl Gay Stolberg and Mike McIntire, "Federal Budget Crisis Months in the Planning," *New York Times*, October 5, 2013, http://www.nytimes.com/2013/10/06/us/a-federal-budget-crisis-months-in-the-planning.html?_r=0.

26: Winning

1. Matea Gold, "Koch-Backed Political Network, Built to Shield Donors, Raised $400 Million in 2012 Elections," *Washington Post*, January 5, 2014, http://www.washingtonpost.com/politics/koch-backed-political-network-built-to-shield-donors-raised-400-million-in-2012-elections/2014/01/05/9e7cfd9a-719b-11e3-9389-09ef9944065e_story.html.

2. Daniel Fisher, "Inside the Koch Empire: How the Brothers Plan to Reshape America," *Forbes*, December 5, 2012, http://www.forbes.com/sites/danielfisher/2012/12/05/inside-the-koch-empire-how-the-brothers-plan-to-reshape-america/.

3. Brad Friedman, "Audio: Chris Christie Lets Loose at Secret Koch Brothers Confab," *Mother Jones*, September 7, 2011, http://www.motherjones.com/politics/2011/09/audio-chris-christie-koch-brothers-seminar.

Appendix 3: Key Events

1. Kenneth P. Vogel, "Secret Koch Memo Outlines Plans for 2016," *Politico*, April 22, 2015, http://www.politico.com/story/2015/04/koch-brothers-2016-election-memo-117238.html#ixzz3Y3llqhb4.

2. Fredreka Schouten, "Charles Koch: We Like 5 GOP Candidates," *USA Today*, April 21, 2015, http://www.usatoday.com/story/news/politics/2015/04/21/charles-koch-on-gop-supports-candidates/26142001/.

ANNOTATED BIBLIOGRAPHY

☆ ☆ ☆

The research in this book includes my review of hundreds of documents in the Legacy Tobacco Documents Library at the University of California, San Francisco; the groundbreaking study by UCSF researchers Fallin, Grana, and Glantz; personal interviews and firsthand experience; and my review of online and hard-copy articles, as noted in order in this bibliography.

The Legacy Tobacco Documents Library. San Francisco: University of California, 2015. http://legacy.library.ucsf.edu/.
Key document links:

http://legacy.library.ucsf.edu/tid/snc37c00/pdf
http://legacy.library.ucsf.edu/tid/tkl95c00/pdf
http://legacy.library.ucsf.edu/tid/dtv34e00/pdf
http://legacy.library.ucsf.edu/tid/xqk92e00/pdf
http://legacy.library.ucsf.edu/tid/eii57d00/pdf
http://legacy.library.ucsf.edu/tid/bub47c00/pdf
http://legacy.library.ucsf.edu/tid/gqg76c00/pdf
http://legacy.library.ucsf.edu/tid/wvx12c00/pdf
http://legacy.library.ucsf.edu/tid/wue07d00/pdf

http://legacy.library.ucsf.edu/tid/uwu47b00/pdf
http://legacy.library.ucsf.edu/tid/oca24d00/pdf
http://legacy.library.ucsf.edu/tid/vbi08b00/pdf
http://legacy.library.ucsf.edu/tid/uvh38b00/pdf
http://legacy.library.ucsf.edu/tid/tcm89h00/pdf
http://legacy.library.ucsf.edu/tid/snc37c00/pdf
http://legacy.library.ucsf.edu/tid/ihi35c00/pdf
http://legacy.library.ucsf.edu/tid/nyn42a00/pdf
http://legacy.library.ucsf.edu/tid/akk16b00/pdf
http://legacy.library.ucsf.edu/tid/xcy72a00/pdf
http://legacy.library.ucsf.edu/tid/rka99h00/pdf
http://legacy.library.ucsf.edu/tid/ypy36c00/pdf
http://legacy.library.ucsf.edu/tid/gpc97g00/pdf
http://legacy.library.ucsf.edu/tid/ykl95c00/pdf
http://legacy.library.ucsf.edu/tid/yqs75c00
http://legacy.library.ucsf.edu/tid/cgg89h00
http://legacy.library.ucsf.edu/tid/lui67c00/pdf
http://legacy.library.ucsf.edu/tid/fnc92b00/pdf
http://legacy.library.ucsf.edu/tid/wnr25b00/pdf
http://legacy.library.ucsf.edu/tid/vtq38b00
http://legacy.library.ucsf.edu/tid/whr34b00/pdf
http://legacy.library.ucsf.edu/tid/iyv72e00/pdf
http://legacy.library.ucsf.edu/tid/tqq88h00/pdf
http://legacy.library.ucsf.edu/tid/pso40d00/pdf
http://legacy.library.ucsf.edu/tid/ytv89h00/pdf
http://legacy.library.ucsf.edu/tid/eqi66b00/pdf
http://legacy.library.ucsf.edu/tid/cdf37b00/pdf
http://legacy.library.ucsf.edu/tid/axi67c00/pdf
http://legacy.library.ucsf.edu/tid/tco60d00/pdf
http://legacy.library.ucsf.edu/tid/oso40d00/pdf
http://legacy.library.ucsf.edu/tid/ykl95c00/pdf
http://legacy.library.ucsf.edu/tid/vbi08b00/pdf
http://legacy.library.ucsf.edu/tid/oca24d00/pdf
http://legacy.library.ucsf.edu/tid/las81f00/pdf

http://legacy.library.ucsf.edu/tid/lkp87e00/pdf
http://legacy.library.ucsf.edu/tid/uar11c00/pdf
http://legacy.library.ucsf.edu/tid/gxs76b00/pdf
http://legacy.library.ucsf.edu/tid/wpb87b00/pdf

Conclusions drawn from my review of Legacy Tobacco Documents Library (also known as the Legacy archive) research:

The Tea Party movement was years in the making. It wasn't a miraculous political virgin birth in the spring of 2009.

Before CSE and the tobacco industry conspired in the early years of the Clinton administration to create antitax front groups in states across the United States to fight taxes of all stripes (obscuring the corporate strategies behind those seemingly grassroots antitax initiatives), the themes and contours of what would become the Tea Party movement were being tested by Ron Paul when he left Congress the first time to become chairman of CSE and simultaneously by smokers' rights coalitions built separately by both Philip Morris and RJR between 1988 and 1993, according to dozens of internal tobacco industry documents archived by the American Legacy Foundation as a result of the massive tobacco litigation settlement that caused several of the tobacco industry's most notorious research front groups to disband. Those thematic and political efforts would start to merge over the next decade or so as industry leaders and surrogates refined them.

While Ron Paul was bracketing his own efforts to create a Tea Party movement—from his first fund-raising pitch for CSE after he'd announced his retirement from the House to, years later, in December 2007, his efforts to bring many of the same concepts outlined in his first CSE fund-raising pitch forward when his presidential campaign held a "Tea Party" money bomb rally in Boston that raised millions for his quixotic presidential campaign—others were testing the same themes.

Beginning in the nineties, Philip Morris began testing its own "Tea Party" themes designed to give its smokers' alliance (orchestrated by public relations giant Burson-Marsteller) something to rally behind that went beyond cigarette-excise-tax fights. "A Tea Party—Boston Style," read the headline from a 1989 issue of *Philip Morris Magazine* that compared opposition to cigarette excise taxes to the Boston Tea Party patriots who opposed taxation "without representation" on the eve of the American Revolution. "The men taking part in this protest of taxation without representation were prominent businessmen and political leaders," said the article. "What they planned was a serious crime under British law. If caught, they risked civil prosecution, imprisonment, or worse."

During this era Rich Fink—serving as president of CSE while ex-congressman Ron Paul was its chairman—first began to work on behalf of the tobacco industry while also working for the Kochs' interests. In the 1980s, for instance, he wrote to Congress, defending both the industry's right to buy tobacco without a "government-backed feudal claim to land" and smokers' rights. He also did the tobacco industry's bidding in fights with Dr. Koop and President Reagan's National Economic Commission, where he commingled the tobacco industry antitax themes with the core elements of the antitax Tea Party movement.

RJR, meanwhile, was busy testing its own Tea Party construct—one that would eventually dovetail with the efforts of Philip Morris, CSE, and two different coalitions at the time: the Coalition Against Regressive Taxation (CART), run by the head of a tiny trade group in DC (American Trucking Associations), and a parallel effort on the deficit-reduction and antiregulatory side called the Coalition for Fiscal Restraint (COFIRE), according to internal tobacco industry memos.

The head of CART, Tom Donohue, would eventually use the tobacco industry muscle and Koch-sponsored framework behind CART to succeed to the helm of the much larger US Chamber of Commerce. The Koch-sponsored antitax group COFIRE was run by Philip Morris and other large corporations, with CSE and other citizen groups out front.

COFIRE was organized by "a group of trade associations, citizens groups and corporations to advocate deficit reduction through restraints on the growth of federal spending, not through an increase in taxes," according to one of its charter documents. COFIRE included CSE and Americans for Tax Reform, as well as companies such as Koch Industries and Philip Morris and a dozen or so business trade groups, and was built to fight tax increases of any sort by opposing federal spending in Washington. More important, it was chaired by a senior adviser to CSE.

In an extraordinary and prescient internal RJR tobacco strategy memo from Tim Hyde (who oversaw all of RJR's public relations campaigns for years before leaving in 1996 to run field operations in all fifty states for the Dole/Kemp presidential campaign, and later becoming a founding partner of the DCI Group) to his boss, Tommy Griscom (who had been President Reagan's director of communications before becoming RJR's executive vice president for external relations), after the midterm elections in 1990, the core of the Tea Party movement concept was drawn out in considerable detail. Hyde and Griscom wanted to build a broad antitax coalition effort that extended from the states to Washington, which would subsume their cigarette-excise-tax efforts in broader efforts, and they were willing to put considerable financing behind it.

"You asked for my thoughts on how we might build broad coalitions around the issue-cluster of freedom, choice, and privacy; and what organizations, interests, and groups might be engaged in such coalitions," Hyde wrote to Griscom before elaborating on what they were already supporting financially and how those efforts could work together.

"Coalition-building should proceed along two tracks: a grassroots, organizational and largely local track; and a national, intellectual track within the DC-New York corridor. Ultimately, we are talking about a 'movement'—a national effort to change the way people think about government's (and big business') role in our lives. Any such effort requires an intellectual foundation—a set of theoretical and ideological arguments on its behalf," Hyde wrote.

"The Reagan revolution didn't happen on election night in 1980 but began in 1960 with Reagan's Republican Convention speech. This movement slowly gained credibility in the 60s and 70s as think tanks and journals in DC began to argue and persuade the rest of us of the perniciousness of high taxes, etc. They provided the intellectual underpinnings for what was happening politically out in America. Simultaneously, these ideas were fermenting at the grassroots level as groups, organizations and individuals struggled on behalf of candidates who embodied them," Hyde concluded, foreshadowing the efforts that would emerge in the coming decade with RJR, Philip Morris, and Koch funding.

Years later, in fact, in another memo to Griscom, Hyde laid out the many successes of RJR's now robust "field program" across the states—including RJR-funded antitax efforts in Georgia, Florida, Iowa, Tennessee, Indiana, New Jersey, Ohio, Wisconsin, New Hampshire, and Texas. Hyde specifically called out the successful efforts of New Jersey Citizens for a Sound Economy to block a cigarette excise tax. "New Jersey CSE helped beat back another effort to raise cigarette taxes in 1996," its state director wrote at the time, according to an archived Internet page. "Pitched as a solution to the very real woes of New Jersey's public school system, the cigarette tax would have been the wrong solution. We launched a campaign to defeat it, including an educational mailing, patch-thru phone calls and paid radio advertising." A 1996 letter from CSE's vice president of development, Michele Isele, to Pat Donoho, a senior vice president at the Tobacco Institute, thanked him for their financial pledge to New Jersey CSE to "promote market-based solutions to economic policy problems."

By the mid-1990s, all of the various antitax Tea Party movement efforts funded by Philip Morris and RJR were in full swing in the states. Its national communications arm—a broad, well-funded media campaign that included elite media in Washington, DC, and efforts in states across the country created by the Tobacco Institute called Enough is Enough—was led by Roger Ailes, a political consultant at the time who would later become chairman of the Fox News Channel.

Enough is Enough began as a Tobacco Institute concept to create local anger against taxes and grew over the years into a robust media initiative surrounding efforts of groups such as CSE and Grover Norquist's Americans for Tax Reform. "Norquist and ATR continue to appear on talk shows around the country," triggering thousands of calls to Capitol Hill to accompany Enough is Enough ads in *Roll Call*, wrote Scott Ehrlich of Ailes Communications Inc. in a campaign-update memo to Craig Fuller, former vice president George H. W. Bush's chief of staff, who had become Philip Morris's top spokesman by the fall of 1993. In another internal Philip Morris memo from David Nicoli (in their Washington office) to Fuller, they explored fully the risks and rewards of continuing Roger Ailes's strategy to use a broad antitax grassroots campaign against Clinton as he ran for president.

"We have conferred on refining and updating the strategy targeting the 'Enough is Enough' generic anti-tax ads," Nicoli wrote. "Due to significant political changes since the presidential election, Roger Ailes' original strategy of targeting an anti-excise tax campaign in the 'marginal' Clinton states from last year's election needs to be modified."

Right about this time, Rich Fink's strategy for CSE to specifically target the BTU tax in Clinton's budget reached its apex—and success. In concert, Nicoli recommended that they keep Ailes's Enough is Enough campaign going in the states. "Executing an anti-excise tax ad campaign in states and districts . . . would keep the 'anti-tax' pressure on those who have already responded to such pressures in the budget battle," Nicoli wrote.

In yet another internal memo at the same time, according to the Legacy documents, Nicoli was even more explicit. "To fight Clinton's proposed 75 cents per pack excise tax increase, we are also working behind the scenes to oppose the Clinton package as a whole," he wrote. "The House Energy and Commerce Committee will be a key battleground over the Clinton health care plan, and we are giving $400,000 to Citizens for a Sound Economy . . . to run a grassroots program aimed at 'swing' Democrats on the committee." It was the lead item on his report for others inside Philip Morris and was explicit in the way in which CSE would fight the cigarette excise tax by attacking Clinton's health care plan and budget.

Outside Washington at the time, meanwhile, the tobacco industry's Tea Party rhetoric was increasingly paired with tax fights at the state and national levels. In Massachusetts, for instance, the *New England Freedom Trail* newsletter for the Burson–Philip Morris coalition drew just such a parallel. "New Englanders don't like unfair taxes—remember the Boston Tea Party?—and they're fighting mad over proposals in Washington to raise the federal tax on cigarettes."

Philip Morris, CSE, and RJR—with Tom Donohue's help at CART—further crystallized the antitax strategy at the heart of the nascent Tea Party movement during the Clinton years. From that first meeting at Philip Morris's headquarters in the spring of 1993, where the construct of state-based antitax groups began to take shape, CSE would go on to receive millions from Philip Morris, until Charles Koch and Rich Fink shuttered CSE and split it into Americans for Prosperity and FreedomWorks in the midst of a fight with former House majority leader Richard Armey.

Shortly before CSE dissolved, the Kochs' organization had become Philip Morris's most trusted outside ally. According to internal Philip Morris memos in the Legacy archive, CSE commanded a $2 million fee for just one effort to mobilize against a Justice Department RICO lawsuit against the tobacco industry and the Tobacco Institute that concluded several years ago with a final judgment against the tobacco companies.

The effort, though, had taken years to refine. At the end of Reagan's term, for instance, CART was careful in its public language. In the draft of a letter to the National Economic Commission at the time, Donohue asked how it could support "your vital and delicate mission of recommending ways of reducing the deficit." CART (which included Philip Morris, RJR, and the Tobacco Institute) represents a "wide variety of industries that are affected by excise taxes on tobacco, beer, wine, distilled spirits, and highway and airways users. We are united in our opposition to increases in excise taxes as a means to reduce the deficit. [It is] broadly and soundly based," he wrote.

But four years later, as the Clinton years dawned, CART had become considerably more assertive in its public posture as it agreed to consider allowing Philip Morris's public relations firm, Burson-Marsteller, to shape the campaign. In a funding proposal from Gary Auxier, who ran Burson's US media campaign for Philip Morris, to John Doyle, media relations director for CART at the American Trucking Associations, the tobacco industry's Tea Party rhetoric and execution took center stage.

"While CART's existing resources are formidable, there is [an] opportunity to identify and mobilize previously unused or unrecognized allies to build these resources into an even more effective political machine. . . . Current anti-tax, anti-government anger can be tapped to support anti-excise tax efforts. [Burson] has in place a national network of public affairs practitioners with experience at the state level on excise taxes," Auxier wrote to CART's leadership in the run-up to the presidential campaign. "One area we would like to explore with CART . . . is the idea of a much stronger, much harder-edged approach to accountability for individual lawmakers who attempt to subvert the tax issue."

At the heart of the Burson–Philip Morris campaign proposal to Donohue's CART was an effort to artificially manufacture a Tea Party movement in the United States—essentially bringing Philip Morris's Tea Party construct into the mainstream of political fights in both the states and Washington. CSE, as their most trusted ally, would help galvanize and carry out these efforts for the next ten years.

"Using the resources provided by state and local member affiliates and their employees, we would use our expertise in grass roots mobilization and experience in campaigning to create highly visible activity at three key [presidential] campaign appearances," Auxier wrote. "Grounded in the theme of 'The New American Tax Revolution' or 'The New Boston Tea Party,' the campaign activity should take the form of citizens representing the widest constituency base mobilized with signage and other attention-drawing accoutrements such as lapel buttons, handouts, petitions and even costumes."

RJR wasn't far behind with its own parallel efforts. Their own US public relations firm—the firm that later merged with the global intelligence firm Stratfor, which was the subject of a massive WikiLeaks hack in 2012 and 2013—masterminded a nearly identical Tea Party effort called Get Government Off Our Back (GGOOB) that organized "regulatory revolt" rallies at a dozen state capitals from Washington to New Jersey in the run-up to Newt Gingrich's Contract with America efforts that caused the House of Representatives to flip in 1994 to the Republicans. The Stratfor-RJR efforts through GGOOB were central to that pact. When the House passed a bill that froze all new federal regulations in 1995, for instance, the text of the bill matched the GGOOB language nearly word for word.

In early 1995, RJR's public relations firm (before it had merged with Stratfor) wrote a follow-up memo, now in Legacy tobacco documents, about GGOOB for RJR executives, explaining that their overarching objective was to "mobilize national and state-level resources to oppose regulations and legislation that is in opposition to RJR's interests. . . . Most important at this time is to expand on and use more effectively the elements that are already in place, specifically GGOOB." RJR executives clearly saw GGOOB's efforts as more effective politically than their own lobbying efforts. RJR sent their paid surrogates, including CSE, out to do their bidding—including to Ross Perot's third-party presidential convention—to sign up attendees for future efforts. Started initially as a grassroots effort with tobacco growers, it had morphed into an effort led by the US Chamber of Commerce and CSE in 1996.

By the end of 1995, CSE had consolidated its position as Philip Morris's preferred antitax ally capable of delivering results in the states as well as the halls of Congress. An October 1995 internal memo from Beverly McKittrick—who'd joined the tobacco giant from CSE earlier that year—listed the Kochs' CSE as its top third-party group that would "monitor and help direct [its] multifront action plan" aimed at discrediting the FDA and its ability to regulate the tobacco companies.

"CSE sits at the table with [John] Boehner concerning Republican priorities. Look for opportunities here for CSE in moving other groups to [oppose] FDA," McKittrick wrote. At the time, Boehner was the head of the House Republican Conference—a post that paved the way to his later election as Speaker of the House. While Boehner may, today, claim independence from the corporate interests behind the rise of the Tea Party that bedevil him in his efforts to corral its faction in the House of Representatives—the tobacco archive documents tell a different story.

Philip Morris and CSE also coordinated their attacks against the FDA's regulatory efforts and budget with the help of David McIntosh, who'd left CSE and won a House seat in Indiana. "Both [Joe] Barton and McIntosh/Shays efforts are ongoing in House. Need media, lobbying and policy support from third-party groups in support of these efforts," McKittrick wrote, referring to successful efforts by Representative McIntosh to hold oversight hearings on the FDA's budget that helped block the agency's abilities to create a unified campus in Maryland. "Preparations needed for FY97 appropriations for House and Senate. CSE should lead here, as they did on FY96 efforts. Need to work with CSE to develop appropriations strategy with teeth."

The Philip Morris–CSE strategy coordinated with McIntosh, Boehner, and Joe Barton in the House was built around "third-party efforts to launch, publicize and execute a broad non-tobacco based attack on the many failings of the FDA," McKittrick concluded in her memo to Philip Morris leadership.

Other memos for Philip Morris's top government affairs official, Steve Parrish, also elaborated on CSE's critical role in the company's antiregulatory efforts. A legal analysis from David Nicoli was even more explicit in the close working relationship. "Rep. Barton/CSE press conference . . . on FDA failings begins running inside-the-Beltway anti-FDA radio and TV ads," Nicoli wrote. "McIntosh . . . hearings on regulatory moratorium focus on FDA/EPA. . . . Prospects look good in House, dicey in Senate. . . . CSE working up, distributing opposition materials to $600 million FDA campus, which GOP is focusing on."

In its most complete listing of its key allies in yet another internal memo called "Tobacco Strategy," Philip Morris summarized CSE's role as its lead organizer of an effort to "show the Clinton plan as a government-run health care system replete with higher taxes and government spending, massive job losses, less choice, rationing of care, and extensive bureaucracies. CSE is taking aim at the heart of the plan—employer mandates, new entitlements, price controls, mandatory health alliances, heavy load of new taxes and global budgets—and, with the program well underway, is by all accounts getting rave reviews in the respective districts."

CSE confirmed its own central role in this drama as well. In its own case study, it said that it had "worked closely with our former distinguished fellow, Rep. David McIntosh (R-IN), on the successful passage of an amendment . . . that froze funding for the FDA's Office of the Commissioner." Legacy documents show that

Philip Morris contributed significant funding for CSE's general operations for more than a decade, until it dissolved to become Americans for Prosperity and Freedom-Works. The tobacco company contributed $500,000 in 1996, according to a letter from CSE president Paul Beckner to Steve Parrish. "It is clear from the legislative events of the past year that public policy is most effectively formulated through the support of grassroots citizens," Beckner wrote.

CSE took on every big fight for Philip Morris throughout this decade. In 1998, it led the efforts to block the Prop 10 cigarette tax effort in California. "Proposition 10 would raise cigarette taxes by 50 cents a pack and is designed to pay for a laundry list of programs supposedly targeted at kids," Beckner wrote in 1998. "A larger government would seem to be the actual target, however. The $700 million annually collected through this new tax would be used to create a mammoth 59 new government commissions, staffed with 8,000 bureaucrats."

A year later, CSE was back at it with a new plan for Philip Morris to block an effort at the end of the Clinton administration to fund dozens of programs with a new excise tax on cigarettes. But the real target, the Legacy documents show, was to serve as the tip of the spear to block a Justice Department lawsuit aimed at the tobacco industry and its research front groups. The price tag for CSE's efforts to lead the mobilization was steep—nearly $2 million. CSE led this effort at the end of the Clinton years—and into the Bush years when the Justice Department's civil service attorneys refused to drop the lawsuit.

CSE was front and center in what became known as the "mobilization universe" inside Philip Morris as it tried to deal with the lawsuit. In an overview budget document, CSE was at the top of Philip Morris's "mobilization" budget, slated for $2 million, while groups such as ATR received $750,000 and the US Chamber of Commerce received $500,000. "They [CSE] are adding this level of value," Philip Morris's chief lobbyist, John Scruggs, wrote to Philip Morris vice president for corporate affairs Tom Collamore. "They have provided significant grassroots assistance, in the nature of several thousand calls to the Hill on the lawsuit [and] direct lobbying on the lawsuit."

By 2002, with the Justice Department refusing to drop the RICO lawsuit, CSE's Beckner wrote to President Bush on behalf of the tobacco industry: "I want to write and offer what I believe are some helpful suggestions on how the Department of Justice can better focus its resources and mission in light of the enormous challenge it faces after September 11." Beckner requested that the White House drop the Justice RICO lawsuit against the tobacco industry: "As we now find ourselves in the middle of an attack within our borders, a war abroad, and an economic recession, I believe that the Justice Department should reallocate the precious resources it has to protect our homeland and prosecute the way against terrorism, rather than pursuing this costly lawsuit."

By the time federal judge Gladys Kessler issued a final judgment against the tobacco industry in the RICO lawsuit in 2006—ruling that the tobacco industry had violated the RICO act by conspiring to deceive the public through the activities and campaigns of the Tobacco Institute and the Council for Tobacco Research; that it should never create such front groups under different names in an effort to deceive the American public; and that it must maintain all internal memos and documents on those efforts in a public database until 2016—CSE had morphed into Americans for Prosperity.

For more than a decade, though, CSE had commingled funds from Koch foundations with the tobacco industry's funding, while they and the business community collectively refined the concept of a grassroots, antitax Tea Party revolution in the United States. In 2002, in fact, CSE created an actual Tea Party Web site—www.usteaparty.com—based on that construct.

"Today, the American tax burden is larger than ever, and the tax code grows ever more complex," reads a Wayback Machine snapshot of the CSE/U.S. Tea Party Web site, complete with a graphic of tea bags dropping from a ship in the Boston Harbor. "Like those patriots in 1773, Citizens for a Sound Economy feels it is time for another symbolic protest in the best tradition of our Founding Fathers. In 2002, our U.S. Tea Party is a national event . . . and open to all Americans who feel our taxes are too high and the tax code is too complicated." While that Web site has disappeared now, the domain name is still owned by the second group, FreedomWorks, created when CSE split in 2004, according to public domain-name records.

Amanda Fallin, Rachel Grana, and Stanton A. Glantz. " 'To Quarterback Behind the Scenes, Third-Party Efforts': The Tobacco Industry and the Tea Party." *Tobacco Control*, TC Online First, February 20, 2013. doi:10.1136/tobaccocontrol-2012-050815. http://tobaccocontrol.bmj.com/content/early/2013/02/20/tobaccocontrol-2012-050815.full.pdf+html.

This groundbreaking study details the deliberate creation and rise of the Tea Party apparatus from the early 1990s through the mid-2000s as a way to do the antitax, antiregulation bidding of the tobacco and oil industries in the states and DC—in a way that masked the money and true intent of the artificially created "antitax" and "antiregulation" network. All of it was strategically planned and funded by Koch, Philip Morris, and RJR.

The UCSF researchers discovered:

- The Tea Party movement was fully fleshed out by both Philip Morris and RJR for a decade or so with CSE and then tested with their help in not one but three different corporate front-group antitax coalitions (including one that made Tom Donohue's career).
- The Tea Party strategy is clearly spelled out by Tim Hyde, Gary Auxier, Roger Ailes, and others in ways no one really knew and then baked into the antitax corporate front groups that the Kochs' CSE mobilized.
- An internal memo from the tobacco industry's principal PR firm (Burson-Marsteller) to Tom Donohue shows that they created the astroturf infrastructure—at a time when Donohue was running the truckers' trade group. The memo lays out the antitax Tea Party strategy to hide the tobacco and oil dollars behind it. This gave Donohue the framework for an antitax coalition in the states, clearly made his career, and allowed him to take this framework to the US Chamber of Commerce.
- A number of internal tobacco memos pin the execution of its Enough is Enough antitax campaign in key states secretly for the tobacco companies to Roger Ailes's firm (called Ailes Communications, which he ran just prior to becoming chairman of the Fox News Channel for Rupert Murdoch).
- A page from Philip Morris's internal magazine placed in the tobacco documents archive in 1999 actually creates the concept of the Boston Tea Party movement to fight all taxes (not just cigarette taxes).
- A Wayback screen shot of the usteaparty.com Web site that CSE created years before (2002–4 time frame), which disappeared by 2009. FreedomWorks still maintained the domain name after they morphed from CSE in 2004.
- Internal memos from both Philip Morris and RJR outlined the creation of the money and muscle in the early 2000s from the tobacco and oil companies to fight their antitax battles secretly through a Tea Party apparatus.

- Internal memos show that CSE received perhaps as much as $20 million from Philip Morris and RJR from 1993 to 2003 to spearhead the antitax front groups that became the nucleus of the Tea Party "revolution." CSE led every tobacco- and oil-related fight against taxes and regulation during this period, paid for either by PM, RJR, or Koch.
- Memos from top PM officials designated CSE—which split its 501(c)(3) and 501(c)(4) into Americans for Prosperity and FreedomWorks in 2004—as their "Category A" coordinator for their growing grassroots antitax coalition designed to hide cigarette- and oil-tax fights.
- An original, signed letter from the president of the Tobacco Institute to Rich Fink as president of Citizens for a Sound Economy thanking him for doing the bidding of the tobacco companies on a key federal tax issue they were trying to block.
- An original memo from the head of Philip Morris government affairs shows that they put CSE on the payroll for $400,000 a year in 1994 to be the grassroots arm of their biggest front group.
- Several memos and e-mails trace a direct route from Big Tobacco through Koch-sponsored groups to the Tea Party movement today. Stratfor (the Global Intelligence files from WikiLeaks) later merged with the PR firm that had created and run another big tobacco front group of the 1990s (Get Government Off Our Back) that had CSE and then AFP at the epicenter. CSE got millions from Philip Morris as part of this, as did CART (Citizens Against Regressive Taxation), which Donohue ran.
- An e-mail shows that Stratfor's biggest client today is the American Petroleum Institute.
- Memos and Wayback screen shots from the two CSE front group state directors in their two biggest states (Florida and Texas) show how they created the Tea Party apparatus for Koch and the tobacco companies years before it seemed to spring from nowhere in 2009. Both morphed into state directors for Americans for Prosperity.

Jeff Nesbit. Personal interviews with those listed below, among others, and firsthand experience revealed four major areas of research and conclusions, presented below in condensed form.

Elsner, Gabriel, Checks and Balances Project.

Fallin, Amanda, Rachel Grana, and Stanton A. Glantz, researchers of the study "'To Quarterback Behind the Scenes, Third-Party Efforts': The Tobacco Industry and the Tea Party."

Graves, Lisa, Center for Media and Democracy.

Jacobs, Larry, Director, Center for the Study of Politics and Governance at the University of Minnesota.

Kessler, Dr. David, former FDA commissioner.

Four major areas reveal the layers of the long rise of the American Tea Party movement in concert with the strategic corporate aims of the Kochs' various front groups and the tobacco industry. All four are supported by reporting and internal tobacco industry memos and documents, which have been reported on in three scholarly journals and are part of millions of documents at the Legacy Tobacco Documents Library at University of California, San Francisco.

I personally reviewed hundreds of those documents and have included the key links to scans of them in this bibliography-and-research section. While it is generally known that Koch-sponsored groups are deeply embedded in the Tea Party movement, its origins with tobacco and Koch money commingled to create the themes and "boots on the ground" Tea Party movement is not known at all.

1. Koch-sponsored groups and Philip Morris created the Tea Party movement together starting in the early 1990s, through Citizens for a Sound Economy. It didn't just leap forth spontaneously in the spring of 2009 as media have always reported. I was in the very first meeting at Philip Morris with CSE in 1993 as they proposed to jointly start antitax front groups in the states, and I watched firsthand when they joined forces with the American Petroleum Institute and targeted the BTU tax to bring down Clinton's first budget.

2. CSE, mostly funded by the Kochs and Philip Morris and RJR, became Big Tobacco's best-funded and most-trusted ally during the next decade, while they tested out all the Tea Party themes and messaging in various corporate front groups. This also included Fox News Channel chairman Roger Ailes and others (such as President Reagan's communications director, Tommy Griscom, who became RJR's executive vice president after leaving the White House). CSE made a seamless transition to AFP in 2004.

3. The Kochs deliberately set out to remake the GOP from the inside out and take over the party through an interlocking "boots on the ground" network. It's all laid out in explicit detail in tobacco-industry documents and in reporting from those inside the Koch network and longtime observers of that network.

The details in the Legacy Tobacco Documents Library and in personal interviews reveal this truth: the Kochs were willing to take anyone's money, from tobacco to oil, to take control of the GOP politically. They are now causing serious, long-term damage to the GOP brand among young people on three key issues for them—health care, immigration, and climate change—but national GOP politicians in Washington, DC, are now addicted to their substantial funding levers. They may not be able to avoid the train wreck headed their way at the national level.

4. The Kochs created and ramped up funding for the five cornerstones of the Tea Party movement (Americans for Prosperity, the Franklin Center, the State Policy Network, the Sam Adams Alliance, and the Mercatus academic network) a full year or so before the so-called virgin birth of the Tea Party.

Not only did the Kochs and major tobacco companies deliberately create the framework for the Tea Party movement, they substantially ramped up their funding for the key pillars of it up to two years before the first year of Barack Obama's presidency—something that directly contradicts the Tea Party creation myth.

After UCSF researcher Stan Glantz and his team reviewed hundreds of internal tobacco documents, they saw clearly that the Tea Party "did not come out of nowhere as a spontaneous reaction to Obamacare," and that the public perception of its uprising in 2009 was completely erroneous. Instead, it was the movement envisioned in the 1990s to "change how people see the role of 'government' and 'big business' in their lives"—all underlined by the concepts of freedom, choice, and patriotism that would rally Americans, who hate taxes in general, to the cause. However, the UCSF researchers proved through their meticulous study of documents that "the Tea Party's leadership's political agenda, and political positions, are actually discordant with what the people they're mobilizing actually think," Glantz says.

Other sources, as listed below:

"About Us." FreedomWorks. http://www.freedomworks.org/about/about-freedom works.

"American Legislative Exchange Council." *SourceWatch*, Center for Media and Democracy. Last modified April 6, 2015. http://www.sourcewatch.org/index.php ?title=American_Legislative_Exchange_Council.

Apollonio, Dorie E., and Lisa A. Bero. "The Creation of Industry Front Groups: The Tobacco Industry and 'Get Government Off Our Back.'" *American Journal of Public Health*. March 2007. http://www.ncbi.nlm.nih.gov/pmc/articles /PMC1805008/.

Carrk, Tony. "The Koch Brothers: What You Need to Know About the Financiers of the Radical Right." Center for American Progress Action Fund, April 2011. https://cdn.americanprogress.org/wp-content/uploads/issues/2011/04 /pdf/koch_brothers.pdf.

Chen, Edwin. "In Shift, FDA Says It Could Classify Nicotine as a Drug." *Los Angeles Times*, February 26, 1994. http://articles.latimes.com/1994-02-26/news /mn-27363_1_nicotine-addiction.

Chet. "The Koch Brothers' Slow Poisoning of America." *NorthDecoder.com*. April 25, 2011. http://www.northdecoder.com/Latest/the-koch-brothers-slow-poisoning -of-america.html.

Continetti, Matthew. "The Paranoid Style in Liberal Politics." *Weekly Standard*, April 4, 2011. http://www.weeklystandard.com/articles/paranoid-style-liberal-politics _555525.html?page=3.

"CSE President Paul Beckner's Response to Remarks Made by Oracle CEO Larry Ellison." FreedomWorks, June 29, 2000. http://www.freedomworks.org/content /cse-president-paul-beckners-response-remarks-made-oracle-ceo-larry -ellison.

David H. Koch Charitable Foundation and Personal Philanthropy, Koch Family Foundations & Philanthropy. http://www.kochfamilyfoundations.org/Foundations DHK.asp.

"David Koch Gives Smithsonian a Record $35M for New Dinosaur Hall." *CBSDC*, May 3, 2012. http://washington.cbslocal.com/2012/05/03/david-koch-gives -smithsonian-a-record-35m-for-new-dinosaur-hall/.

Dickinson, Tim. "How Roger Ailes Built the Fox News Fear Factory." *Rolling Stone*, May 25, 2011. http://www.rollingstone.com/politics/news/how-roger-ailes -built-the-fox-news-fear-factory-20110525.

"Donors Capital Fund." *SourceWatch*, Center for Media and Democracy. http:// www.sourcewatch.org/index.php/Donors_Capital_Fund.

Edwards, Lee. *Leading the Way: The Story of Ed Feulner and the Heritage Foundation.* New York: Crown Forum/Crown Publishing Group/Random House, 2013.

Erlandson, Dawn. "The BTU Tax Experience: What Happened and Why It Happened." *Pace Environmental Law Review* 12, no. 1 (Fall 1994). http://digitalcommons.pace.edu/cgi/viewcontent.cgi?article=1528&context=pelr.

Estes, Jim. "How the Big Tobacco Deal Went Bad." *New York Times*, October 6, 2014. http://www.nytimes.com/2014/10/07/opinion/how-the-big-tobacco-deal -went-bad.html?_r=0.

"Exposed: The State Policy Network." Center for Media and Democracy/ALEC Exposed, November 2013. http://www.prwatch.org/files/spn_national_report _final.pdf.

Fang, Lee. *The Machine: A Field Guide to the Resurgent Right.* New York: New Press, 2013. http://www.thenewpress.com.

Fisher, Daniel. "Inside the Koch Empire: How the Brothers Plan to Reshape America." *Forbes*, December 5, 2012. http://www.forbes.com/sites/danielfisher /2012/12/05/inside-the-koch-empire-how-the-brothers-plan-to-reshape -america/.

"Frequently Asked Questions." John Birch Society. http://www.jbs.org/about-jbs /frequently-asked-questions.

Friedman, Brad. "Audio: Chris Christie Lets Loose at Secret Koch Brothers Confab." *Mother Jones*, September 7, 2011. http://www.motherjones.com/politics /2011/09/audio-chris-christie-koch-brothers-seminar.

Gibbons, Gene. "Statehouse Beat Woes Portend Bad News for Good Government." *NiemanReports*, December 15, 2010. http://niemanreports.org/articles/statehouse -beat-woes-portend-bad-news-for-good-government/.

Gold, Matea. "Koch-Backed Political Network, Built to Shield Donors, Raised $400 million in 2012 Elections." *Washington Post*, January 5, 2014. http://www .washingtonpost.com/politics/koch-backed-political-network-built-to-shield

-donors-raised-400-million-in-2012-elections/2014/01/05/9e7cfd9a-719b-11e3
-9389-09ef9944065e_story.html.

Goodman, Andrew. "The Billionaire's Party: David Koch Is New York's Second-Richest Man, a Celebrated Patron of the Arts, and the Tea Party's Wallet." *New York,* July 25, 2010. http://nymag.com/news/features/67285/.

HuffPost's Eyes & Ears Citizen Journalism Unit. "Anatomy of the Tea Party Movement: Sam Adams Alliance." *The Blog, Huffington Post,* March 18, 2010. http://www.huffingtonpost.com/alex-brantzawadzki/anatomy-of-the-tea-party_b_380662.html.

Hurst, Dustin. "Underage Tanning Could Mean Misdemeanor, $1,000 Fine." *IdahoReporter.com,* February 16, 2012. http://idahoreporter.com/19276/underage-tanning-could-mean-misdemeanor-1000-fine/.

"John McManus at the Rally for the Republic (Part 1 of 2)." YouTube, uploaded September 4, 2008. https://www.youtube.com/watch?v=obgsT03oqS4.

"John McManus at the Rally for the Republic (Part 2 of 2)." YouTube, uploaded September 4, 2008. https://www.youtube.com/watch?v=fiI25K78X7M.

Kelly, Jim. "Koch Classic." Style, *Vanity Fair,* June 2014. http://www.vanityfair.com/style/2014/06/daniel-schulman-koch-brothers.

Koch, Charles G. "Charles Koch: I'm Fighting to Restore a Free Society." Opinion, *Wall Street Journal,* updated April 2, 2014. http://www.wsj.com/news/articles/SB10001424052702303978304579475860515021286.

———. *The Science of Success.* Hoboken, N.J.: John Wiley & Sons, 2007. http://www.amazon.com/The-Science-Success-Market-Based-Management/dp/0470139889.

———. "Why Koch Industries Is Speaking Out." Opinion, *Wall Street Journal,* updated March 1, 2011. http://www.wsj.com/articles/SB10001424052748704288304576170974226083178.

"Koch on Campus: Polluting Higher Education." Greenpeace/Greenpeace USA. http://www.greenpeace.org/usa/en/campaigns/global-warming-and-energy/polluterwatch/koch-industries/KOCH-POLLUTION-ON-CAMPUS-Academic-Freedom-Under-Assault-from-Charles-Kochs-50-million-Campaign-to-Infiltrate-Higher-Education/.

Kopan, Tal. "Report: Think Tanks Tied to Kochs." *Politico,* November 13, 2013.

http://www.politico.com/story/2013/11/koch-brothers-think-tank-report-99791.html.

Kosterlitz, Julie. "Conservative Watchdogs Awake." *National Journal*, December 12, 2009.

Kroll, Andy. "Exposed: The Dark-Money ATM of the Conservative Movement." *Mother Jones*, February 5, 2013. http://www.motherjones.com/politics/2013/02/donors-trust-donor-capital-fund-dark-money-koch-bradley-devos.

Levinthal, Dave. "Koch Foundation Proposal to College: Teach Our Curriculum, Get Millions." Center for Public Integrity, September 12, 2014, updated September 16, 2014. http://www.publicintegrity.org/2014/09/12/15495/koch-foundation-proposal-college-teach-our-curriculum-get-millions.

Limbaugh, Rush. "Scott Walker's Opponent Fired by Her Own Family." *Rush Limbaugh Show*, October 29, 2014. http://www.rushlimbaugh.com/daily/2014/10/29/quick_hits_page.

Liversey, Bruce. "How Canada Made the Koch Brothers Rich." *National Observer*, May 5, 2015. http://www.nationalobserver.com/2015/05/04/news/how-canada-made-koch-brothers-rich.

Mantyla, Kyle. "The Emerging Right-Wing 'Resistance.'" *Right Wing Watch*, November 19, 2008. http://www.rightwingwatch.org/content/emerging-right-wing-resistance.

Mayer, Jane. "Covert Operations." *New Yorker*, August 30, 2010. http://www.newyorker.com/magazine/2010/08/30/covert-operations.

———. "Is Ikea the New Model for the Conservative Movement?" *New Yorker*, November 15, 2013. http://www.newyorker.com/news/news-desk/is-ikea-the-new-model-for-the-conservative-movement.

Mencimer, Stephanie. "A Secret Tea Party Donor Revealed." *Mother Jones*, October 28, 2010. http://www.motherjones.com/politics/2010/10/tea-party-donor-patriot-one-raymon-thompson.

Monroney, Michael. "You Call This Fiscal Restraint?" *Christian Science Monitor*, December 17, 1990.

Moore, John W. "Wichita Pipeline." *National Journal*, May 16, 1992. http://www.precaution.org/lib/wichita_pipeline_national_journal_19920516l.pdf.

"#9 Charles Koch: The Forbes 400 Richest Americans 2009." *Forbes*, September 30,

2009. http://www.forbes.com/lists/2009/54/rich-list-09_Charles-Koch_Z9KL
.html.

Oldham, Taki. "The Billionaires' Tea Party—Trailer." https://www.youtube.com
/watch?v=uB2d-1PRvO4.

Oppenheimer, Laura. "Anti-Spending Crusaders Gain Steam [Americans for Limited Government Convention]." *Free Republic,* September 5, 2006. http://www
.freerepublic.com/focus/f-news/1695774/posts.

"Partisan Aim Denied by Liberty League; Founded to Defend Constitution, Organization Declares in a Statement." *New York Times,* April 20, 1936. http://query
.nytimes.com/gst/abstract.html?res=9C01EED9173AE33BBC4851DFB266838
D629EDE.

Perlberg, Steven. "Rick Santelli Started the Tea Party with a Rant Exactly Five Years
Ago Today—Here's How He Feels About It Now." *Business Insider,* February 19,
2014. http://www.businessinsider.com/rick-santelli-tea-party-rant-2014-2.

Phillips, Kate. "The Sam Adams Project." *New York Times,* July 19, 2008. http://
thecaucus.blogs.nytimes.com/2008/07/19/the-sam-adams-project/?_r=0.

Phillips-Fein, Kim. *Invisible Hands: The Businessmen's Crusade Against the New Deal.* New
York: W. W. Norton. 2010. http://books.google.com/books?id=g0tCwOhyl7MC
&pg=PA20&#v=onepage&q&f=false.

Pilkington, Ed, and Suzanne Goldenberg. "State Conservative Groups Plan US-
Wide Assault on Education, Health and Tax." *Guardian,* December 5, 2013.
http://www.theguardian.com/world/2013/dec/05/state-conservative-groups
-assault-education-health-tax.

PRW Staff. "How a Right-Wing Group Is Infiltrating State News Coverage." Center
for Media and Democracy's PRWatch, July 12, 2012. http://www.prwatch.org
/news/2012/07/11636/how-right-wing-group-infiltrating-state-news-coverage.

"Robert Brulle: Inside the Climate Change 'Countermovement.'" *Frontline,* PBS,
October 23, 2012. http://www.pbs.org/wgbh/pages/frontline/environment
/climate-of-doubt/robert-brulle-inside-the-climate-change-countermovement/.

Santelli, Rick. Speech. February 19, 2009. http://www.huffingtonpost.com/2014
/02/19/tea-party-santelli_n_4815941.html.

Sassoon, David. "Koch Brothers Positioned to Be Big Winners If Keystone XL
Pipeline Is Approved." Reuters, February 10, 2011. http://www.reuters.com
/article/2011/02/10/idUS292515702420110210.

Schouten, Fredreka. "Charles Koch: We Like 5 GOP Candidates." *USA Today*, April 21, 2015. http://www.usatoday.com/story/news/politics/2015/04/21 /charles-koch-on-gop-supports-candidates/26142001/.

Schulman, Daniel. "Charles Koch's Brain." *Politico 50*, September/October 2014. http://www.politico.com/magazine/politico50/2014/charles-kochs-brain .html#.VUuZbWd0yfA.

———. *Sons of Wichita: How the Koch Brothers Became America's Most Powerful and Private Dynasty*. New York: Grand Central Publishing, 2014.

"The Science of Success." Koch.com. http://www.kochind.com/MBM/science_of _success.aspx.

Scott-Farnsworth, Darrick. "Taxes Are Focus of April 18th Rally." *LPM Online*, April 17, 2007. http://michiganlp.org/ENewsletters/N20070417.htm#News211.

Seymour, Julia A. "Santelli: Five Years After His Rant Launched Tea Party." *MRC-Business*, February 19, 2014. http://www.mrc.org/articles/santelli-five-years -after-his-rant-launched-tea-party.

Stolberg, Cheryl Gay, and Mike McIntire. "Federal Budget Crisis Months in the Planning." *New York Times*, October 5, 2013. http://www.nytimes.com/2013/10 /06/us/a-federal-budget-crisis-months-in-the-planning.html?_r=0.

Tesler, Laura E., PhD, and Ruth E. Malone, PhD, RN. "'Our Reach Is Wide by Any Corporate Standard': How the Tobacco Industry Helped Defeat the Clinton Health Plan and Why It Matters Now." *American Journal of Public Health*, July 2010. http://www.ncbi.nlm.nih.gov/pmc/articles/PMC2882403/.

"Tobacco Farmers Stage 'Tea Party' Protest." *New York Times*, June 10, 1994. http:// www.nytimes.com/1994/06/10/us/tobacco-farmers-stage-tea-party-protest .html.

Vogel, Kenneth P. "Secret Koch Memo Outlines Plans for 2016." *Politico*, April 22, 2015. http://www.politico.com/story/2015/04/koch-brothers-2016-election -memo-117238.html#ixzz3Y3llqhb4.

Wilson, Bill, and Roy Wenzl. "The Kochs' Quest to Save America." October 13, 2012, updated August 13, 2014. http://www.kansas.com/news/special-reports /koch/article1100675.html.

Wren, Adam. "The Week Mike Pence's 2016 Dreams Crumbled." *Politico*, April 1, 2015. http://www.politico.com/magazine/story/2015/04/mike-pence-indiana -2016-116569.html#.VUuMnGd0yfA.

INDEX

☆ ☆ ☆